W9-BMU-574

ADOPTION DIGEST

ADOPTION DIGEST

Stories of Joy, Loss, and the Journey

Tim O'Hanlon and Rita Laws
Foreword by Ann M. McCabe

BERGIN & GARVEY
Westport, Connecticut • London

Library of Congress Cataloging-in-Publication Data

O'Hanlon, Tim.
    Adoption digest : stories of joy, loss, and the journey / Tim O'Hanlon and Rita Laws;
foreword by Ann M. McCabe.
      p. cm.
    Includes bibliographical references.
    ISBN 0-89789-669-6 (pbk. : alk. paper)
    1. Adoption—United States—Case studies. I. Laws, Rita, 1956– II. Title.
HV875.55 O45 2001
362.73'4'0973—dc21   2001035724

British Library Cataloguing in Publication Data is available.

Copyright © 2001 by Tim O'Hanlon and Rita Laws

All rights reserved. No portion of this book may be
reproduced, by any process or technique, without
the express written consent of the publisher.

Library of Congress Catalog Card Number: 2001035724
ISBN: 0–89789–669–6

First published in 2001

Bergin & Garvey, 88 Post Road West, Westport, CT 06881
An imprint of Greenwood Publishing Group, Inc.
www.greenwood.com

Printed in the United States of America

The paper used in this book complies with the
Permanent Paper Standard issued by the National
Information Standards Organization (Z39.48–1984).

10 9 8 7 6 5 4 3 2 1

Dedicated to the memory of Jimmie Williams and Emily Babb

And to Mr. Samuel L. Laws, 1925–2000,
father, grandfather, great-grandfather, and adoption advocate

CONTENTS

Contents

FOREWORD

Throughout my work in adoption and foster care over the past twenty years, I have been struck by how child advocates and workers can get polarized in what is commonly known as "the child's best interest." I have participated in case-planning meetings where a lead social worker has declined to send birth family photos with a child being placed in a new adoptive home, believing that the siblings' smiling faces in the picture may interrupt the bonding process with the adoptive family. Strange to some, others view this choice as a caring intervention.

When I was adopted in the early 1950's, the best interest of the child was thought to be achieved by a veil of secrecy. Today we advocate for openness, though some remain skeptical. Through the honesty of adult adoptees returning to the system, we have learned that adoption is a life-long process and that legal realities do not erase the relational realities of birth and history.

This information has challenged all of us working in adoption to rethink past practices, some of which left children in the middle of loyalty conflicts for their entire lives. Like the scarecrow in the classic story, *The Wizard of Oz*, who declared; "Then they took my arms and threw them over there and took my legs and threw them over there," children can feel the emotional disconnection when families are not helped to honor all the relational connections that children carry.

Relationships formed through adoption are like any other relationship, only more so. It is this more so that is captured so poignantly in the *Adoption Digest: Stories of Joy, Loss and the Journey*. Story after story, we ride the roller coaster of emotion, experiencing the hopes and dreams, joys and sorrows of these real people. We gasp with Liz, the 40-year-old biology professor, as she learns for the first time at a family reunion that she is adopted. Later we try to hold back the tears as we read about Charlie, an abused boy who grows up in a time when foster parents cannot adopt, yet who as a young adult of 19 is adopted by his devoted foster sister after the death of their parents.

This book is not meant for the faint hearted though. Tim O'Hanlon and Rita Laws unflinchingly and skillfully touch on some negative aspects of the adoption process and how agencies, like other institutions, can turn away from the people they were created to serve. Time and again the reader will cheer for ordinary people who face the most challenging life events with extraordinary courage.

These stories will resonate with those who have had a personal experience of adoption but will appeal to readers unfamiliar with adoption. All will be touched by the universal themes of loss, injustice, commitment, and home-coming, wherever home may be.

The authors applaud and encourage families to always be their child's best advocates. Using their knowledge and expertise in adoption policy, process and law, the authors have brought these heartfelt stories to life. Tim O'Hanlon and Rita Laws have outdone themselves in bringing this well-balanced and candid approach to the complexities of adoption.

—Ann M. McCabe

PREFACE

"And how long will you keep working in adoption?"
Until there are no more waiting children.

When it comes to the stories in this book, the authors want the reader to know:

- In writing this book, we drew on personal, professional, and volunteer experience and the experience gained assisting thousands of other families over the last two decades. The families and people described are composites of many real-life individuals with details changed to protect the privacy of all, and especially to protect the privacy of the children.

- This book was written to illustrate, celebrate and encourage adoption, especially the adoption of children with special needs, and to share the fascinating stories of American families.

- Every effort was made to portray adoption realistically and honestly and from many different viewpoints, but such is the nature of adoption—there will be those who think the book too positive and some, too negative. Hopefully, as with the bowls of porridge in the Goldilocks fairy tale, experienced adoption sojourners will find the temperature to be just right.

- We live in a time of revolution, as far as adoption is concerned, so a book like this might read quite differently in another decade or two. Things are changing rapidly, from societal attitudes, to social work practice, to federal law. What matters is that new state and federal laws are making adoption easier for typical American families to seriously consider. What counts is that the adoption of children from foster care is becoming more commonplace each year, and we are setting annual records for the number of children removed from foster care and placed into new permanent families. The process is maturing, becoming better, more humane, and more in touch with the true needs of foster children and the people who open their hearts and homes to them.

- We do not identify states by name because state laws and adoption procedures change so rapidly. What's true today in a certain place can be totally different tomorrow. A state in violation of federal adoption law this year may be the state with the best regional compliance or most innovative new adoption law next year.

- As these stories are composites based on hundreds of families, any similarity to actual persons, living or dead, is simply coincidence.

ACKNOWLEDGMENTS

We would like to thank Greenwood Publishing's Lynn Taylor, our prepublication reviewers, Matt O'Hanlon, Ann M. McCabe, Jeanette Wiedemeier Bower, L. Anne Babb, Maryann Brunasso, Shelley Linsday, and Barbara Leiner at Fosterparents.com for help with the manuscript.

Tim would like to thank Nancy and Matt for their love. They are my constant blessings. They are my family. Matt O'Hanlon, journalism graduate, also happens to be one of the best copy editors anywhere. He found mistakes that Sherlock Holmes would have missed, made sentences flow better, and acted as my sounding board. His talent and dedication improved the manuscript in a thousand different ways both big and small. To my mother Connie for her amazing faith in her eldest, her boundless enthusiasm for life, and her big heart. And Rita, my friend, writing partner, and constant inspiration.

Rita would like to acknowledge the priceless ongoing support of her mother, Nancy Laws, and her children and to thank her co-author, Dr. Tim O'Hanlon. It is a joy to write with him. A special thank you to Mr. Shawn McBroom, college student and respite care provider, without whose aid this book might not have happened. For wading through piles of clean laundry yet to be sorted, for making peanut butter and jelly sandwiches without the jelly, for teaching Rita's younger children how to putt, dunk, and play soccer, and for being a mentor and role model, too.

1

ADOPTION AS JOY

Joy (noun): Exhilaration of spirits, jubilation, to rejoice, to exult, full of joy

INTRODUCTION

As with childbirth, the adoption process is rarely easy or painless, but when it culminates in the arrival of a child, there is great joy. Unlike childbirth, the rejoicing has many facets because the new child or children may be of any age from newly born to adult!

To rejoice is "to cheer, to triumph, and to express joy." This dictionary definition is an ideal way to describe adoption joy. We cheer as a society because another child without a family to grow up with now has one. The parent or parents have triumphed over the arduous homestudy and the complex adoption bureaucracy. And everyone who knows the family blessed with a new child or sibling group expresses joy at the wonder and miracle of growing a family through adoption.

And it is a miracle. Children born in our hearts, not from our bodies, children given a second chance for permanency within a functioning family, children loved by their first families, by their former foster families, and by their new forever families, too.

People who parent both children born to them and adopted children will tell you that the processes are different, but the bonding is just as intense and the joy, every bit as sweet with all of their children. There is no "second best" way to become a parent.

Children are children, and joy is joy.

The Tale of Tomas

If Debbie Santos had ever been more anxious in her whole life, she could not remember when. Her entourage had arrived at the Baptist Children's Home much too early—the agency would not even open for forty minutes. So Debbie's husband, Jose, and her father took her to a coffee house for breakfast.

As she watched them eat eggs and waffles, the 28-year-old marveled that they could eat at a time like this. Had they not, after all, been trying to adopt a baby for three years? And now the baby was here, just 6 weeks old, and they were about to meet him. No photos, just come and get your baby tomorrow, Mr. and Mrs. Santos, and congratulations. She wondered how he would look, being Puerto Rican, African, and German. She'd never known anyone before who was triracial. And she wondered if the cocaine found in his blood at birth would be totally out of his system yet, or if he would still be in withdrawal.

The idea of prenatal drug exposure had left them paralyzed with fear the first time they heard about it. But the social worker had given them several magazine and journal articles to read. They had learned that while damage from prenatal alcohol exposure is usually permanent, exposure in the womb to other drugs, like cocaine and heroin, had a more unpredictable outcome. Some babies had problems, even serious ones, and others did not. Still other exposed children outgrew their difficulties or learned to compensate for them. No one could predict the health or learning problems, if any, that this baby would experience. It was a gamble, but one they were prepared to take. So far the baby appeared to be healthy but very colicky.

As she watched the two men eat breakfast, Debbie's anticipation turned to severe anxiety. What if the baby hated her? What if she could not bond to him? What if . . . She jumped up and called the agency, and even though they were not supposed to be open for another ten minutes, her social worker, Marlene, answered the phone. Debbie was surprised to hear how nervous her own voice sounded. "We are just two blocks away from the agency," she explained, "but I was wondering if, I mean, what, how . . . does the baby look like?" She was horrified. Her question sounded so superficial. She wondered what Marlene must think of her.

But Marlene just laughed. She'd heard placement jitters before. "Debbie," she said slowly and deliberately and with complete sincerity, "don't tell anyone else this but Jose. I've personally placed dozens of children, and I can honestly say that your new son is the most beautiful baby I have ever seen!"

An hour later, the foster mother walked into the presentation room at the agency and handed a ten-pound blue blanket-wrapped bundle to Debbie. Jose and her father pressed in on both sides of her as she pulled the blanket away from his face. And what a face! Debbie actually gasped.

He was indeed a beautiful baby with the roundest brown eyes, blinking questioningly at them, a rosebud-shaped mouth with a drop of formula visible in the center of his pursed lips, silky milk chocolate skin, and big black curls framing his tiny face. The baby quickly moved his gaze to his new grandpa, who was cooing at him, and smiled. "See?" exclaimed Debbie's father, "he likes his grandpa best. What a smart young man!"

Debbie never heard the laughter this comment created. She saw only the face of her son, heard only the sound of his breathing. She was aware of nothing else in the world. This was the moment she had dreamed of for years. There are no words, she thought, to describe such joy, such wonder, such contentment. She was a mother at last, and her baby was the only child on the planet. The long struggle was over.

They were a family of three, as they had always hoped they could be. Tears flowed down her face and blurred the sight she had so longed to see. She handed the baby to Jose and plucked a handkerchief from her purse. She'd never seen her husband's eyes radiate with such pride and jubilation. Could there be a happier moment in the human experience than this?

The foster mother spent time explaining how to deal with the baby's colic. It was hoped that the worst of the drug withdrawal was over, but Tomas still cried a great deal. Papers were signed, and the family headed for their car and the new infant car seat they had installed the day before. As they left the building, with the baby asleep in Debbie's arms, the new mother suddenly had an overwhelming sense of unease. Would the agency change its mind and take the baby back? Did she and Jose really know how to take care of a baby? Why did she feel like a kidnapper? It was as if the social worker read her mind. "Many people feel anxious with their first adoption," Marlene said. "They wonder if it's all too good to be true. And since they have not had time to develop a sense of entitlement, they may feel like they are going to lose their new child or that they will never bond. These feelings are normal and temporary. As you bathe and feed and rock your son, your sense of entitlement will grow. In a short while, it will feel natural to be called 'mom' and 'dad' and you will not only wonder why you ever worried about this, you will be unable to remember what your life was like before you were parents!"

Tomas slept most of the way home, exhausted from the excitement of the day, but began crying loudly as soon as they arrived. As Debbie prepared the bottle, Jose tried to comfort the baby, but his cries quickly turned to screams. "Pronto!" said a worried Jose. Debbie was right there with the bottle but Tomas continued to scream, and even though he eventually drank all of the formula and burped three times, he kept on screaming. They tried the techniques the agency had described, Debbie's dad came over and walked the floor, and still Tomas cried. After a sleepless night, they took him to the family doctor who had the baby's birth and medical records faxed to her office. After examining the baby and reading the records, she explained that Tomas was a "high needs" baby by temperament. This was exacerbated by a possible slow, ongoing withdrawal from the drugs he was exposed to prenatally. He also seemed to have some difficulty digesting the proteins in the formula, what was once called colic, so she gave them samples of other types to try.

All of the things that typically comfort most other babies made Tomas scream more, such as the white noise of a vacuum cleaner, a ride in the car, rocking, walking. Tomas cried more than half of the time he was awake, but he cried less when he had two things, two arms wrapped snugly around him and a bottle or pacifier in his mouth. The doctor had warned them never to let him "cry it out" as this could lead to emotional problems later. So they took turns holding and feeding, singing to him in between his screams, and hoping they would all survive their "high needs" experience.

They gave up trying to put him to sleep in a crib. Tomas slept in their arms, and they took turns sleeping in the rocker-recliner. They never went anywhere together because the movement of the car terrified the baby more than anything else. Tomas' crying disrupted church service so much, they asked the parishioners to pray for them and said they would not be back for awhile. Debbie was granted first one and then two extensions on her family leave time from work, and the next six months passed in a blur.

Since baths in the sink made Tomas shriek with fear, Debbie and Jose developed a new way to bathe him. They took turns sitting in the bathtub with the baby and literally bathing him in arms. He tolerated the water a bit at a time this way, but he did not like it. They learned how to change his diapers while he lay in their laps because putting him on the changing bed made him hysterical. They eventually gave up on encouraging him to scoot or crawl—he was determined never to leave their arms.

In spite of everything, however, they could not have loved him more, so they simply molded their lives to the care of Tomas and to his preferences. In weekly checks, his weight and growth showed average or better, but the doctor was concerned about his ongoing fear of everything away from his parents' bodies.

He was not making the developmental milestones like other babies in the typical range. For example, he was barely trying to say "ma-ma" or "da-da." The doctor decided to schedule him for a battery of tests at a university child study center to look at the potential for conditions like autism, developmental disabilities, and certain nervous system disorders.

Two days before the tests were scheduled to take place, Jose took Tomas to the bathtub for a bath while Debbie was cooking dinner. A few minutes later, Debbie heard Jose screaming her name. His voice was loud and strong, but not frantic. He sounded happy or excited, but shocked. She ran to the bathroom, flung the door open, and was immediately taken aback by the sight that greeted her. She had to rub her eyes to be sure she wasn't dreaming.

Just three feet in front of her, her husband sat cross-legged in the tub. Water droplets covered his face and dripped off his chin. Tomas was not held tightly in his arms while the water was introduced to his skin an ounce at a time. Tomas was not crying, sobbing or screaming. Instead, their baby was standing—a bit unsteadily but standing—in the tub with warm water up to his waist, legs wide apart, knees bent, one hand holding on to the edge of the tub, and one hand happily splashing water into his dad's face. But the really shocking thing was that he was smiling, a big ear-to-ear smile, the likes of which they had never seen before.

And he was laughing and making giggling sounds as he splashed. He looked and sounded like any other 7-month-old baby who loves bath time! It was as if someone had turned on a switch in his brain, and the world was no longer terrifying. The world was fun! And wet! Their son had just been re-born. Debbie knelt next to the tub, and the three of them splashed and laughed until everyone was soaked and their finger tips all looked like prunes.

A subsequent battery of testing showed a baby in the average to slightly below average range of development and in good health. No other conditions or disorders were identified. Tomas still had a bad night once in awhile, but from that day forward, he was much easier to care for. He began to vocalize and crawl, walked on time, and ran on schedule. He was in remedial reading until third grade, but once he caught up, he never needed special education again.

Debbie and Jose called it a miracle. Their doctor was pleasantly surprised but said that such developments were not unheard of. It is possible that Tomas' brain and nervous system just needed more time to mature and adjust to the world outside the womb. Perhaps his brain was rewiring itself, in a sense, in the early months to overcome the effects of prenatal drug exposure. It was rare for improvement to occur as suddenly as this did, but it happened. What really matters, continued the doctor, is that Tomas had patient, loving round-the-clock care during his difficult first half year. Without that, he could never have come through it with such a sweet and trusting personality. Debbie and Jose laughed to think that at one point they did not feel entitled to the names of "Mom" and "Dad." They certainly felt entitled now. Love at first sight had long ago grown into a deep and comfortable bond between parents and child.

The adoption of Tomas Santos was finalized when he was 10 months old, and when he was 5 and in kindergarten, he became a brother. His parents adopted a 4-year-old sister, Josefina, for him to play with and torment.

The family has a pool now in the backyard, and splashing Dad remains a favorite family activity.

ço oco

Extending Family

"I'm sorry, Terrie," said Ms. Frye, her social worker. "Jillian and Ellen have gone to a married couple that put their homestudy in at the last moment. I'm sure you understand that most agencies prefer to place children with couples, when at all possible. In this way, the children will have a mother and a father."

Terrie understood all right, all too well. This was the third time in as many months that she had been matched to a waiting sibling group and then lost the children to a late-applicant married couple before the first visit could take place. This last time, she had gotten very close to placement. The state had even sent a detailed file on the children's history in order to better familiarize Terrie with their needs. She had taped one of the five photographs of the girls above her computer monitor, where she could see their bright smiles often. Terrie returned the file and four of the photos but kept one. She told Ms. Frye to remember her if the adoption with the couple did not work out for Jillian and Ellen.

Couples preference runs strong. It often means that single adoptive parents may only adopt children with more severe disabilities and older children, like teenagers. It is ironic, mused Terrie, that the very people who were least able to deal with the most challenging children, parents with no spouse to help them, are the ones who are most likely to be offered such children for adoption. She understood the need for two parents for every child but couldn't help feeling a bit of resentment. She disliked being considered a "last resort" for children when she had so much to offer.

Terrie lived with her divorced mother and two older brothers. The three youngest in the family of six children had never married, but her happily single state had never dampened Terrie's desire to parent. As a self-employed attorney making a good living, she could provide all kinds of material advantages for a child or two. And her home was full of family. Her retired mother, who was almost as excited about the adoption as Terrie, was a built-in at-home baby-sitter, and her two brothers, Marcus and Paul, who owned and operated a small construction business, would provide the full-time male role models as uncles.

All she needed now were kids.

No sooner had Terrie grieved the latest loss than Ms. Frye called again with a new match. There were two children in the sibling group, a boy and girl, ages 6 and 7, Caucasian, abuse survivors, stable, and living in the same foster home, their first foster home, for the last three years. That was a good sign. When children have been in the same foster home for several years, it is an indication that they are somewhat emotionally and behaviorally healthy.

The siblings had been removed from their birthhome originally due to ne-glect. Their birthmother had turned to alcohol after the death of their father and her continued active alcoholism made foster care necessary.

Parental rights had been terminated when the birthmother disappeared from a treatment center and never came back. There was no other family available to adopt the kids. Dion had asthma and a reading learning dis-ability. Carolyn suffered from depression but was responding well to coun-seling and low doses of medication.

The foster parents had intended to adopt the children but changed their minds, opting instead to move to Florida and retire. A file was on its way, overnight mail, describing the life history of Dion and Carolyn, and she could meet the children in one week if she wanted to. The foster home was only a few miles away!

Terrie and her family read the file so many times, they had practically committed it to memory. They knew that Carolyn hated to wear her glasses and Dion had a million techniques to avoid doing his homework. There was nothing in the file that discouraged them. They had spoken to the children and to the foster parents by phone several times. Carolyn, who loved computers, had even e-mailed her new future mom. But Terrie de-cided to go alone to meet the kids, so as not to overwhelm them. If the day-long visit went well, they would start spending weekends with Terrie's family until move-in, and placement, occurred.

As Terrie maneuvered her four-wheel-drive SUV onto the street where the foster family lived, she suddenly realized she had not rehearsed anything to say. What do you say to your children the first time you meet them? "Hi. I'm your mother. Nice to meet you. How do you do?" Somehow, that didn't sound right. There were no traditions or rules to govern such an event. Her mind raced back to what she had said to her older sister's first baby on the day of her birth. As the wrinkled, bright red, squinting newborn was placed in her arms, Terrie had blurted out, "Oh! You are so beautiful!"

As she struggled to find the right words of greeting, she found herself pulling up into the driveway of the three-bedroom brick home. Before she could even get out of the car, Dion and Carolyn, who had been watching for her, burst from the house, ran across the front lawn, and almost knocked her back into the car with their welcoming hugs.

"Hi, Terrie," the kids cried in unison. "Come meet our foster parents!" As they dragged her toward the house, time seemed to stand still for a moment. How long Terrie had planned for this event! The children, no longer just photographs and voices, stood before her in 3-D. At last! Dion was tall and slender with straight dark brown hair that hung down to his eyebrows, and matching color eyes. Carolyn was more small-boned but just as tall as her brother. She had a lovely smile with perfect teeth, but her hair, the same color as Dion's, was curlier and thicker. Without even thinking about her words first, Terrie exclaimed, "Oh! You're both so beautiful!" And then she chuckled at the familiarity of the comment.

The foster parents, determined to see the children adopted by a wonderful family, relaxed as soon as they got to know Terrie a little better. They peppered her with questions about her home and family and gave her a list of the children's favorite foods and activities. They chatted over coffee for several hours until Dion asked if they could go out to lunch. "Sure," replied Terrie. Then Dion pushed the envelope a bit. "Can I drive your wheels around the parking lot?" he asked hopefully. Her first test as a mother. "Nope," she smiled, "maybe when you're 16." Terrie had passed her first mom test.

The following weekend, as the children prepared to return to their foster home for their last week there, Carolyn spontaneously called Terrie "Mom" and Dion soon followed suit. After move-in, Terrie found that frequent family meetings helped the kids learn the rules, adjust to the changes, and communicate clearly. But Terrie quickly learned to keep the meetings brief, for her brother, Marcus, cracked up the kids with mocking facial expressions if Terrie droned on too long for his tastes.

In no time at all, the children grew used to living with four adults and learned to rely on each for different needs. Terrie did parent things, like tucking them in at night and making their school lunches. Grandma taught them all kinds of cool stuff, like how to make a bed military style, so a quarter flipped on to it would bounce, and how to recycle soap chips. Uncle Marcus loved horseplay. From him, they learned arm wrestling, thumb wrestling, and flag football. He was a master of rainy day sports, too. He taught them how to play basketball indoors with just a laundry basket and some balled up socks. Marcus could make ten different kinds of paper airplanes and two kinds of paper helicopters. Finally, from Uncle Paul, Carolyn and Dion learned how to manage their allowance for maximum returns. He bought them stock for their birthdays and made them learn Quicken on the home computer before he would buy them Doom II. He also helped them start coin collections for their investment potential.

The adoption made the formerly quiet and well-ordered home noisy and disarrayed, but only Paul complained, and not very loudly or very much. Terrie had been well prepared and found motherhood a joyful experience.

No one can predict older child outcome. Every case is unique, but in Terrie's case, the adoption process turned out to be no more challenging than the children's adjustment. Perhaps it was because she had wanted motherhood so long and so much, or maybe it was the presence of her wonderful mother in the home, or possibly, Terrie was simply well prepared and patient. Whatever the reason, parenting was a great deal more fun than it was challenging. The children tested the rules and broke the rules, too, but they responded well to consequences.

When it came time to finalize eight months later, Ms. Frye joined the whole family in the judge's chambers at the county courthouse. Terrie was able to do the legal paperwork herself without hiring an attorney. After the judge signed the finalization papers, Dion asked if he could try on her long black robe. It reminded Terrie of a request by the same child, about one year ago, to drive her SUV. "Still pushing the limits, eh, son?" she teased.

Leaving the courthouse brought with it a rush of euphoria that reminded Terrie of her feelings when she first laid eyes on her children. What joy to have the adoption finalized and official! No more homestudies or home visits, no more paperwork. She breathed a sigh of relief and gave her son and daughter a huge hug.

But Carolyn and Dion were a little bit distracted. They wriggled out of Terrie's grasp and ran to join Uncle Marcus, who was balancing himself on the edge of the large stone basin water fountain in front of the courthouse. Within moments, the three of them were racing around the edge, arms extended like planes taxiing before take off, trying to balance well enough to stay dry. Terrie's eyes filled with tears at the sight of two formerly parentless children now doing something very important and utterly normal—being everyday carefree goofy kids.

Marcus, however, decided Terrie, would never be quite normal. And that was okay, too.

Adult Adoption: Charlie's Turn

Charles was born in 1968, a normal healthy baby who went home with his mother from the hospital at age 2 days. The baby's father refused to help support him and moved away. The mother, Duray, was poor and living on disability due to chronic depression and cognitive difficulties, but she was dedicated to her only child, and with a little help from a caring landlord, she took good care of him.

Right after Charlie's second birthday, Duray met a man at the supermarket and began dating him. Within three weeks, he had moved into their small, one-bedroom mobile home and had taken over every aspect of their lives from what they ate and when to how the disability check would be spent. Ironically, his name was Charles, also, but everyone called him Chuck.

The worst change was that Charlie could no longer sleep with his mom. He now slept on the sofa with an assortment of stuffed animals. It felt so much colder on the sofa. And his mother was now obsessed with pleasing Chuck. Her whole life revolved around making him happy and, especially, about making sure he never became angry.

Chuck had a bad temper. When life did not go his way, he took it out on Duray with his fists and on Charlie with his boots. Charlie learned to fear cowboy boots because when Chuck pulled them on in the middle of a temper tantrum, Charlie knew he would get kicked in the head and back again and again as he lay curled up on the floor. By the time Social Services became involved via a phone call from the concerned landlord, Charlie had already suffered brain damage from the abuse. The toddler was placed in foster care and saw Duray regularly. But no matter what the department did to keep Duray and Chuck apart so that Charlie could go home, it didn't work. Duray was determined to go on seeing Chuck and had even secretly married him. After eighteen months of foster care, it was determined that Charlie could not ever go home. Duray had made her choice, and Charlie had lost. Eventually, she stopped showing up for visits.

Under today's laws, parental rights would have been terminated sooner, Chuck would have been prosecuted for his violence, and an adoption permanency plan would have been made up, but in the early 1970s, the removal process took longer. Long-term foster care was the department's choice for Charlie. Today, foster parents are encouraged to adopt their kids if they want to, but it wasn't always that way.

The foster home Charlie was placed in was the home of Mr. Wayne and Mrs. Lavinia Smith. Wayne and Vinnie were a retired couple with a daughter, Jolene, long grown, who had wanted to open their comfortable home to a single child who needed them. Jolie technically lived at home with her parents, but her career in the Air Force kept her on the go most of the year. She traveled from base to base, checking quality control procedures for various jet maintenance crews.

Jolie and Charlie bonded instantly. The first thing she taught him was how to execute a sharp formal military salute. He was much more of a son than a foster brother to her. She brought him toy jets and planes from every city and country she visited. They kept in weekly contact via letters. The beatings had cost Charlie thirty to forty IQ points, but they never dampened his ability to love. Vinnie did the typing while Charlie dictated the adventures of the week to his big sister.

It didn't take long for the Smiths to make a commitment to Charlie. The couple devoted every aspect of their lives to his care. They told the social worker that she must never move him to another foster home. Wayne, especially, was determined that Charlie would not get lost in the system. "He's kin now as far as we're concerned," Wayne said with a smile. "We are the only family he knows and it should stay that way." They never bothered to ask about adoption because they had been told long ago that foster parents were not allowed to adopt. Just asking about it in those days could result in the child's immediate removal from the foster home.

Years passed. Jolene had married and then divorced, but her career was nothing but successful. Soon after she achieved the rank of colonel and Charlie had turned 16, Wayne died in his sleep of a massive coronary. If there had been any warning signs that he had heart disease, Wayne had suffered them in silence.

Jolene had already been granted a transfer to the Air Force base near her home and a reassignment of duties so that she would no longer be traveling regularly. And it was a good thing. The tremendous strain of Wayne's death seemed to hasten the progress of the Alzheimer's disease Vinnie had recently been diagnosed with, and within a year of the funeral, Vinnie was no longer capable of taking care of herself, much less of Charlie. Suddenly, Jolene was part of the Sandwich Generation, caught in the middle between caring for a medically fragile parent and a dependent child, in this case a foster brother.

The transition was tough at first for Jolie, who was used to caring only for herself. She had gone from a well-ordered military life of living alone to having full responsibility for her mother, a house, and a developmentally delayed teenage brother.

She coped two ways; first, by delegating. Her father had left a nice-sized nest egg for his wife and foster son, and Jolie used this to hire daytime help in two shifts. The first shift came in after Jolie got Charles off to school and cared for Vinnie until Jolie got home. The second home care helper came in for a few hours in the evening to help a restless Vinnie get to sleep.

Jolene's second coping mechanism was what she called "P & Q," the peace and quiet of doing normal stuff. Jolie and Charlie spent many quiet evenings just watching TV, chatting on the back porch, and doing homework. The slower pace helped both of them adjust to the changes and losses in their lives.

Soon, Charlie chose a career path. In his junior and senior years of high school, he spent half of his day in high school lab classes and the other half at the vocational technical college learning how to be a house painter.

Vinnie passed away the day after Charlie turned 19, while he was at work as an apprentice for a local painting contractor. Charlie clung to Jolie during the funeral, in part because she was the last family member he had on this earth. Over the next few weeks, his newfound sense of vulnerability would express itself as a lack of appetite, confusion, and loss of sleep.

Jolie was concerned about her brother, for his present state, but mostly for his future. Her parents' deaths had created in her a keen awareness of mortality. What would happen to Charlie, she wondered, if something should happen to her? Who would care for him, and how? Jolie visited a base attorney for help with her new will.

"This will is not as secure as it could be, you know," said Cecelia Bettis, the Air Force lawyer. "Since Charlie is not your legal relation, one of your cousins, for example, could contest this will, especially since the life insurance policy is substantial."

Jolie scoffed at this. "Charlie is my brother, Mrs. Bettis, and has been since the age of 4."

"A foster brother, Colonel. And now he is an adult, albeit a dependent adult. There is no legal relationship here. Unless you wish to adopt him."

Adopt. The word jumped out at her. Of course! Such a simple solution and a perfect one. Jolie had not had any idea that adult adoption was even an option, legally speaking.

Mrs. Bettis noted the smile on Jolie's face and continued. "Adult adoption is one of the simplest legal processes of all in this state. No homestudy, no six-month waiting period, no birthparent relinquishments. Just a little paperwork and a visit to the judge's chambers at the county courthouse. The judge will want to be sure that you are not adopting Charlie for an improper reason, for example, to get at a fortune he may own. But once satisfied that the adult adoption is being requested for a sound reason, it's a green light."

That evening after dinner, Jolie and Charlie sat on the back porch for a chat. "Charlie," Jolene began, "You know that I have always loved you like a brother and like a son, too, don't you? I mean, I'm more than twenty years older than you."

"Sure, Jolie," replied Charlie, "I love you, too. We're always going to be together, right?"

"That's what I am trying to be sure of, Charlie. I spoke to a lawyer today who said it would be better for us if I adopted you, in court, now that Vinnie is in heaven. Then, legally, I would be your mom for always, not just your sister. Would that be okay with you, Charlie?"

Charlie's eyes were already sparkling with excitement. The fear and insecurity that Vinnie's death had put into his heart was vanishing. He hugged Jolie tight and said, "You bet! But what will I call you after this, Jolie?"

Jolie couldn't resist an old joke. She replied, "Call me anything you like, Charlie. Just don't call me late for supper!" The atmosphere in the judge's chamber was one of restrained jubilation. Charlie, dressed in a new three-piece dark blue suit, and Jolie, in her formal dress military uniform, stood in front of the judge and swore to tell the truth. The judge remarked that it was the first time he had ever finalized an adoption where the child was taller than the mother!

Charlie answered every question with enthusiasm, and within fifteen minutes, the judge was convinced that the adoption was a good idea. Papers were signed and exchanged between the judge and Mrs. Bettis, and then the judge turned to the parent/child duo.

"It is with great pleasure, Colonel Smith, that I now pronounce you a mother and you, Mr. Charlie Smith, her son. Congratulations!"

Charlie turned sharply toward Jolie and saluted her as he had practiced in front of the mirror for days. Jolie saluted back and then burst into very maternal and nonmilitary tears.

୧ංৎ৴

Billy's Movie

One nurse was kind and one was hostile; of this much Daniella Washing-ton was aware. Having adoptive parents present at the birth of a child was not something nurse number two was used to or liked. Her attitude and voice tone made it clear that she thought of the adoptive couple as little more than a pair of vultures circling the laboring victim, ready to scoop up and run away with the newborn as soon as possible.

Nurse number one, however, was going out of her way to make everyone comfortable in what was a unique situation. Her sister had relinquished a baby for adoption years ago in an open adoption when such placements were still rare, so she had an idea of the emotions present on all sides.

Rosa King, the birthmother, age 22, was in the final stages of labor. Her mother, acting as labor coach, was holding her hand as she pushed. Daniella, the adoptive mom, was on Rosa's other side, giving her ice chips and wiping her forehead with a damp cloth. Daniella's husband, Billy, stood near the door of the delivery room filming the birth from behind Rosa's head.

The Washingtons and the Kings had grown close over the last six months, ever since Rosa handpicked the Washingtons from a pool of sixteen home-studies provided by the private adoption agency. Rosa chose Daniella and Billy because of the similarities between them and herself. They were also African American, Baptist, well-read, and they loved learning. Rosa did not wish to stop her graduate school studies and raise a child as a single parent. And her own mother's heart problems prevented her from helping much. The baby's father, a fellow student at the university where both Mr. and Mrs. Washington taught English courses, had signed away his parental rights and returned to his African homeland for good.

But even though Rosa had made an adoption plan, she saw no good reason why she should be separated from her child forever or cloak an adop-tion in secrecy. So she approached the small agency with her request and was delighted to learn that most of their newborn placements were now open adoptions to some extent. Some families used intermediaries for con-tact, some had contact only by mail, and others were completely open.

Rosa wanted the last type. She craved an honest trusting relationship with the people who would adopt her baby. She wanted to feel confident that the adoptive parents would honor the openness agreement even after the adoption was legally finalized. She hoped the Washingtons were the best choice.

The Washingtons agreed to an open adoption because they saw no reason why a stable, intelligent, loving person like Rosa should not be involved with her child's life. They signed an agreement allowing Rosa to visit the child at least four times a year for up to six hours at a time and allowing for contact by telephone, email, and letters as desired. This was a minimum. Everyone was hopeful that the relationship among the parental trio would continue to be positive so that visitations would eventually feel more like those of an aunt instead of something that was stiff and required.

Some of Daniella's and Billy's friends criticized them for this choice, but Daniella had done her homework. She'd read every book she could find on the subject, and she saw no danger of harm to the child or the parent-child relationship resulting from such an arrangement. Her main concern now was what would happen after the baby's birth. Would Rosa change her mind? Legally, nothing was stopping her from doing so.

With one final long push, a healthy 9-pound newborn girl came into the world. She had mounds of thick black hair on top of her head, slightly almond brown eyes like Rosa, dark brown skin, and a good strong voice. The two families had already chosen the name Jasmine for her. The nurse-midwife scooped the squalling baby up, cut the cord, wrapped her in a white blanket, and handed her to nurse number one, who then placed her into Rosa's outstretched arms.

Rosa kissed her daughter's soft cheeks and said loud enough for all to hear, "God loves you, Jasmine. His name is the first word you heard. Walk with God, and know that all of your parents will love you forever." Then, with a tear-streaked face that looked surprisingly at peace, she turned to Daniella. "Hey, Mom," she said, "meet your baby!"

Daniella had been watching Rosa to this point, not knowing for sure how she would react after the baby's birth, and what she saw filled her with relief and gratitude. They had all known this would be difficult for Rosa, painful beyond pain, but her eyes showed a clear determination to follow through with her carefully made plans. Now, at last, Daniella could risk a peek at the baby.

Daniella cried out unconsciously, "Oh, my Lord!" She was so happy and so much in awe, it was tough to take in enough air. Slowly, she raised her arms toward Rosa, keenly aware that they were shaking slightly. Daniella had held many nieces and nephews, but she'd never held her own baby before. She momentarily wondered if her arms would cooperate fully.

Rosa's eyes locked on to Daniella and shone with tears that spilled out of both eyes simultaneously. She blinked them away and laid her arms on top of Daniella's. For a moment, their arms touched and locked, as if one mother was transferring an energy and a strength to the other mother. Daniella's arms stopped shaking. She willed her own tears away, as she was determined not to be blinded at this, the most important moment of her life. Slowly and silently, Rosa withdrew her arms from Daniella's, leaving Jasmine behind, cradled securely. Jasmine was no longer crying but was alert, almost as if she knew this was a momentous event in her life.

Nurse number one had dimmed the lights so that Jasmine would open her eyes and look around. Newborns don't like bright lights and loud sounds. They are used to darkness, muffled sounds, and tight spaces. Daniella, aware of this, pulled the baby in close and spoke to her in hushed tones. Jasmine's eyes popped open and locked on to Daniella's immediately. Daniella felt as though her heart would burst with love. She had wanted a baby for so many years, and every fertility treatment had failed. She'd actually become pregnant twice, but she miscarried before the third month each time.

Now, finally, she was a mother, entrusted to raise a little angel. Jasmine was the most perfect and most beautiful human being she had ever seen. A daughter. A daughter!

Minutes passed in silence, all eyes on the baby. With just a twinge of regret, Daniella realized that she needed to give Billy a chance to hold his daughter. Nurse one had already taken the videocamera from him in anticipation of his holding the baby.

But as Daniella turned to hand the child to him, nurse number two stepped between them and took the infant out of Daniella's arms. "Time to weigh her," she said brusquely and headed toward the incubator and scales at the other end of the room.

"Stop, please," said Rosa. "Unless the baby is having difficulty, I would appreciate it if you would not take her away right now. Her father wants to hold her." She put a special emphasis on the word "father."

Reluctantly, nurse two handed the baby to Billy.

Billy had never held a newborn before, but he wasn't nervous. He was delighted by her delicate hands, her two adorable chins, and her perfectly formed toes, the smallest of which was almost too small to be seen. Like his wife, he was filled with so much love, his chest hurt as if he would explode with joy. He couldn't believe that he had once doubted his ability to love an adopted child. At that moment, he could not have loved any baby, any person, more than he loved Jasmine. "Welcome to the world, Jazzy," he whispered into her ear. "We're not going to spoil you. Much."

Daniella had been attending La Leche League meetings for months, and with Rosa's encouragement, was planning to breastfeed Jasmine. As with open adoption, the more Daniella had read about this time-honored worldwide practice, the more sense it had made to her. Breastmilk is best for human babies. Why not give her baby the best? Using an electric breastpump several times a day for ten minutes each session, Daniella had already established a modest milk supply. She'd saved a couple of dozen ounces of breastmilk in the freezer at home. On the second day, when they brought Jasmine home for the first time, Daniella nervously prepared to nurse her.

She sat down in her grandmother's rocking chair, where both she and her mother had once been nursed, and offered Jasmine her breast. The baby latched on almost immediately and nursed vigorously and expertly for fifteen minutes before pausing. Daniella was delighted that she could offer her baby mother's milk. She loved breastfeeding and found it convenient, as well, especially in the middle of the night.

Daniella knew from talking to the hospital lactation consultant and from her friends in the league that she could be sure if the baby was getting enough breastmilk by weighing her and by counting the number of wet diapers she produced each day. Jasmine was producing more than enough of them and gained weight steadily with only a small amount of supplement required. Daniella gave her this through a tiny feeding tube attached to her breast. In this way, the baby was getting nourishment through the slender tube even as her nursing stimulated Daniella's body to produce more milk for the next feeding. Once Jasmine was a few months old and "nipple confusion" was no longer a risk, Billy gave her the supplements in a bottle after some of the breastfeeding sessions.

The adoption proceeded on schedule, and the Washingtons kept to the letter and the spirit of the agreement between them and Rosa. Rosa said that seeing the baby lessened her grief and brought her great joy. She always snapped lots of photos at the visits.

Daniella stopped working for a couple of years, so she did not see Rosa as often, but Billy did. He almost always had a new Jasmine story to tell her. Rosa finished her master's degree with honors. She would later marry and raise three more children, including a stepson.

Jasmine grew up calling her parents "mom and dad," calling Rosa by her first name, and introducing her matter-of-factly as "my birthmother."

Every other year or so, Jasmine still sits down with her mom and dad and watches the tape of her birth and the creation of her family, the film Billy had so carefully created.

In eighth grade, in her last year of middle school, Jasmine wrote an essay that would be duplicated and become a cherished possession of all the parents. She called it "Blessings." She concluded it by saying, "No one can be loved by too many people. Many kids don't even have one parent, but I have three in my life, and a wonderful step-birthfather, too. And all of them love me for who I am. How lucky, how blessed, can one kid be?"

ᖆᖆᖆ

Jerry's Spark

"So is Carter my brother, or what?" asked 12-year-old Mike of his longtime volunteer "Big Brother," Jerry.

"Yea, sure, Mickster, in there," responded Jerry pointing to Mike's heart. "What else could he be? Ready to head to the airport to fetch him?"

As Mike kissed his mother good-bye, she handed him a bag full of cookies baked the night before and a reminder to make Jerry bring the baby inside when dropping Mike off later that evening. "We're dying to see him!" she said excitedly. She neglected to add that a surprise baby shower was being prepared for Jerry and his new son, Carter, at that very moment.

For the last five years, Jerry had thought about special needs adoption more and more. He'd always loved kids and wanted a house full of them. Before his parents died in a commercial jetliner crash, they had encouraged his dream to father lots of kids. He felt the presence of his folks now more than ever.

Jerry had been working as a junior high school science teacher since college graduation and had even signed on with the local "Big Brother" program for parenting practice. He had enjoyed spending one or two weekends a month with Mike, a young man growing up in a single parent home without a father or father figure.

Mike had lost his dad in a motorcycle accident when he was only in second grade. Part of the special bond between Jerry and Mike was that both of them knew what it was like to attend the funeral of a parent. Mike was excited about Jerry's upcoming adoption and had even attended several support group meetings with him. As far as Mike was concerned, baby Carter was his kid, too.

Single parent adoption isn't easy, but it's even tougher for men than it is for women. Homestudies are more rigorous, motivations more closely scrutinized. Everyone at the state agency had to be sure Jerry would be a good father. They wanted to see what kind of support network he had created to help him with the child. After all, there would be no grandparents unless he married someday. Jerry had his two younger sisters, both married and mothers, and Mike's mom, Clare, would be there for him. And then there were his fellow teachers and the friends he'd made at the adoption support group.

After the homestudy, Jerry found 14-month-old Carter online at the photolisting web sites. Carter had been diagnosed with severe cerebral palsy (CP) shortly after birth. His photo showed a smallish baby with bright shining eyes, wisps of blond hair, and a huge smile. He had photobonded at first sight. "This is my kid," he thought.

And he was. But there was a problem. Carter was in Arizona and Jerry was in Kansas, and Jerry didn't—couldn't—wouldn't fly. He was understandably nervous around airplanes. And a long drive wasn't conducive to initial bonding and attachment. So the Arizona adoption worker was flying Carter to Jerry.

Jerry's mind was reeling as he drove. The adoptive parent support group had warned him about last-minute doubts, and now they were upon him. His firm resolve and dogged determination were suddenly replaced with doubts. Am I crazy? What am I doing here? What do I really know about cerebral palsy?

The last question surfaced even though Jerry had read seven different books on cerebral palsy, watched three videos, and even interviewed a doctor who specialized in treating kids with CP. Jerry had felt ready to parent Carter and help him achieve in every area. But as he approached the airport, he was not only filled with last-minute worries; the sight of the airport itself unnerved him. He hated airports.

Mike was full of nervous energy as they settled in at Gate 27-B to wait on the "baby plane." He left Jerry downing one cup of coffee after another and wandered over to Gate 29-B, a flight arriving from Dallas. Mike noticed someone like Jerry, a man, obviously nervous, absent-mindedly rocking an empty stroller. When he heard the woman with him say something about adoption, he told them all about Jerry two gates down.

There were two couples, both waiting on a flight that had originated in Korea, a jet that was bringing each of them a child. Since they had arrived at the airport two hours early, (in case of flat tires, traffic jams, and the odd earthquake that might delay them!) the two couples and their families and friends wandered down to Gate 27-B to give Jerry some moral support.

"Storks don't deliver babies," Marie Kowalski said to Jerry. "Airplanes do!" The Kowalskis were expecting a baby girl, about Carter's age. They showed him the same photo, but blown up into four different sizes. This was the only picture they owned of their first child.

Mr. and Mrs. Warren were expecting a daughter, too, age 3. Mrs. Warren had her photo in a gold locket around her neck. The new daughter would be joining their family of four sons, who had been born to them. As Mr. Warren said, "We love our boys, but we were determined to have a girl, and this was the most sure-fire route we could find!"

A few minutes later, Ty Kilmer of the Arizona agency walked down the ramp with Carter in his arms. All of Jerry's fears vanished in a flash as he saw his son. Carter couldn't hold his head up too well yet, so after a welcoming hug, Mr. Kilmer helped Jerry hold him with his legs facing outward and his head resting on Jerry's chest so that Carter could see everyone. Jerry's heart filled with an indescribable joy. Mike was just staring at the baby in awe. "He's cute, Jerry! When can I hold him?"

But Jerry was not ready to let go yet. He sat down, turned his son around, and looked Carter over. There was more blond hair now—it was growing out. And his eyes were a beautiful hazel, something that had not shown up in the photolisting. Carter was a little fussy but quieted down as soon as Jerry gave him a bottle of apple juice. The new dad could not have been more relieved that his last minute doubts were nothing after all. Carter felt like his son immediately.

Ty Kilmer was not scheduled to fly out until that evening so he stayed with the new family until the stork visited Gate 29-B as well. Mr. and Mrs. Kowalski both burst into tears of happiness when their plump baby girl was placed in their arms. "In one instant, I'm a mother," exclaimed Mrs. Kowalski, "and it only took two years!" Everyone on the plane was aware of the pending adoptions, and most of them stood around after departing the flight to watch the youngsters meet their new families. There was enough happiness and euphoria for everyone to share, friend and stranger alike.

The sobs of the Kowalskis were drowned out by the cries of the Warrens' new toddler. She had not enjoyed the long plane flight and was tired and cranky. Mrs. Warren tried in vain to soothe her with a bottle and then with a toy. Finally, Mr. Warren walked her up and down the airport aisle singing her the same song he had used to calm his sons when they were her age. Within ten minutes, she had quieted and fallen asleep on her new daddy's shoulder, her long black hair dangling down his back.

The air was thick with joy and celebration. Jerry's perception of airports was forever changed from a place of family loss and grief to a place of family growth and joy. As the three family groups left the airport together, they knew their special bond would last forever. Everyone exchanged phone numbers and promised to get together regularly—to commemorate this unforgettable day. And Mike managed to keep the baby shower a secret all the way home. Jerry was completely surprised and totally delighted.

After Carter's adoption was finalized, Jerry became active in a local adoption support group for single parents called SPARK (Single Parents Adopting and Raising Kids). Eventually, he was elected president, a title he held throughout Carter's childhood. SPARK hosted an annual picnic with other groups in the area, including the international adoption support group that the Kowalskis and the Warrens belonged to.

Carter's physical therapy helped to maximize his abilities, and he was eventually able to walk with the help of special leg braces and modified crutches. With an above average IQ and a love for science, Carter thrived in school. And he liked having his dad the teacher nearby when he went to middle school.

Jerry's "little brother," Mike, grew up, went to college, and became a teacher, too. He never lost contact with Jerry and Carter.

Shortly before Carter graduated from high school, Jerry married a woman he had met at SPARK meetings. She was the adoptive mother of a sibling group of three sisters. Overnight, the men were outnumbered by females in their home, 2 to 1.

Last anyone heard, however, they were holding up just fine.

2

ADOPTION AS LOSS

Loss (noun): having lost something, being lost, the value of the thing lost, defeat, the number of dead, wounded or captured

INTRODUCTION

Just as a coin has two sides, so does adoption. Every adoption creates joy but comes about as the result of loss. Birthparents experience the physical loss of precious children. Adoptees sense the loss of the family they were born into, regardless of their ages at placement. Adoptive parents who come to adoption through infertility, as most do, have to first grieve the loss of the biological children who will never be.

Some people think we should celebrate the joy of adoption and ignore the losses. But adoption is not a one-time event; it is a lifelong process, and loss is a part of it that demands recognition and attention. More important, there is much to learn from loss and how people use it to grow. These stories are full of pain, but there is achievement, too. Valuable lessons can be learned. People sometimes turn the sourest of lemons into the most delicious lemonade. Loss is a teacher, if we will but pay attention.

What Kind of a Woman . . .

Had she not run to the bathroom at full speed, Wilma Lee Cho would have caused quite a disturbance in class. The attacks of nausea were sudden, severe, and occurred most frequently between 9:00 and 9:30 in the morning, chemistry lab time. The gifted college junior had suspicions that she might be pregnant, but she was embarrassed to go see her gynecologist.

After all, she asked herself, what kind of woman does not remember whom she had sex with, or why, or where?

Wilma had never been a party goer, so it was ironic that this began with a party. She liked to study and to learn and was dedicated to an accelerated course of study that could net her a Ph.D. in chemistry before the age of 25. Her parents, both scientists and researchers, were thrilled with her choice to go into the family "business" even though they had long expected she would pursue her love of music professionally. Wilma was a talented clarinet player as well as a science prodigy.

The last round of midterms had been particularly brutal. She was taking a heavy course load of twenty-one hours, fifteen of which were advanced classes in her major. Her refuge from the pressure was concert band where she could relax, tickle her clarinet, and revel in the serenity of music.

After the last midterm, the percussion and flute sections kidnapped quiet, shy Wilma and whisked her off to one of the infamous off-campus band parties. In three years, she had never attended one of these highly unofficial events. Tonight, unwinding, she felt entitled to some craziness. After unknowingly drinking two cups of vodka-spiked punch, Wilma remembered downing a few vodka "shots" and trying desperately to forget what she had learned from chemistry about alcohol poisoning.

What happened next was nothing but a thick fog in her mind, but she knew she left the party with an outsider, a stranger, not a student. It was raining heavily. Was he tall, short, interesting, dull? Wilma had no clue. She awoke back in her dorm room with no memory at all about how she got there. Her keys were by the bed, her money still in her pocket. Her clothes were damp and covered with mud. Shoes gone. Within a few weeks, she had morning sickness. A pregnancy test followed. And so did Wilma's tears of anguish.

She prayed for a natural miscarriage that never came, rejected the idea of abortion once she saw the incredibly tiny fetus in ultrasound, and carefully examined her remaining options. Even though her parents had offered to help her raise the baby, she had no desire to do two challenging things—raising a child and earning a Ph.D.—simultaneously. Instead, the driven young woman wanted to give her full attention to one or the other.

Also, she had never pictured herself as a very young mother. She had been born to her parents when they were in their early thirties, a parenting choice she had long wanted to emulate. She felt that she had nothing to give a child at this point in her life—financially, emotionally, or in any other way. Wilma Cho had never failed to meet a goal, and she simply could not envision derailing her entire life to be a mom.

An adoption plan was made, a local agency contacted, and a Chinese American family, like her own, located to adopt the baby. As kind as the agency was, Wilma was too ashamed for words. She declined all counseling and support services again and again. What kind of a woman, she thought, did not know the race of her baby's father? What kind of woman could give her baby away? Her silent self-torment knew no bounds.

The baby, a son who looked very much like her, was born to Wilma the following summer after a relatively short and easy labor. Lots of straight coal black hair, round pink cheeks, and a tiny mouth. He was healthy and perfect, but Wilma could hardly stand to look at him in the delivery room. It broke her heart to think of what he might one day think of her.

No one, not even her parents, could convince her to at least hold the baby and say good-bye. The hospital social worker came by her private hospital room and tried to speak to Wilma, but the new mother only stared at the walls of her room. Finally, the social worker said, "Wilma, I am clearing this room and leaving your son in the bassinet, right here next to your bed. I will be back in a few minutes. While I am gone, talk to him, please. Say good-bye. Talk from your heart. If you don't, you may regret it—no, you WILL regret it—for the rest of your life."

Everyone left. The only sound was the ticking of an old electric clock on the opposite wall. Wilma glanced at the baby. To her surprise, he was looking right at her. She thought about picking him up but changed her mind. Something told her that if she held him, she would never put him down. She leaned over the bassinet. His eyes looked for her face and found it again. He gazed at her intently, as if thinking about her every word.

"Hi . . . son, my son," she said hesitantly. "Your mother is going to be a doctor. You will be proud of me someday, very proud. Somehow, we'll find each other again . . . I want you to know that I . . . that I really do love you, but all I can give you right now is a new family."

After the relinquishment, Wilma asked not to be contacted. Even a photograph would be too painful to see. She threw her energies into her studies and tried never to look back. She never went to another party. In fact, she never played her clarinet again. Music held no joy now, only an association of emotional agony.

Graduation day dawned bright and sunny, the happiest day of Wilma's life and her crowning achievement. But when Wilma Cho finally walked across the stage to receive her doctorate, she was surprised to realize that her first thought as she left the stage was of the baby. As she looked at the diploma, it suddenly and inexplicably seemed to her that she had traded her flesh and blood for a roll of printed sheepskin and a satin ribbon. What should have been the best day of her life was instead full of intense and completely unexpected mourning. Securely locked emotional gates had burst open, spilling their emotion. At last she would grieve. She could not put it off anymore.

Where Wilma the birthmother had not allowed herself to cry before, now Dr. Wilma Lee Cho cried every day for three months, unable to work, barely able to get out of bed. Her self-esteem disintegrated. What kind of a woman, what kind of a doctor, had no control over emotion, she wondered. She refused counseling, determined to beat the blues all by herself. What kind of a person could not stop crying simply through self-control? But the self-control was elusive.

It was a brief story on the news that turned her life around, a film clip about a recent reunion of former Peace Corps volunteers. It gave Wilma an idea. Peace was exactly what she needed. Perhaps she could find peace in her soul by helping others in the Peace Corps. Almost a year to the day later, and after an intense study of the language, she was in the Philippines as a Peace Corps volunteer. She worked fifteen-hour days helping farmers increase their yields through the environmentally sensitive use of chemistry and natural substances. She loved the work, the people, and the challenge.

Eight months into her tour of duty, Wilma was giving an open-air talk to a group of farmers about organic fertilizer when she heard a somewhat familiar sound in the distance. It was a clarinet, but being played very badly. She winced twice—once at the screeching noise, and once at the thought of what the instrument itself was suffering at the hands of the incompetent attempting to play it. When her lecture ended, as soon as she could, she went off seeking the offender.

One block away, she found him, all 3 feet,10 inches of him. Name of Junior. No more than 8 or 9 years old. The black instrument was old, scratched, and dented but immaculately clean. The bamboo mouth reed was split in several places. Wilma introduced herself to Junior and promised to buy him a whole box of new reeds if he would promise not to play his clarinet until he had a proper reed in place. They shook on the deal and went off to find a music supply store in town.

On the way, Wilma found out that Junior lived at a nearby church-run orphanage. He had no memory of his family but was told he had been brought to the orphanage at age 5. Sadly ironic, Wilma thought, to be named Junior and to have no Senior around to parent you. He had swept floors at a local market for several months to earn enough money to buy the instrument from the market owner. Junior had dreamed of being a musician his whole life. Wilma liked him immediately. She enjoyed his sense of humor, his easygoing personality, and his quirky way of looking at life. Junior loved to say, "If there's enough rice to eat today, I don't have nooo problems!"

Within days, Wilma was playing the clarinet again. It wasn't a conscious decision or a difficult one; she simply started playing again because it felt right. Within a week, she was giving lessons to Junior and five other children in the orphanage. Within a month, she was scouting every village and town for miles around looking for used musical instruments to buy. By the end of her first year in the Philippines, she was spending every spare moment with her fifteen-member Children's Center Classical Music Band. Junior was her star pupil and the apple of her eye.

The decision to try and adopt Junior came as naturally to her as her resumption of clarinet playing. One day she simply voiced a thought: "Hey, Junior, would you like to come to America as my son—and stay with me?"

Junior flashed a smile and replied, "Yes, Wilma! Yes!" And then he added mischievously, "As long as there's enough rice at your house for me, too, I don't have noooo problems!"

Wilma's parents, unsure at first about her decision to adopt Junior, soon came around. The paperwork would prove formidable. Junior's ultimate adoption by Wilma would take the combined efforts of her mother and father, the attorney they hired, the Peace Corps, the local politicians (who were leaned on by Wilma's grateful farmers), her US congresswoman, and the nuns working in the children's center. But it happened.

When Wilma finished her tour of duty and headed home, she was accompanied by a backpack full of souvenirs, a battered old clarinet, and a very happy little boy named Junior Cho, who now called her "Mommy."

Dr. Cho smiled to think about the odds of such a thing happening. What kind of a woman leaves the country alone and single and comes back two years later with a son and no husband in sight?

In this case, a very happy woman, who is, at last, at peace with herself, her life, and her expectations of what she should be and is. Wilma did not adopt one child to replace another. No child can ever be replaced in a parental heart. Instead, she connected to a child who had suffered the loss of the flesh and blood closest to him, a loss she knew, too. Together, they would navigate this thing called life.

Someday, Wilma knew, she would search for and reconnect to the son she had relinquished. And maybe someday Junior would get a daddy and Wilma would give birth again. Maybe. But for today, they had each other, a couple of clarinets, and plenty of rice in the house. They had nooo problems.

ೞ☙

The Poor Little Rich Girl

Dianna Carlisle was born with a silver spoon in her mouth. As sole heiress to what became the Carlisle software empire, she never knew want during childhood. She only had to whisper the name of a toy to her dad, and it was delivered the next day. Dianna was bright and kindhearted when she wanted to be. She was also a bit spoiled. But events would conspire to humble her, a grief so great that there are few experiences in the human life span that cause more emotional anguish. Dianna would spend the first twenty years of her adult life struggling to have a baby.

Dianna, married right out of college to her childhood sweetheart, Emerson Dane III, couldn't wait to have a baby to lavish her love and attention on. But the Marquis de Sade himself could not have designed a more painful battle with infertility than what she and Emerson would endure.

It began with a false sense of security. Dianna was pregnant within three months of their first effort to have a baby. But she miscarried in the ninth week. Doctors assured her that, statistically speaking, a miscarriage in the first pregnancy was so common, it did not even lessen her statistical chances to carry another baby to term. One doctor insisted he did not start worrying until a woman's third consecutive miscarriage.

The second pregnancy developed just as easily but failed in the fourth month. The third pregnancy took longer. They tried for almost a year, and this loss would prove the most painful. The baby's heartbeat could not be found midway through the seventh month. An ultrasound confirmed that the Carlisle-Dane baby, a girl, had died.

The couple went home to wait for contractions to begin. It was almost forty-eight unimaginably horrible hours before labor was underway. When Dianna gave birth to 2.5-pound Baby Darling, as they had nicknamed her, she asked to hold the baby to say good-bye. Darling, tiny but perfectly formed, looked like she was simply sleeping. There was a peacefulness in her face, as if she had been delivered to heaven by angels. Dianna didn't even cry until the funeral. She could only feel a dullness, a numbness in her heart. She handed Darling to her husband. Emerson kissed his daughter on the forehead and dressed her in the pink sleeper outfit she would never take off.

By the time they buried Darling, Dianna had a new resolve in her heart. She would be a mother someday, no matter what it took. She whispered into her father's ear, "Can you help me get a baby?" And as he had always done, George Carlisle set about to make his daughter's wish come true. Dianna, her parents, and her husband were about to become experts in the technology of infertility by living it.

She and Emerson submitted to dozens of tests at the best fertility clinic her father could find. They wanted to find out why they could not carry a baby to term before trying to become pregnant once more. The source of the problem was unclear. Dozens of experts, from gynecologists specializing in the treatment of infertility to psychologists, went to work on the couple. The tests and treatments and experimental techniques took over their lives for the next three years. A fourth pregnancy never occurred. At one point, a therapist asked them about adopting.

Emerson liked the idea of adopting. Anything was better than going through infertility treatments. Dianna, too, was agreeable, but as an only child, she really wanted to give birth to at least one biological child to please and honor her parents. So the idea of adoption was put on the back burner.

Thrice weekly visits to the clinic continued, but no explanation for the miscarriages and the stillbirth was ever discovered. Eventually, the couple, now in their thirties, was given two options, try pregnancy again or hire a surrogate mother who would carry a baby conceived in vitro with Dianna's egg and Emerson's sperm. They chose to try again by themselves and to consider the surrogate option later.

Years passed. No pregnancy. Infertility hung over their heads like a permanent storm cloud. They tried to ignore the gloom that followed them everywhere, but it was always there, hovering.

Finally, they agreed to a new type of in vitro procedure for Dianna. But tests performed before harvesting the eggs revealed more bad news, the very early stages of ovarian cancer. Dianna's ovaries were removed, and two more years passed while she underwent cancer treatment and recovered emotionally. Fortunately, the cancer treatments were very successful and she remained in remission.

But at this point, the couple wondered aloud whether or not God was "trying to tell us something." They sought the counsel of Emerson's childhood pastor, an elderly minister who was close to retiring from the pulpit. Already somewhat familiar with their list of tragedies, Reverend Osborne listened intently as Dianna and Emerson explained their long difficult story of the pursuit of parenthood.

"Are we being punished," asked Emerson, "for something we did to someone in another life?" Dianna wanted to know if this was God's way of teaching her that some things in life don't come so easily. "Am I being scorned by God because my family is wealthy?" she cried.

Reverend Osborne shook his head from left to right. "No, no, no. I don't believe that your troubles are the result of either of those things. Look at what happened to Lot, in the Bible. He did nothing to deserve his suffering, but by keeping faith, he was blessed many times over. You see, when people don't lose their faith in God's plan, bad things have a way of making good things happen that otherwise could not have occurred."

The minister stopped to light a cigar, his "favorite vice," and went on. "For example, last year, my 90-year-old father passed away after a long battle with emphysema. You'd think a man my age could get along pretty well without his daddy, but his death devastated me.

"I felt completely alone and a little terrified without his counsel, without him. Remember? I took a month off from the ministry because I felt so ineffective. During that month, I spent lots of time with other family members I had lost contact with. I reconnected to cousins and second cousins and my dad's youngest sister, who has always been one of my favorite aunts. I emerged from this period of grief feeling emotionally strong and as though I had gained a whole new family. True, no one can replace my father, but do you see my point? Something good eventually came out of something bad."

"Yes, Reverend, I see your point," said Dianna, "but our pain is so immense! Proverbs says that the barren womb is never satisfied. How well I understand that! What good can possibly come out of two miscarriages, a stillbirth, ovarian cancer, and almost two decades of wanting, desperately wanting an infant?"

"My child," replied the minister, leaning forward to take her hands in his, "my loss does not compare with your tragedies in the scope of its horror, but I assure you that when I heard the news that my father had died, I could not imagine any good coming from it. All I can do is remind you of God's promise. If we keep the faith, eventually we will know what to do next. He will light up the path."

Adoption resurfaced as an option soon after that discussion, and to Dianna's delight, her parents and her parents-in-law all supported the idea enthusiastically this time. Mr. Carlisle hired the best independent adoption facilitator in the state. Money was no object. He had spent more than a quarter of a million dollars on the infertility tests and treatments. Another $30,000 to $50,000 to adopt a healthy newborn would not be a problem. The homestudy was written in just a few weeks.

The birthparents located by the facilitator, Phyllis and David Dwyer, ran a small coffee shop below their apartment. They chose Emerson and Dianna as their favorite adoptive couple because they were drawn to their personalities during an interview. However, they wanted to know them better before placing with them. They wanted the couple to meet their whole family, too.

The facilitator drove Dianna and Emerson to the downtown business district where the Dwyers lived and worked. The coffee shop, part of Mrs. Dwyer's inheritance, had to be fifty years old. It was tiny but very clean. No more than twenty customers could be served sandwiches and drinks at the same time. The upstairs apartment was more spacious, running the length of several businesses below it, and sparsely furnished. There were seven people and an elderly yellow cat named Dandelion living in the three bedrooms. When Phyllis had become pregnant again, just one year after her last birth, they decided on an adoption plan. They did not want more than five children because they could barely afford to raise the kids they had now.

Mrs. Dwyer explained to Dianna that most of the women in her family were "superfertile," and managed to become pregnant repeatedly no matter what kinds of birth control methods were used. Mr. Dwyer was scheduled for a vasectomy in the near future, since everything else had failed them.

As she looked around the apartment and at the children, Dianna could not help but marvel once more at how unfair life can be. She could not have even one baby in spite of Herculean efforts, but this couple could not prevent pregnancy no matter what they tried, had more babies than they wanted, and were relinquishing one. But she would not give in to bitterness. She tried to remember Reverend Osborne's admonition to never lose faith. Everything was part of God's plan, she reminded herself.

Dianna and Emerson enjoyed meeting the Dwyer kids. They were smart, verbal, curious, and very polite, especially the oldest, Tom, age 8. The couple was peppered with questions about how they would raise "our baby brother." When Tom had been unable to talk his parents out of the adoption, he focused on the openness agreement. He wanted to know how Dianna and Emerson felt about it. Could he, for example, talk to his little brother by telephone on Christmas morning to find out what he got?

Months passed and Dianna and Emerson visited with the Dwyer family several more times and had the Dwyer family over for supper, too, at their place. The more they got to know the children, especially the charming and engaging Tom, the more excited they were that their child would share these characteristics. And they were very comfortable with the idea of keeping the adoption open.

Phyllis had obtained excellent prenatal care, and the last month of the pregnancy went flawlessly. One morning, about a week after her due date, Emerson received a call from the facilitator.

Baby Boy Dwyer, he said, now named Jeremy, had been born at 2:05 A.M. and was healthy and hearty. Phyllis was fine, too. But there was just one problem.

Somehow, perhaps from the somber voice tone, Emerson knew what it was before he ever heard the words: "They have changed their minds. I'm so sorry, Emerson."

No one had called them to come to the hospital, because Phyllis had decided against the adoption plan with the very first labor pain. David had been having doubts for weeks but didn't voice them until Phyllis talked about her own change of heart. Both of them felt awful about the pain this would cause for their new friends. No one was more surprised than they that they had changed their minds. Adoption had felt so right for so long. But now, suddenly, it was the last thing on earth they wanted.

"Just one of those things that happens in independent adoption. Happens all the time. Some couples lose five or six healthy newborns in a row before an adoption happens," said the facilitator. Once again, Dianna and Emerson faced loss, a bottomless pit of sorrow and pain so black and cold that they had to cling to each other for fear of being swallowed up in it.

Days passed and Dianna thought back on Reverend Osborne's words. Could good ever come of this? What should they do next? She decided to think about it, to do something simple. She would buy a pillow and embroider that last part of his advice. It would become her daily prayer, "Lord, show us the way."

After more grieving, they looked into international adoption—$20,000 to go to Russia, but just $15,000 to go to Korea, a six- to twelve-month process. They looked into adopting a sibling group with special needs through the county adoption agency. No charge, roughly the same length of time. They attended an adoption support group meeting, read brochures, and looked at some videos, but both of them were tired, tired to the marrow of their bones. In the end, they decided to take a break from the business of babies, kids, and adoption. They celebrated their twentieth wedding anniversary by taking a long, relaxing, carefree cruise to South America and back.

Near the end of the cruise, feeling refreshed, Dianna decided to finish embroidering her pillow. Emerson helped by picking the colors for the words and designing the border around them. The small pillow, covered in blue cotton, had the words "Lord, Show us the way" embroidered in multicolored thread. The border, a series of small flowers and leaves entwined on a vine, was done in greens and pinks.

As Emerson and Dianna arrived home from the cruise, the phone in their penthouse apartment was ringing. Throwing down their suitcases, Emerson picked up and listened for a couple of minutes, saying only, "Yes, it is," and "Yes, we are," and "Yes, all of them, yes! Absolutely!" Then he motioned frantically for Dianna to pick up the extension on the other side of the room. She stopped the unpacking and ran for the cordless phone.

"I hope you don't mind a call from out of the blue like this, but I understand you already have a homestudy, so I thought it would be alright. After all, it is not an easy thing to find one home for six children, and Tommy said you were—well, his exact words were, 'Pretty cool!' "

Mr. and Mrs. Dwyer had been killed in a tragic automobile accident a few days prior, while returning from a night of dinner and dancing to celebrate their own anniversary. It had been raining heavily, and while swerving to avoid an animal in the road, their car had gone over a bridge and into a rain-swollen creek. This left all six of their children orphans, with no relatives willing to adopt them all together. They were about to be split up three ways among two sets of very reluctant aunts and uncles and one foster home when Tommy remembered Dianna and Emerson.

"Emerson and Dianna have an apartment big enough for all of us, a room already set up for a baby like Jeremy, and they have enough room for Dandelion, too," Tommy had declared to the state social worker. "And neither one of them is allergic to cats."

"Well, what do you think so far?" asked the county social worker. "Could you bring a copy of your homestudy to my office immediately? We don't want these children to spend one more night in the emergency children's shelter than necessary."

Emerson looked a few feet away to his wife, whose eyes were glistening with happiness as she clutched the phone and whose many losses were suddenly a fading memory.

She said nothing but plucked a certain blue pillow from the top of her suitcase where it had been laying and threw it at her spouse. It hit him in the head and bounced into his arms. He laughed. "We'll be right over. Just tell us your street address, ma'am," he replied, "and I assure you that the Lord will show us the way!"

❦

The Wisdom of Solomon

Rebecca Solomon grew up knowing she was adopted, but she never felt a strong curiosity to know why, or who her birthparents were. For a long time, she thought she might be abnormal in this regard, but she eventually met enough adoptees to realize that everyone handles being adopted in their own way.

Her parents adopted her when they were in their late forties, and she was just 2 years old. They had heard about her from their rabbi. Rebecca would be their only child. She majored in business in college and, soon after graduation, went to work in her father's retail outerwear business. She was the new advertising and marketing manager. She loved using her imagination and artistic skills to sell the coats and jackets her father designed and her mother made.

On the night of her twenty-fourth birthday, Rebecca tossed and turned. Sleep would not come near her, and when she did doze off, she always awoke, terrified, a few minutes later. But she couldn't remember the nightmare. Finally, she headed to the kitchen for a glass of milk. Her mother was there looking similarly sleep-deprived. Mrs. Solomon had also had trouble sleeping that night. She could not remember her nightmare either, but only knew that sleep was not being friendly that evening. Over their milk, they discussed what to do if their bad dreams returned.

"If you can remember the dream, perhaps you can conquer it. To remember your nightmare," said Mrs. Solomon, "do what my mother taught me. Say three times out loud, 'I will remember my dream,' and say it right after you close your eyes to sleep."

Rebecca tried it and it worked, but as it turned out, remembering the dream did not bring her understanding about it. Her nightmare's setting was a pitch blackness, out of which wafted a feminine voice calling her name, a voice she had never heard before but that sounded familiar anyway. When she woke the next morning, her first thought was to find her birthmother, and she did not know why.

Carefully, she broached the subject of a search to her parents and was delighted to discover that they had been trying to find a way to suggest to her that she think about it! "We love you so much, Rebecca," said her father, "that we are naturally curious about your birthparents. We want to meet them, too!"

Mr. Solomon asked his brother, Uncle Mort, a police captain, to help them search, and to their surprise, it only took Mort a few days to come up with a phone number. He used the original birth certificate, which the agency had given them at the time of placement, and checked some old phone books from the local library. The Gold family had moved a few times but not out of state.

By now, Rebecca could think of little else but her birthfamily. Would she have siblings? Would her two sets of parents like each other? Would she finally discover which relative gave her those too-short, funny-looking toes on the end of her feet?

The phone number rang at a house just one county away. A woman, sounding like she was in her forties, answered the phone. Rebecca's hand was shaking, and her voice followed suit. "Is this Mmmm, Mrs. Gggg, um, Mrs. Gold?"

"Yes, it is," replied the voice. "Who's this?"

"My name is Rebecca Solomon, and I'm looking for my birthmother, Alice Gold. Are you—"

"Just a moment," said Mrs. Gold, "I need to put you on hold."

The phone went silent so fast, Rebecca wondered for a moment if it had been hung up. This was not the reaction she had expected. She had prepared herself to hear sounds of joy, a shocked silence, even a denial, but she hadn't expected to be immediately put on hold. What did that mean? Did her birthmother not to wish to speak to her? Moments passed like months, but a male voice picked up the phone after awhile and said, "Are you still there, Rebecca?"

"Yes," she spoke in a whisper, afraid of what he would say next, "I'm still here."

"Rebecca, I'm your birthfather, Donald Gold. I'm surprised, but happy that you found me. The woman who answered the phone is my wife, Betty, your, well, your birth-step-mother."

"Hello, Donald. I'm glad that you are happy about this. I've been anxious to meet you and my birthmother. My parents are, too. They helped me with this search, you know. . . . Do you . . . know where . . . my birthmother is?"

"I do," replied her birthfather, "but I can't tell you on the phone. Can you and your parents meet me for dinner tomorrow? I'll bring you some photos, too."

Rebecca did not sleep a wink that night. Why could he not tell her? Was her birthmother a criminal? Was she on the run? Was she mentally ill and living in an institution? Donald had said he couldn't tell her. What prevented him from doing so? It was a mystery with no answer that she could fathom. Finally, the hour arrived for their meeting. The location was a local French restaurant. Rebecca's parents ordered her some soup and a salad to eat, but she knew she was much too nervous to think about food.

She knew Donald the moment he walked in, and he walked straight toward her. He looked just like her! There was her jutting chin, her good posture, her perfect ears, and her sandy brown hair. She would have to fight the temptation to ask if she could see his toes! Betty, who looked about a decade younger than Donald and had a large brown bag slung over her shoulder, let go of his arm so that father and daughter could embrace. Before a word was spoken, everyone present had tears in their eyes.

Immediately, Betty pulled a small photo album out of her shoulder bag. It was full of photos of a lovely young woman with Rebecca's eyes. Several of the pictures showed her sunbathing at the lake. Stifling a laugh, Rebecca saw some odd looking toes. Well, that mystery was solved.

After introductions and orders for the waiter, Donald took Rebecca's hands in his and told her what she wanted to know without waiting to be asked. "Rebecca, I'm sorry to tell you that your birthmother is dead. She died right before I relinquished you for adoption. As you might guess, it is because of her death that I gave you up for adoption. There were no grandparents to help me raise you, and I didn't think I could do right by you all alone. Fortunately, the adoption agency said they knew of a couple who attended a nearby temple. They called the rabbi, and the rest, you know."

Dead. No wonder he had wanted to tell her in person. Death was the one scenario Rebecca had not allowed herself to consider. Perhaps this was one reason why she never thought of searching as a child. Perhaps she knew somewhere deep in her heart that her birthmother was gone. "How did she die? Was it an accident of some kind?"

That question caused a cloud to come into Donald's eyes and a look of confusion. "Cancer," he mumbled, looking deflated and sad. "I thought the agency had told you about your own risk of cancer. She was just 25, about your age. It was the same damn breast cancer that took her mother, too, and one of her aunts. Since some breast cancers have a strong genetic component, I had asked the adoption agency years ago to forward a medical history to you. I guess they failed to do that or that, for some reason, you never received it."

"We never saw any medical history!" said a horrified Mrs. Solomon. "We have to get you into the doctor's office right away and discuss this family history with her!" Rebecca was a little surprised to see such concern in her mother's eyes. But then, Rebecca didn't know the first thing about breast cancer.

Another sleepless night, and Rebecca underwent two different mammograms the next day as a precaution. The doctor ordered tests with two different technicians so as to be able to have lots of film to study. The first mammogram was negative, but the second one resulted in a call-back, an ultrasound, and eventually a small lumpectomy. Normally, a biopsy would precede a lumpectomy but the suspected tumor was so small, the surgeon took it all.

Rebecca had breast cancer, all right, but it had been caught in the earliest possible stages, a tumor too small to be seen with the naked eye. Her doctors were thrilled and highly optimistic that Rebecca would beat the cancer. She was young, healthy, and the cancer had just formed and had not spread beyond that single site. She had everything in her favor.

Various other treatments followed surgery, all with good results. At her first follow-up visit, Rebecca sat with her mother while the oncologist gave her the good news: "No sign of cancer."

As they prepared to leave, a nurse said, "You know, most 24-year-olds don't come in for mammograms, especially when they have not experienced any symptoms or felt a lump. What made you come to us?"

Remembering her nightmare and believing it to be a message from her birthmom, Rebecca squeezed her other mom's hand and explained, "Well, you see, my two mothers made me come. It's tough enough to say no to one mom, but it's impossible to deny two of them!"

With her cancer in remission, Rebecca Solomon vowed to devote her spare energy to raising money for breast cancer research. She became active in breast cancer support groups. And she started giving talks to groups of young women about the importance of early detection.

"I suffered the loss of my birthmother twice," she told them. "I lost her to breast cancer when I was two years old, and as a grown woman wanting to find her, I lost her again when I learned of her death. However, from loss came my personal survival. In a sense, I lost her twice, but she gave me life—twice."

❧

A Photobonding

"But all children need the unconditional love of a real family, Lou, and besides, does this baby not have just as much of a right to a happy, normal family life, regardless of how long he might live?" Edie had thought long and hard about this. Urgency shone in her eyes as she attempted to convince her husband to just consider this child. That's all; just think about it.

Lou Francis already knew deep in his heart that his wife of twenty-five years was on to something. He was fighting the idea of adopting a baby with a terminal condition only because the idea of burying a child was almost too much to contemplate. But then this cross was not much to bear considering what the baby himself had to carry. Jeremiah had been born with a rare condition called annencephaly. Most of his brain was missing, had never formed. The brain stem kept the child alive by performing automatic tasks like breathing, blinking, and digesting. No one knew how long he could or would live—maybe months, maybe years—but there was no way he could have a normal lifespan. Miah, as the nurses where he was born had nicknamed him, was blind, deaf, mute, and, of course, profoundly retarded, but there was more to him than just his near-fatal birth defect.

Everyone who knew him swore he had an endearing spirit and a personality, a sweetness. His pediatrician called the child completely unresponsive, but those who took care of him saw something else. They could feel his muscles relax when he was touched. They could sense that he knew when he was rocked and that he liked it. The neonatal intensive care unit nurses said that caring for Miah was a joy, plain and simple.

The more the case worker told Edie, the more she knew that Miah was the perfect child for them. Caring for a terminally ill child was a difficult calling, to be sure, but it was not without its rewards. The dying are closest to God and to heaven, after all, and she wanted to help Miah on his journey to eternity. She wanted to help him enjoy every moment he could have on Earth. The more she prayed about it, the more she knew that the joy of parenting this child while alive would greatly outweigh their grief at losing him.

Lou admitted that it wasn't as though the Francises had not enjoyed the typical parenting experience. They had raised two biological sons and a daughter to adulthood and watched them go to college and become productive citizens. They had also fostered five different children over the years on a short term basis for a local adoption agency. It wasn't so easy to let go, even when a foster child was going into a good adoptive home or to a loving relative, but to lose a child to death would be tougher.

Still, Lou's heart beat a little faster when he thought of this tiny infant and how much he needed to feel loved by a forever family. His prayers led him to conclude that not only did they have a calling for this child, but it would be a privilege to usher him into the next life.

The Francises concluded, after lots of contemplation, that children like Miah were a good match for people like them. As soon as they told this to their social worker, she e-mailed them five scanned Polaroids. Miah was a beautiful baby with clear skin and lots of straight dark brown hair. He was half Caucasian and half Japanese. His birthparents, both high school students, had planned to relinquish their baby for adoption all along. When the full extent of Miah's problems was discovered, the prospective adoptive couples lined up to apply for him vanished. The state agency was now forced to look out of the state for a family.

And it was time for Miah to leave the hospital. Who would take him home? Mr. and Mrs. Francis were the only ones to step forward, and with each passing hour, their excitement grew. A baby in the house again! Edie grabbed the basket of baby clothes from the top shelf in her bedroom closet and began sorting out the smallest sizes.

An adoption specialist by the name of Katrina Givens called Edie on a Friday morning to tell her that Miah would be ready to leave the hospital on Monday. Could she and Lou be ready to fly to Detroit from their home in Houston by Monday? Yes, they'd be ready. Lou immediately got online to find airline schedules, but no sooner had he disconnected from the Internet than the phone rang again. It was Katrina with an important question.

Miah's doctor had just told her that the baby would need a fairly simple operation in the next two weeks to repair an umbilical hernia. He could do the surgery on Tuesday and Miah would be ready to fly home a few days after that, or the couple could come to Detroit on Monday and then take Miah to their local hospital for the surgery. "Which scenario do you prefer, Edie?" asked Katrina. "It's up to the two of you."

"Well . . ." replied Edie slowly, "Lou and I have always made tough decisions by asking ourselves which path is best for the child. Seems to me that Miah would be happier being taken care of after surgery by people he already knows and that he'd be better off being operated on by the people who have cared for him since birth. As much as I want that beautiful angel in my arms right now, I think it might be better for him if he has the surgery there on Tuesday."

"You know, those are good points," said Katrina. "I like the way you think."

It was decided that Edie would fly out on Monday anyway and stay nearby to be with Miah until he was able to come home. Lou would take off work and join her at the end of next week so that they could bring Miah back home together. While Edie spent the next two days preparing a diaper bag and a nursery in the spare bedroom and packing her own clothes, Lou stayed busy e-mailing photos of Miah to dozens of different friends and relatives. Their kids rushed home to hold the photos of their new baby brother and to help ready the house. The entire weekend passed in a flash of excitement, celebration, and preparation.

Lou returned home from the airport on Monday tired but happy. Edie had been glowing that "pregnant glow" as she boarded the "Adoption Express" to Detroit. He stretched out in his favorite chair for a nap, but the phone rang before sleep took him over.

It was Katrina and she sounded somber. "I'm so sorry, Mr. Francis, it is my sad duty to tell you that Miah passed away on the operating table a few minutes ago. His heart simply stopped, inexplicably, and would not start up again. Has your wife already left for Detroit?"

Lou fell back into his chair and wondered which horrible thought to think first, how to deal with losing a son he'd never met or how to console his wife who would be hundreds of miles away from him when she heard the devastating news. His mind raced to find some way to help Edie.

Automatically, he said a silent prayer, and then an idea formed in his mind as if coming out of a fog and revealing itself. Quickly, he shared it with Katrina, who was immediately enthusiastic and promised to implement the plan as soon as she could call her supervisor. Lou called his kids and told them to come home and wait with him by the phone. Edie would be calling them in a few hours, and she would need their love and support more than she ever had before.

Katrina shared the sad news with Edie at the airport a few hours later, although Edie could have guessed it by the sorrow and tears-induced redness in the social worker's eyes. The mother asked only two questions: Did Lou know, and could she see Miah to say good-bye? Katrina answered yes to both. All the way to the hospital, Edie wept quietly into a handkerchief, saying nothing.

Miah lay in a little glass bassinet in the morgue, wrapped tightly from the neck down in a blue hospital blanket. Edie was grateful that they had not put the baby on a cold steel slab. His face, eyes shut, was a portrait of peace. She picked him up and held him close, kissing his cheeks several times. To say good-bye, she did the same thing she had done with her other babies to say good night—she sang him a lullaby. Then she asked for a small cup of water and baptized him by pouring it slowly over his forehead and saying the age-old sacramental words.

"Lou would want me to do this," she explained to Katrina. It's what we believe."

Lou had wanted something else done, too. He had asked Ms. Givens to make sure that Miah's organs were donated to any other children who could use them. Katrina's supervisor signed the consent forms, and every usable organ had been harvested before Miah left the operating room. When Katrina told this to Edie, she broke down and wept loud and long, holding Miah in her arms while Katrina held Edie in hers.

They were tears of gratitude. "Now this baby will not only live on in my memory and in heaven; his organs will live on in other children. That's a blessing if ever there was one."

Photobonding is a process by which an adoptive parent falls in love with and bonds to a child they have never met, a child they have only seen in a photo or, in some cases, only read about. It is a process many people cannot understand and one that psychologists have not yet studied adequately. But for people who have experienced photobonding, it is very real and very powerful. Miah's adoption was never finalized in a court of law, but it is a forever thing in the minds and hearts of the family who loved him completely and lost him too soon.

৩৯৽৵

An Ordinary Family

Jim Chaney and Ryan McLaughlin had been together for eight years. They owned and operated a successful sporting goods store in a large midwestern city. Ryan was a talented runner who often placed in his age group in regional road races. Ryan's status and the store's sponsorship of running clinics and races drew runners from all over the area.

Jim discovered he had a flair for marketing and ran the financial side of the partnership. In his spare time, he indulged his passions for cooking and music. He was a fair piano player and could play a mean blues harp. Jim and Ryan were members of the local chamber of commerce and parishioners at a downtown church. The men were quite sure that there were elements of the local citizenry who disapproved of their union, but during their four years in town, no one had gone out of his way to express those views. Both were active in Stonewall Union, an advocacy organization, and once a year they participated in the gay pride parade. For the most part, however, they lived a quiet life, and their cordial relationship with customers, neighbors, and business associates was primarily due to the fact that Jim and Ryan seemed like nice guys, like regular people.

Life was good for Jim and Ryan, but it had not always been that way. Ryan had grown up with a sister in a middle-class family. As a boy, he played sports, made good grades in school, and had the usual number of friends. But for as long as he could remember, he felt different from other kids. In the midst of a family gathering or field trip, this funny feeling would come over him, like these familiar people were suddenly strangers. The episodes left him vaguely disturbed and frightened, but he couldn't figure out why. Thankfully, they didn't occur that often, and most of the time he managed to push them aside and carry on as a regular suburban kid. As an adult, he looked back on his childhood as a happy one.

In high school, Ryan's small stature was balanced out by success on the cross country and track teams. He had a quiet, gentle voice, but no one thought he acted "gay." Ryan took a date to the junior prom and joined his friends in fag jokes. He continued to do well in his studies. Outwardly he was fine, but the dark feelings of estrangement began to occur more frequently and Ryan went through periodic bouts of depression.

Ryan discovered his sexual orientation when he went away to college, and it filled him with a powerfully mixed sense of liberation and fear. After a difficult freshman year, things got better with the help of the campus gay, lesbian, and bisexual student group and an empathic counselor at the campus health center. But halfway through the second semester of his sophomore year, the big question still loomed. Should he come out to his family? The counselor encouraged him but didn't push. One weekend, on a visit home during the spring, he went out shopping with his older sister Karen. On the way home, they decided to grab some coffee and take it to a nearby park overlooking the river.

"There's something I want to tell you," said Ryan. His throat was so dry, he could barely get the words out and his heart was hammering in his chest. After a few false starts, he told her his secret in a halting voice. His sister didn't say a word but stepped forward and hugged him. "I kind of suspected you were going to say that, but for a minute you had me going. I thought maybe you had cancer or something serious."

"You mean . . . you . . . knew?"

"Not for sure. But I wondered from time to time. I figured if you were gay, you'd tell me when you were ready."

Tears of relief ran down his face and for a few minutes he couldn't speak. Later, they talked about coming out to the rest of family.

Two months later, Ryan sat with Karen and his parents at the kitchen table. Jerry and Cheryl McLaughlin felt the usual waves of conflicting emotions: fear, disappointment, fierce protectiveness, and love. Like most parents of gay children, their first impulse was to question their own responsibility in shaping their son's sexual orientation. "Was I too distant or too affectionate?" "Was I a bad role model?" "Too strict, too soft?" "Too masculine, too feminine?" In time, they would realize that they had little to do with Ryan's sexual orientation, only with his capacity to love and treat other people with respect.

Ryan knew that his father would have a harder time accepting it than his mom. His mom did most of the talking. His dad remained silent, with a look on his face that registered pain and confusion. Finally, he got up, walked over to his son, grasped his hand, and kissed him gently on the forehead. "I can't say that this isn't gonna take a little getting used to," he said, "but it seems to me that, that you're basically the same young man now that you were yesterday, a young man I'm proud to call my son."

"A year later, Cheryl McLaughlin was elected vice president of the local PFLAG chapter (Parents and Friends of Lesbians and Gays). Jerry McLaughlin was lower keyed, but he never wavered in his commitment to Ryan. Later, Ryan's parents became very close to Jim, especially Jerry, who, as he neared retirement age, developed a passion for Cajun cooking. Jim was as fanatically interested in cooking as Ryan was addicted to running.

To Jim, it always seemed like he'd been switched with some other kid in the nursery and dropped into the wrong family. He resembled his father and two older brothers, but the physical similarity only served to heighten the differences between them. Jim's father, Frank, was a strapping man, a high school football and baseball star, peewee league coach, and big time sports fan. Walt and Vince, his brothers, were always chosen first in neighborhood games and carried their father's athletic legacy into their teen years. Walt quarterbacked the district championship team his senior year and earned an athletic scholarship to a small school in the Southeast. Vince started as an outside linebacker as a sophomore on that same championship team.

Everyone expected Jim to follow the Chaney tradition. But where Walt's and Vince's size was a source of speed and power on the athletic field, Jim's large body seemed to rebel against his every move. He tried baseball and football in an attempt to please his dad and brothers, but the harder he tried the worse he played. Jim was bigger than most of the other kids but had few aggressive instincts, which made him even more conspicuous and embarrassed.

Jim's size and gentle disposition identified him as a target of opportunity for neighborhood and school bullies. The very traits that would make him a popular businessman, an ideal neighbor, and empathic friend in adulthood, branded him as easy prey as a kid. By middle school, taunts of "fag," "homo," and "queer" became a normal part of his day. Jim wasn't the mincing stereotype of homophobic movies and TV, but he lacked the testosterone swagger favored by adolescent boys. Fueled by confusion and insecurity about themselves, middle school predators recognized something different in Jim, even if they didn't know what it was. Frank tried to teach him to fight back, but it was no use. Frustrated by his inability to protect Jim and shamed by the prospect of raising a sissy, Frank failed to see how much courage it took for his son to get through the day.

By the age of 14, Jim knew that the taunts were true. He was gay. He was a fag. Years later, Jim would tell Ryan that in some ways he always knew he was gay. Jim could still see the pain in his parents' faces as they sat in the den that night, tears streaming down his mother's cheeks. They loved him, they truly did, but they believed that homosexuality was a sin and perversion and told him so because they honestly feared for his soul. "The choice is yours," his father finally said. "You can be a homo. I can't stop you. But not under this roof. If you decide to live a homo lifestyle, then you are not a member of this family."

Three days later, he took off. He landed in a large city a hundred miles away and soon exhausted his paltry resources. For several horrible weeks, he lived on the street, hung around gay bars, and had several sexual experiences with older men. One night, he tried to kill himself with a combination of pills that were as available as chewing gum.

He woke up in the psych ward of a local hospital. That afternoon a man walked into the room and introduced himself as Paul Beck. Beck was director of an organization for gay teens called Kaleidoscope. The agency operated a residence for runaway teens and a mentoring program for gay teens living at home. Jim was too depressed to say much that day, but Beck came back the following afternoon.

As he took a seat by the side of Jim's bed, a news program showed footage of a gay pride parade held in the city the previous weekend. The camera panned to a small knot of demonstrators. One held up a sign proclaiming "GOD HATES FAGS!"—the same slogan that would appear at the funeral of Matthew Shepard some years later.

"Do you believe that?" asked Jim pointing at the picture on the screen.

"Do you?" asked Beck.

"I think my parents do," said Jim sadly.

"Well, I always get a little nervous around people who proclaim to have a corner on the mind of God. It's hard for me to believe that God hates anything, let alone His own creation. You ever think that maybe God doesn't really care about who we love, but only how much we love and that we love."

Jim looked at Beck. "I would have given anything to have been more like my dad and brothers," he said wistfully.

"Did you wake up one morning and decide that you were going to be gay to spite your family?"

Jim laughed for the first time he could remember. He thought a lot about what Beck said over the next year. As a 16-year-old, he was eligible for the state's independent living program and moved into Kaleidoscope House. Beck and a child welfare caseworker contacted Jim's parents to let them know he was safe. After two months at the house, Jim began writing letters home but received no replies, except for a brief note from his mother saying that she was praying for him. He had a few awkward phone conversations with his mom during his senior year but was never invited home, even for Christmas. The only thing he heard from his brothers were angry letters blaming him for upsetting their mom and breaking their father's heart.

Jim continued to grieve over the loss of his family during his early years in college, but he was also traveling his own road to self-acceptance. With Ryan and his parents, he found a new family. The McLaughlins had loaned them the money for the store. Jim sometimes thought, with a mixed sense of irony and sadness, just how stable his life had turned out in comparison to his two brothers. Although they rarely communicated, Jim knew that Vince was going through a bitter divorce after five years of marriage, and his oldest brother, Walt, had been married three times.

Something, however, was still missing in their lives as they left their twenties behind. Gradually the men realized that the something was kids. They wanted kids. They were ready to be dads and to pass on to children what they had learned about the world and about life.

At first, Jim and Ryan tried not to dwell on their unfulfilled need more than necessary. Jim spent more time volunteering with the youth group at church. There, he was a mentor to kids. Ryan spent more time with his sister's twins, taking them to the zoo, to work, to the movies. But spending time with kids made them want kids of their own all the more. It was Ryan who suggested adoption and showed Jim the web site where all of the waiting foster kids in their area were listed.

Jim was drawn to the photolistings of Marcos and Ramon, 9- and 10-year-old brothers. Marcos had an 85 percent hearing loss, and Ramon, a 90 percent sight loss. The brothers supplied the eyes and ears for each other and were inseparable, physically and emotionally. Jim knew both the trauma of losing a family and the joy of finding one. The boys' devotion to one another in the face of their own losses touched him deeply. His imagination raced with ideas of becoming their father and modifying their home to make it a safe and happy place.

But first things first. No social worker will discuss placing waiting kids with a prospective family that has not had a homestudy completed and approved. Homestudies, far from being tools to locate perfect people, are designed to weed out adults who are not ready to be parents or who would not be good parents. Jim and Ryan knew they would have no trouble passing a homestudy if they could surmount just one obstacle: finding an agency that would work with a gay couple.

Adoption agency A said they would allow either man to fill out an application to adopt as a single parent but would not work with them as a couple. Agency B was sympathetic but pointed to their charter as an agency affiliated with a church that did not allow openly gay or lesbian members. Agency C was willing to work with them as two individual applicants each adopting a different child as long as they did not discuss their relationship as being anything other than roommates and business partners. Agency D wouldn't talk to them at all and quickly showed them the door as soon as Ryan referred to Jim as his "life partner."

Jim went online to look for resources and was thrilled to discover half a dozen support groups for gay and lesbian adults wishing to adopt kids. In no time at all, the two men found all the help they needed. There was one more option: a new private, nonprofit special needs adoption agency less than sixty miles away who would work with otherwise qualified couples that happened to be gay or lesbian. Only one man would be officially home-studied for adoption in a legal sense, under state law, but the homestudy would describe their relationship as committed and would include the other man as a member of the household. They liked this honest approach best of all.

Five months later, Ryan and Jim were holding a copy of their highly detailed homestudy, complete with criminal background checks, fingerprint checks, FBI clearance, and multiple positive recommendations. Ryan had been approved to apply for sibling groups "of no more than three members" in any age range they chose.

Rushing back to the waiting child web site, they were disappointed to see that Marcos and Ramon had found adoptive families. But their disappointment did not last long. After all, the kids had families now. They had to be happy for them.

After a few days of scanning web sites, they had collected fifteen different phone numbers to call on fifteen different sibling groups in twelve states. The next few days consisted of contacting social workers, faxing an unofficial copy of their homestudy for consideration on a certain sibling group, and then repeating the process with a different set of children.

Their support group had told them it wouldn't be easy. They would be rejected many times simply because of their sexual orientation. But if they continued trying, they would find a match sooner or later. Not only are there social workers that will work with gay couples because the workers themselves are gay, but there are also many experienced heterosexual social workers that know that sexual orientation, per se, has nothing to do with good parenting.

By carefully following their support group's suggestions, Jim and Ryan were matched to a sibling group much faster than they had hoped. It took only four months and thirty-seven faxed homestudies. The children, a brother and two sisters, were ages 5, 7, and 8 and named Lamar, Lavonne, and Lakeshia. This would be a transracial adoption, as the dads were Caucasian and the children were biracial: African American and Caucasian. They liked to be called Lamar, Vonnie, and Keshia.

Jim and Ryan talked well into the night about the pros and cons of two gay men adopting children who regardless of their mixed ancestry would be considered black. Was it fair to subject them to the inevitable insults the children would endure? Some African American children would reject them because their parents were white. Having two fathers would bring more curiosity and hostility into their already troubled lives.

They talked it over with adoption workers, African American friends, black clergy, and an African American psychiatrist friend. In the end, it came down to the fact that the children had been in foster care for four years and had no other prospects of adoption. The siblings had worn out their welcome in a number of foster homes and were finally placed in a residential facility for children with emotional and behavioral problems. They had only recently been placed back in a therapeutic foster home. It was a tough call, but to Jim and Ryan it seemed that Lamar, Vonnie, and Keshia needed the stability of a family more than insulation from intolerance.

An exchange of scrapbooks, phone calls, and videos eventually led to three weekend visits, and then the children moved in. The therapists and staff at the treatment facility, along with the foster parents, worked closely with Jim and Ryan to prepare them to parent the siblings. They warned the prospective parents that the children had serious problems and that it would take time for them to give back emotionally. Their affection would be superficial for some time, and their behavior, manipulative. They would need ongoing therapy. Lamar would need to keep taking calming medication for severe hyperactivity, and Keshia would eventually need medication to control mood swings due to possible depression.

They would have to get rid of their dog. Lamar was terrified of animals and had a tendency to treat them with great cruelty. Jim's German shepherd, Atilla, went to the McLaughlin's house.

The official diagnoses on the children's records read like alphabet soup:

Lamar: ADHD [Attention Deficit Hyperactivity Disorder], RAD [Reactive Attachment Disorder], LD [Learning Disabilities], ODD [Oppositional Defiant]
Vonnie: RAD, ODD
Keshia: RAD, ODD, possible clinical depression.

Jim bought armfuls of books on attention deficit hyperactivity disorder, reactive attachment disorder, learning disabilities, oppositional defiant disorder, and depression. In no time at all, he was a walking encyclopedia on the latest research, medication, and therapeutic techniques for each disorder.

What it all means, he explained to Ryan, is that these kids had been severely neglected and abused early in life, when babies are supposed to learn to trust adults to meet their needs. They began life at the bottom of Maslow's Hierarchy of Needs and stayed there, crying and crying, without a response from anyone. As a result, their emotional behavior was severely arrested. They trusted no one and nothing, and they looked out only for their own needs. Attaching emotionally to a parent was a skill that was beyond them but one they might get closer to with lots of therapy. The bottom line? These children would challenge them like nothing and no one ever had before. They would test them to the extreme. But the potential for rewards was there, too. If they could help these children back to emotional good health, meet their needs through a normal family life, it would be the toughest job they ever had but also the best. The two men did not take up the challenge lightly or without misgivings. More than most people, they knew the importance of belonging to a family.

The first month was what the social worker called the "adoption honeymoon." The children were on their best behavior for the most part and seemed anxious to please and ready to mind their new parents. For Jim and Ryan, it was one of the happiest times of their lives. They enjoyed every aspect of parenting, from breakfast to bedtime stories.

Lamar, the youngest, was a rail thin tornado of a child. He had been a "failure to thrive" baby and still gained weight slowly. His hyperactive nature meant that he burned the few calories his dads could get him to eat long before the intake had a chance to be stored as fat. On orders of the family pediatrician, they put melted margarine into Lamar's milk shakes, gave him bacon and French fries and anything he would eat that was high in calories and at least somewhat nutritious. They weighed him weekly and every ounce gained was a victory.

Ryan and Jim loved Lamar's bright smile and ability to make friends easily. They worried about his inability to focus, pay attention, and stay with a task, even while on ADHD medication. Personal hygiene was a big problem. Lamar refused to brush his teeth on his own, comb his hair, change his clothes, or wash his hands before eating. Bath time was a nightmare, not because Lamar refused to get into the tub, but because he splashed and romped and refused to sit still long enough to get clean. The sides of the tub as well as the bottom had to be padded with suction cupped rubber bath mats to keep Lamar from hurting himself.

Vonnie and Keshia were better about their daily hygiene, but Jim and Ryan couldn't turn their backs on them for a second. Vonnie loved to take and hoard food in every hiding space she could create in her bedroom. She rarely ate the food. She just hoarded it and let it spoil. Daily explorations of her room for the new jar of peanut butter or the recently purchased bag of apples became routine.

Keshia, the oldest at age 8, was used to the role of surrogate mother and argued with Jim and Ryan about nearly every decision they made. She was never happy with what was served at meals, although she ate well. She expected Vonnie and Lamar to give her blind obedience but questioned every directive given her by her new dads. If Jim reminded her to wear a sweater before going to school, she'd say, "Why? I don't need it," and then stand shivering at the bus stop.

There were happy moments. Lamar's eyes lit up when Ryan brought him a soccer ball. The little boy slept with it like a teddy bear when he wasn't kicking it over and over into the garage door. Vonnie and Keshia had been so neglected before coming into the system that the idea of having a toy box was totally new. Vonnie refused to take most of her toys out of their original boxes to play with, preferring instead to simply gaze at them in their new condition and imagine playing with them. Keshia was rough on her toys but thoroughly enjoyed throwing herself into the toy box and wading around for something new to play with.

Taking the children shopping was always a delight, whether it was for shoes or food. Everything thrilled them. Giving a neglected child normalcy is an immense pleasure for most adults, and it was no different for Jim and Ryan. They were seeing the world again through fresh eyes, and it was an unforgettable experience.

Vonnie and Keshia were good students when they could be compelled to complete homework assignments. Their oppositional behavior was most apparent after dinner, when their dads sat them at the kitchen table to do homework. Keshia was supposed to be starting her multiplication tables, but she fought the idea of doing schoolwork at home with all of her might. Ryan, determined to be more stubborn than his daughter, sat up with Keshia until midnight several times before she finally cooperated with the math drills.

Lamar was another story. He had writing, reading, and math learning disabilities. Combined with the hyperactivity and oppositional behavior, he could not even begin to function in a regular kindergarten classroom. An individualized education plan was written for him; it consisted of half-day lab class for children with learning disabilities, lunch and recess with his peers, and an afternoon consisting of speech therapy, psychological counseling, and playtime at an after-school program.

The after-school program did not last long. In less than two weeks, the director asked Jim and Ryan never to bring Lamar back. He simply had no idea how to interact with other children appropriately. He hit, pushed, punched, and kicked to get at his favorite toys, urinated openly on the playground, refused to sit still at snack time, and refused to do anything asked of him, from washing his hands to putting away toys. He acted as though he couldn't hear commands, and when he did comply, he created more messes. The only time Lamar washed his hands when told, he also attempted to flush the bar of soap and the hand towel down the toilet.

Vonnie and Keshia bonded slowly but steadily to their two dads. Vonnie almost never watched TV unless she was sitting in Ryan's lap. Keshia enjoyed private walks with Jim around the perimeter of the backyard. In time, she opened up about many of the sorrows in her past. Jim was a very good listener. The four of them loved cooking together, whether over a large brick grill built into a backyard patio or in the kitchen. Vonnie loved baking and Keshia preferred chopping and mixing. Cooking became their time to be a family—to talk, laugh, argue, and plan the next day.

Predictably, the children had to deal with the cruelty of schoolmates. Jim and Ryan spent hours with them after bad days, soothing hurt feelings and planning strategies for dealing with ignorance. Some kids were not allowed to play with them, but essentially the school was very supportive, and many of the students were friendly. The insults of a few students or neighborhood kids were pretty small potatoes compared to the deprivation the children had already experienced in their young lives. Vonnie, Keshia, and Lamar were slow to adopt the turn-the-other-cheek-response recommended by their fathers. Although Ryan and Jim discouraged it, each of the children was prone to answer taunts with a swift punch in the mouth. The word spread fast that messing with them was very risky business.

Being the adopted children of two gay white men made their lives harder sometimes, but they got through it, aided by a community of family and friends. In time, Vonnie and Keshia made friends who accepted their unusual family and enjoyed eating over and spending the night. None of the three children regretted being adopted. Life in a family was a lot more fun than the residential treatment facility, and most important, they were loved.

Father's Day was a big deal. First, the whole family went to see Jerry McLaughlin and took him a homemade cake with five layers. "There's one layer for everyone in the family," said Vonnie proudly. Then they went to the zoo for a few hours and snapped a photo of every single type of mammal there for Keshia's science report. A big dinner at their favorite restaurant and a movie topped off the day. The children presented Jim and Ryan each with a handwritten card and a gift. Jim's was addressed to Dad 1 and Ryan's to Dad 2. The cards read: "Roses are red. Violets are blue. We love you daddy one and daddy two." The gifts were identical bottles of after-shave, although Ryan's was half empty. "Lamar tried to drink it," explained Keshia. Ryan said, "It is still the nicest gift anyone ever gave me."

For every bit of progress the girls seemed to make, Lamar seemed to take a step backward. His constant disobedience, destruction, and out-of-control behavior sometimes caused his sisters' behavior to go downhill, too. Consequently, the girls behaved much better at school, when they were away from their brother, than they did at home. Jim and Ryan rarely had a calm day.

Four months into the placement, Ryan started keeping track of Lamar's behavioral outcomes. His statistics were shocking, even to himself. Lamar averaged ten time-outs per hour, or one every six minutes, up to twenty rules violations every waking hour, and at least one out-of-control, violent, or destructive tantrum each day. An "out-of-control" was a temper tantrum in which Lamar lashed out violently at anyone or anything he could reach. There was no pattern. He was as likely to go ballistic after being reminded to brush his teeth in the morning as he was after being encouraged to drink a bedtime high calorie milk shake. Ryan recorded a list of the following items that Lamar destroyed or damaged beyond repair in a single one-week period:

1 telephone cord (used as a leash to drag toys)

2 video game controllers (used as ropes to climb chair "mountains")

2 soccer balls (one apparently destroyed with a claw hammer)

5 toothbrushes (2 missing, 1 flushed down the toilet eventually resulting in a substantial plumber's bill)

1 new pair of shoes (toes worn through from repeatedly kicking concrete wall at school)

1 fitted bed sheet and one pillowcase (poked holes with a fork and then shredded them by tearing)

3 t-shirts (from sucking on the neckline or poking holes over the stomach and tearing)

2 action figure dolls (demolished by banging them into each other hour after hour)

1 TV remote control (not sure, but may have dunked it into a glass of milk)

1 storm door (threw a wooden rolling pin at it and cracked a glass panel)

1 bedroom door (kicked a hole in it, actually, that door now has 4 similar holes)

Half a dozen miscellaneous kitchen dishes and glasses (will be buying all plastic in near future)

1 backpack (dragged repeatedly through gravel at school).

Six months into the placement, the social worker mentioned that they could now go to court and finalize the adoptions if they felt ready to. Jim and Ryan had real doubts about Lamar. They had great hopes for the girls because they could maintain their behavior well enough at school to stay in regular classes and out of serious trouble. They could spend a weekend at a relative's house or, with careful supervision, could be left for short periods with a babysitter. Their dads could find some brief respite from their huge emotional needs, allowing them to recharge their parental batteries.

It was different with Lamar. Lamar did not even sleep in a little bit on the weekends. He hit the floor running before 6:30 every single morning and had to be carefully watched at all times. Since he was behind a closed door while in the bathroom, the dads had to take everything out of the bathroom and dole out toilet tissue, as each child needed it. They had to lock up everything sharp. Only spoons were left in kitchen drawers. More and more, they felt like Lamar's prisoners, living in a twenty-four-hour nightmare of "What will he do next?"

They took their son to a child study center at the local university, where he spent the day being exhaustively evaluated by a team of professionals, including medical doctors, psychologists, speech therapists, and psychometricians. Two weeks later, Jim and Ryan were asked to come in to hear the interdisciplinary report on Lamar, including his diagnoses and the prognosis for his future. The news was devastating. Dr. Renee Kozlowski spoke for the team as she handed the men a copy of their twenty-page report. "Jim, Ryan, first we want to say how impressed we are with your parenting skills. We have no major recommendations for you, just a few minor things, as far as changing how you parent Lamar, and this is rare. We can tell you did your homework and that you are consistent and loving but firm. Unfortunately, we don't see Lamar's behavior problems getting better anytime soon. Reluctantly, we would advise you to consider finalizing the adoptions of your daughters and request to be kept in contact with Lamar. He needs to be in a residential treatment facility because he needs the kind of structure and supervision not available in a typical family home setting. Unless the state is willing to pay for that as part of an adoption assistance contract, there is no way you can afford this in the long term."

She sipped a cup of coffee and continued. "In comparing Lamar with his sisters, we find two important differences. All of the children are attachment disordered and oppositional. By themselves, these diagnoses are more than most parents can handle in one child, much less three. But Lamar is also severely impulsive from ADHD and learning and developmentally disabled. His IQ, at 71, is a full 30 points lower than his sisters' IQs. He lacks the ability to concentrate on a task, the ability to look ahead to how present choices impact on the next moment, and the brain power to comprehend why he should behave differently. He does not learn from his mistakes like most children and, so, is prone to the same dangerous behaviors again and again, even when they cause him pain and harm.

Emotionally, psychologically, behaviorally, and educationally, this child needs a twenty-four-hour a day staff, working in eight-hour shifts, to meet his needs. If he were your only child, and neither one of you had to go to work, you might be able to raise him. Lamar is so needy that he is the human equivalent of a black hole in outer space. You can't do enough for this child at this point. No one can. And he is incapable of giving anything back, like love or trust or loyalty or gratitude."

Ryan asked the first question, "What will happen to Lamar if we don't adopt him? We love him, you know, in spite of everything, and the girls love him, too." Jim thought about his time on the street, the despair. The thought of rejecting Lamar filled him with guilt and terrible sorrow.

"That's a good question," replied Dr. Kozlowski. "A good residential treatment facility can help Lamar find the right combination of medication and therapy to stabilize him sufficiently enough so that he can learn. He may have all the contact with his sisters that you can cope with and that will not endanger his gains. In time, hopefully, he might even be ready to spend summer vacations with you or at least occasional weekends.

But remember, his progress will depend in large part on the consistency of the structure and routine around him. Surprises set him off. Routine calms him down. It may be years before he is doing well enough to leave what will become the security of the treatment center. His sisters will miss him at first, but they are also tired of his extreme behaviors, whether they know it consciously or not. In time, life will be so much improved for all of you that the girls will be happy with the change."

Ryan and Jim knew the team was right, and the social worker and her supervisor were in agreement. Only the girls could be adopted at this time, but that didn't make the decision easier.

Perhaps Lamar could join them later, but not now. The unanimous nature of the decision to disrupt or end Lamar's adoption should have given the men solace, but it did not. Disruption feels like death, even when limited contact is ongoing. It meant the death of their dream to raise a son, maybe the only chance they would ever have. Jim knew that Lamar was emotionally incapable of responding to them, but he couldn't escape the self-accusation that he was abandoning a child who was no more responsible for his demons than Jim was for his sexual orientation.

Ironically, Lamar himself seemed totally unconcerned about moving to a residential treatment center. He had never attached emotionally to his dads anyway. To him, all adults were interchangeable, even the ones called "parents." He was more distressed at leaving his sisters behind but brightened when promised that he could speak to them on the phone every single Sunday. After all, Lamar loved to take apart telephones.

It would take years of therapy before Lamar could understand and then verbalize his feelings about the disruption. Sometimes he expressed great affection for the family that still came to visit. At other times, however, he was filled with a rage he did not understand, bitterly angry that he had not been adopted. Although Lamar could not live in their home, Jim and Ryan maintained their commitment to him. They gradually mastered the art of staying in contact with him without letting the child's limitations drive them into depression. They tried to look at the bright side. Lamar was safe. He was getting intensive therapy. He was learning to be less destructive and oppositional, and he still had the love of his sisters, too. Lamar would never be adopted, but he still had a family who would never desert him. With medication and support, perhaps he could learn to rein in his impulses and function in society. Without the love of his family, Lamar had little chance of staying out of prison, the ultimate fate of so many abused and neglected children.

Three months after the adoption disruption, the adoptions of Vonnie and Keshia were finalized in court. The family celebrated with a big party at home with the McLaughlins and lots of friends in attendance. Attila the dog, back home for good now, strolled into the house, upset the dining room table, and flipped the cake onto the floor. Jim and Ryan both laughed. The one positive legacy of their disruption nightmare was that they would never again sweat the small stuff.

ADOPTION AS FAMILY

Family (noun): parents and their children, the children of the same parents

INTRODUCTION

For many parents, adoption is first experienced as a powerful, often mysterious calling. Because it so often forges lifetime bonds among adults and children with separate histories, adoption invites us to reexamine our beliefs about families and "family values." The stories that follow portray both the great diversity and common experiences of adoptive families.

Granny Grinch

"Guenivere Delores-Joan Parker Davis, I did not carry you for nine months, give birth to you after twenty-seven hours of excruciating natural labor, pay for five thousand dollars worth of orthodontia, and put you through four years of Notre Dame on the humble profits from my catering business just so you could give me a handicapped grandchild!"

Gwen Davis pulled the phone receiver three inches away from her ear as her mother ranted. She covered the mouthpiece and whispered to her husband, Devon, "She must be really upset. She didn't mention the ten thousand-dollar wedding after the Notre Dame bit this time." Devon had to stifle a hearty laugh. Mrs. Parker was a follower of the mythical "Better Mothering Through Guilt" philosophy.

"You are my only daughter and my only hope of ever having a grandchild, unless the Pope decides to allow your brother the priest to marry!"

"Well, actually, mom, the Vatican does allow priests and nuns to adopt children with special needs these days. Hundreds worldwide have done so, so you could, technically, get a grandchild from my brother, the father."

"Shut your mouth; don't even think of such a thing! Why, Frank is the assistant pastor of one of the largest and oldest churches in Boston. Where is he going to find the time to raise a handicapped child? And why would he want to? Guenivere, why are you and your brother so intent on solving everyone else's problems? What about my problem? I'm 60 years old next month, although everyone tells me I don't look a day over 42, and yet I have no grandchildren to bake cookies for. Do you have any idea what it's like to go to bridge parties and to be the only woman with no grandchild photographs to pass around with the onion dip? Can't you just have one baby? For me? I need an heir, a legacy, someone to teach. I want a grand-baby! But I would prefer to have one that has my eyes and nose, thank you very much."

Gwen smiled. Her mother had long ago decided to deal with the fact of her interracial marriage by using a technique called Total Denial. Yet again Gwen reminded her mother that even if she and Devon did decide to get pregnant, instead of pursuing a special needs adoption, the baby would not look like its maternal grandmother as much as she might like. After all, Devon was African American, Jamaican by ancestry, and Gwen was Irish American.

"I'm not worried about Devon's influence, dear," replied her mother. "After all, the children in my family tree always look more like their mothers, and besides, Devon is part French, too. All Jamaicans have French blood, don't they? That means European blood on both sides of the family!"

Gwen just sighed deeply ending the conversation with "I'll call you later, Mom," and hung up.

They were celebrating their fifth wedding anniversary, and Devon remained in awe about the process that produced two people as kind and warm as his wife and his brother-in-law, Father Frank, when they had been born to and raised by someone as cold and closed-minded as Lucille Parker. It would make sense if their late father, who died from a stroke within weeks of his retirement, had been a giving kind of person. But his reputed attitude of intolerance made his wife look positively generous.

Gwen and Frank always gave credit for their attitudes to the brothers and sisters of the Franciscan order that taught them throughout their school years. In the summer, the children attended camp with the Franciscans as well. In fact, it was at camp that Frank first heard his calling to become a priest.

Devon had an additional, more evolutionary explanation. "Years from now," he told his wife, "geneticists will find out that grinchiness runs in families but skips a generation in each cycle. That will explain you and Frank. And it is an extra incentive for us to adopt, too, come to think of it."

"Grinchiness?" asked Gwen. "As in the Dr. Seuss book, *How Granny Grinch Stole Christmas?* I love that book. Frank and I watched the TV show every year when we were growing up."

"Exactly," continued Devon in a mock scholarly tone. "Dr. Seuss was a visionary when it came to the study of hearts that are 'two sizes too small.' If he had known your mother, the book may have been called *How Granny Grinch Stole Christmas.* What was it she said last week about adopting a child with special needs? Oh, yeah, her exact words were, 'Why would you want to adopt someone else's mistake?' As if a child created by God and in God's image could ever be a mistake!"

Gwen rubbed Devon's shoulders. "Don't let Mom get to you, honey. We've been talking about adopting a waiting child for four years. We've done the research, we've gone to the classes, and we have a homestudy. We know what we want and what we are doing. And we have tried to get Mom's blessing. If we can't get it, so what! At least our child will have his Uncle Frank, and Frank could not be more supportive."

Devon was an orphan. His parents had died trying to bring him to America on an old boat from Jamaica. When it sank near the U.S. coastline, their last efforts were aimed at fastening one of the few life preservers to his little body. He was pulled from the water by the U.S. Coast Guard and, after a lot of red tape, grew up in U.S. foster care. His third foster home "stuck," and he stayed for thirteen years with Miss Jenna, a career foster mother. From her, he learned to love God above all else, to believe in himself, and to work hard. Miss Jenna lived in a rest home now, recovering from a stroke, and Devon and Gwen were frequent visitors. Devon was sent to Notre Dame on a scholarship for gifted foster children, and he met Gwen when he stood up at a party and asked if anyone else present was from Boston. Their friendship blossomed into love and they married one year after graduating. Devon was now in the Coast Guard himself, a captain, the realization of a lifelong dream. Gwen worked as an accountant. In addition to their love of Boston, they shared a passion to help kids, to give something back, and to give of themselves.

The toughest thing for their friends to understand about their decision was their fertility. Or, rather, their lack of infertility. Devon and Gwen had no reason to believe they were not fertile. They could try to have a baby at any time, and they might someday. But at the moment it made sense to them, on a very personal and spiritual level, to parent a child that was already born instead of bringing another baby into a world that was already overpopulated.

Someone had plucked Devon out of the ocean, had given him a chance to show what he could do. They were excited about plucking a child out of the foster care system and seeing what he or she could be with the support of a loving and permanent family.

Gwen kept hoping she could communicate her feelings about adoption to her mother. She had been working on Lucille for months. But even their carefully prepared carrot analogy had not impressed the wannabe grandma.

"Mom, if I want a carrot right now, and my neighbor has grown more carrots than he can use, why should I drive to the market and buy a carrot when he is willing to give me a perfectly good carrot for free?"

"Because," Mrs. Parker had answered testily, "you don't know what kind of fertilizer your neighbor used, what kind of insecticide, or if the soil is any good. I'd rather see you go to the health food store and pay any price for an organic carrot. Or better yet, grow your own darn carrot!"

As Devon put it, to some people, a carrot is a carrot. But not to everyone.

Now they had decided to proceed with an adoption and pray that Lucille would "come around." Many relatives soften up after the child arrives, according to their social worker.

For the next several months, the Davises poured over hundreds of photolistings, new and old. Unlike the other members of their adoption preparation class, they had no clear idea of the kind of child they wanted to adopt. They had no gender or race preference, any age up to about 12 sounded fine to them, and they weren't frightened by most disabilities. Gwen knew she wanted just one child for now. She wanted to lavish her attention and love on just one. And Devon was sure he wanted a child who was quick, bright, and resourceful, maybe even a little precocious. Like he had been as a child. He would know how to shape such attributes and how to guide the child toward setting educational and career goals and away from any desire to use his or her intelligence to hustle people for a living.

They kept telling their social worker to send more listings. "We'll know our child when we see and read about him or her." They checked out the photolistings on the Internet. They looked at photolistings of children waiting in Haiti and Jamaica as well as in the U.S. foster care system. But none of these listings made their hearts jump to their throats. None of them brought tears of recognition to their eyes or the words, "This is it!" to their lips. Frank gave them an offbeat prayer to recite as they waited for the right child to come along. It never failed to bring a smile to Gwen's mouth when she said it: "Lord, give me patience as I wait, but please give it to me right now this minute!"

The Grinch went on complaining loudly and long to anyone who would listen. She clipped a newspaper story about a murderer who was described as an "adoptee" and sent that to her daughter. Gwen sent an Internet article back to her with a list of prominent people throughout history who were adopted, from Moses to Nat King Cole to President Clinton.

It was Uncle Frank who made the match. One of his parishioners was fostering a 10-year-old girl named Luz. "Sis, I had no idea she was a foster child until recently. I found out when I gave last rites to her birthmother at the hospice center. Luz is one of my favorite kids—bright, funny, creative, kindhearted. And she loves to play basketball, sew her own clothes, and cook, too! Her foster parents tell me that she will be eligible for adoption soon. Why don't you call her social worker? If it's okay, I could arrange for you guys to meet briefly after mass tomorrow over juice and donuts in the parish hall. Oh, and by the way, Luz means "light." My prayer now is that this little girl is the light at the end of your tunnel."

If Frank liked her that much, she had to be special. That much Devon and Gwen were sure of. The social worker gave her blessing to a meeting but asked that they refrain from talking about adoption because Luz had not yet been prepared for the process. While she was on the phone with them, she gave them more background. Luz had lived in her present foster home for five years. Her single mother, Gloria, had been battling AIDS for that long, but was now dying of AIDS-related cancers that would not go into remission. Luz had maintained a close relationship with her mom during her entire foster care stay and was devastated to be losing her. This was a child who eventually would go into an adoptive placement in the middle of a long grief and loss process. Her adoptive parents would need to work very closely with her foster parents to create a sensitive transition, one with full and ongoing access to the foster home.

During mass, the Davises scanned the church for any sign of a little girl who might be the one. Frank and the social worker had failed to describe any of Luz's physical characteristics, and Devon and Gwen had not thought to ask. Now their curiosity was about to consume them.

As Father Frank stepped into the center aisle of the church to wait for the parishioners who would be offering the gifts that day, he glanced at his sister and nodded slightly toward the back of the church. The signal was clear. Luz would be one of the people coming up the aisle with the bread, the wine, and the donation basket. Gwen's heart almost stopped.

Moments later, the procession was near the front of the church. An elderly African American man carried the basket, a woman, perhaps his wife, carried the wine offering. And in a small wheelchair with pink tires, wearing a dress of the same color, was a pretty girl holding the bread. Father Frank accepted the gifts, and the procession turned to go back down the aisle. The Davises saw Luz up close at last, and she even glanced their way and smiled. She had long braids cascading down from the top of her head in every direction, a round face with enormous dark brown eyes, high cheekbones, and delicate bone structure. She was very slender, but her upper arms and shoulders were well developed. Her skin was the color of dark chocolate. They were drawn back to her eyes in the few seconds they saw her, eyes full of intelligence, mischief, and wonder. As she went past, Devon gave his wife a look that said, "This is it." They had no more glimpse of her than they might have of a child in a photolisting, but it was enough to know that this child might well be the one.

Orange juice and donuts stretched out into a two-hour visit as Gwen and

Devon visited with the foster parents, who turned out to be the couple in the offertory procession with Luz. She was an amazing little girl who loved to talk, sing, swim, and show off her basketball skills. (The parish hall doubled as a gymnasium.) At one point, in an intensely competitive ten-point duel with Father Frank, she purposely ran over his toe to halt his concentration. When he cried foul, she suggested sweetly that her wheelchair had a mind of its own. Frank reached up, grabbed an imaginary halo hanging over her head and threw it to the ground, making a shattering noise at the same time. "I know you, Luz," he said. "You may be an angel everywhere else, but on the basketball court, you sprout horns!" The duel ended with Luz winning by a point and an exhausted Father Frank begging for a glass of water. Luz quickly wheeled to the kitchen area and got him the water. There was almost nothing she couldn't do all by herself.

They would find out later that her spine had been broken in a diving accident when she was just 6 years old. She had gone camping with some friends of her mother and dove into a pond without knowing a large boulder lay below the surface. By the time she reached a hospital, the spinal cord injury had left her paralyzed from the waist down. The accident had not dampened her love of the water, and although she could no longer dive, she loved to swim. Outside of the water, she could get around on crutches, but she preferred her wheelchair, which she had learned to manipulate with amazing expertise.

Luz's birthmother went into a coma that very night and died the next day. After the funeral of her birthmother, which Father Frank officiated at and Gwen and Devon attended, the Davises visited Luz more and more over the course of two months. When Luz herself said she was ready, she moved into their home as their adopted daughter. Luz and Miss Jenna hit it off immediately and became good buddies. Luz loved to bake goodies on Saturday to take to Miss Jenna and the other rest home residents.

A few weeks later, after Luz had figured out how to access every part of the house and yard, they began preparing her to meet her grandmother. Devon had referred to her as Granny Grinch. Luz took it in stride. She was used to people making inaccurate assumptions about her based on her use of crutches or a wheelchair or based on the fact that she was African American or a child. She was quite accustomed to waiting patiently for people to get to know her, and the truth, simultaneously.

Gwen decided that since her mother was probably going to be rude no matter what, they would not even bother to try and prepare her slowly. They simply invited her over for dinner, and when she walked in and put her famous potato and cheese casserole down on the kitchen table, Luz wheeled in.

Gwen slipped an arm around her mother's waist to give support and swallowed hard. "Mother, I would like you to meet our daughter, Luz Davis. Luz, this is your Grandma Lucille."

Lucille's mouth dropped open as she shook hands with a smiling Luz. She said very little, except to announce her intention to rewarm the casserole before dinner. As she went to the kitchen, Gwen and Devon collapsed on the sofa, relieved that there had not been a scene. Luz followed her grandmother and began to describe a casserole with similar ingredients that her birthmother had loved to make. At first, Lucille tried to ignore Luz. She turned on the oven, removed the glass cover, and placed the casserole inside.

"Aren't you going to sprinkle on bread crumbs or parmesan cheese before warming that up?" asked Luz innocently. "A crunchy topping would be perfect."

"And just what do you know about cooking?" said Lucille, with exasperation in her voice. "Do you run a catering business out of your kitchen like I do? Or are you just a little pipsqueak?"

"I may be a pipsqueak, Granny Grinch," replied the child fearlessly, "but I can bake circles around you when it comes to, well, when it comes to oatmeal cookies. Go ahead, ask your son what happened when he challenged me to a basketball free throw contest. Even with Uncle Frank, I take no prisoners!"

"Granny Grinch, eh?" snarled Lucille. "So you have a mouth on you, too. Fine, you're on, Pipsqueak! I'll accept that challenge. Oatmeal cookies, it is. But don't go crying to mommy and daddy when I make the best darn cookies you've ever eaten, and yours are still sitting on the baking sheet, getting cold."

For the next hour, Devon and Gwen avoided the kitchen, the racket of bowls clinking, mixers whirring, and kitchen cabinet doors slamming. They could hear arguing, and louder arguing, and then they could smell cookies baking. Father Frank arrived with an appetite but quietly took his place on the sofa, too. Somehow they knew the kitchen was barely big enough for the two people there right now. It was best to avoid "Main Street" until the high noon shoot-out had been decided.

Lucille arranged the two types of cookies on two plates and then blindfolded the three judges before giving them one of each to try. The final score was Lucille, one, Luz, two.

Luz screamed in triumph and jubilation and exchanged high fives with all of the judges. Lucille said nothing but slowly ate one of Luz's cookies. Then she raised one eyebrow and extended her hand to Luz. "Not bad, for a kid."

"You mean a pipsqueak, right?" Luz shot back.

"I'll tell you what," said Lucille with a smile spreading slowly and completely across her face. "You call me Grandma Parker or just plain Grandma, and I'll call you Luz, or maybe even Lucy, since I plan to make you my protégé. After all, I have to have a grandchild to leave my business to because your parents and your uncle can't cook their way out of paper bags!"

By the end of the evening, Luz was sitting in her grandma's lap showing her photos of her birthmother. After they shared a good cry, Luz told her favorite jokes. Devon had never heard his mother-in-law laugh so much. As a matter of fact, he had never heard her laugh before at all.

Before Lucille left, she made arrangements to have Luz spend the next weekend with her. "I'm going to rearrange the kitchen so that Luz can reach things more easily. And then we are going to cook up a storm. The ladies are dropping by for bridge, too, and I'm going to have a granddaughter to show off! Finally! Luz, you know how to play bridge?"

"Of course, Grandma," said Luz, "and I'm good, too!"

But the best part of the evening was what was overheard as Lucille put her coat on, lifted Luz up, and gave her a good-bye hug. She said, "I just knew your parents would find me the perfect grandchild. And it's about time, too. You know I'm 60 years old, although I don't look a day over 42. We are going to have such great times together, Luz! This is one of the happiest days of my life!"

No sooner had she closed the door behind her than the whole house erupted with laughter. Devon had the last word.

" 'And in Whoville, they say that the Grinch's heart grew two sizes that day!' "

❦

The Invisible Father

Dominic Wallace whistled as he maneuvered his twenty-year-old pickup truck through the downtown streets of Dallas, Texas. He had just closed an important deal for his small tree trimming company that would give him enough work to last the rest of the year. Now he could devote his energy to his upcoming dog shows and litters instead of to finding enough work to keep his two dozen blue ribbon German shepherds fed.

Tree trimming was enjoyable work, a craft he had learned from his own father, but dog breeding was his hobby, his vocation, his passion. His dogs had the best of everything, from veterinary care to dog food. There wasn't a flea or tick anywhere on his ten-acre miniranch. His dogs didn't chew on rawhide. They chewed on hand-selected dried pigs ears. They didn't sleep in doghouses. They slept on and around Dom's king-sized bed. His casa was their casa.

The only number on Dom's speed dial was Dr. Laura Montez, his veterinarian. She was the only person he'd ever met who loved dogs as much as he did. He always told her that if she wasn't married, he'd steal her heart the way she steals all his money.

Dom figured he spent the first almost forty years of his life trying out various things and would spend the next forty enjoying all of the things he had found out that he loved.

Marriage. Not for him. Kids. Probably not in the cards. Nine-to-five job. Hardly. Living anywhere but Texas. Never.

Sharing his life with dogs. Definitely. Earning just enough to pay the bills instead of working himself to death. Absolutely. Trimming trees. Yes, for sure. A simple life, but a very happy one.

His longest learning process was his marriage. It lasted ten years, until he was thirty-five, which was about eight years longer than it should have. She didn't dislike dogs, but she didn't love them quite as much as he did either. When, in an argument, she yelled, "Choose—the dogs or me!" and he yelled, "Bye, bye, honey!" the marriage hit the rocks.

Dom liked to name his studs after presidents and his bitches after first ladies, so when he called Laura one afternoon to tell her that Eleanor was in labor, the first pup was a footling breech, and he needed help, she was able to pull that dog's file by looking under "R" for Roosevelt.

Eleanor was one of his older dogs. This was her final litter before she would be spayed and allowed to enjoy a carefree retirement. A quick examination showed a pup with a good heartbeat, but Eleanor seemed unusually tired and her contractions were weak. Laura rolled up her sleeves and prepared for a long afternoon. Dom did what he could to help, but the waiting and the worry made him so nervous, he couldn't stop twisting the corner of his t-shirt. It wasn't the additional mouths to feed. He had every one of these pups sold, because Eleanor and Franklin were two of his show champions, but what he worried about was Eleanor's life. He couldn't bear the thought of losing her. She slept on his feet. She was the one who woke him each day. She was, in many ways, his oldest and most devoted friend. Nervously, he paced the living room floor.

He spotted the old TV in the corner, rarely used because he despised TV (yet another factor that doomed his marriage—his ex had been a soap opera addict). Now, he switched it on, hoping it would take his mind off of Eleanor.

High Noon, Dallas was on, a local talk show that highlighted political and news items for thirty minutes each day. He glanced at his watch: 12:05. Just in time to find out what the topic would be. The host, Vance Lance, called it "The Invisible Parent." The show was about birthfathers, the little recognized, almost forgotten fourth parent in the adoption triad that included adoptee, adoptive parents, and birthparents.

"We are bombarded," said Vance, "with images of birthmothers and scenes of reunion. We hear plenty about fathers, adoptive fathers, even stepfathers, but the birthfather is the one we ignore. Sometimes birthfathers don't even know they are birthfathers until their grown children seek them out! Our guests today are three local residents, all "reunited adoptees" who have met their birthmothers and are now searching for their birthfathers.

Take a minute and meet these young people. Maybe *you* can help them in their searches."

Each guest took a turn offering information about herself and her un-found birthfather and asking for help. The second young adult, a 20-year-old named Serena Hill, caught Dom's attention immediately because she was wearing a t-shirt with a Doberman pinscher's bust splashed across it. When her turn came, she gave Dallas as the name of her lifelong residence and mentioned a birthdate. "I don't want to violate my birthmother's privacy," Serena said, "but I do have her permission to show a photo of her, since my birthfather may not remember her by name. We hope that if he is watching, he will recognize something in this photo—their relationship was brief—and maybe he will see something familiar in me, and he will find me. You see, my dad died when I was a baby, and I was raised by my mom, who never remarried. And while I think she is absolutely the best, I have always wanted a daddy. I want to find him so much!"

Serena's photo did not ring any bells with Dom, so he jumped up and went back in to check on Eleanor. "I was just about to call you," said Laura. "The pup is fine and so is mom. The rest of the puppies should be born without incident. Eleanor was lying on her side, nursing her firstborn and wagging her tail, a silent request for Dom to scratch behind her ears. As he complied, he said, "Thanks, Laura, once again. You know how I feel about Mrs. Roosevelt. Hey, are *you* still married?"

"Cut it out, Dom," Laura warned in a mock serious tone. "Even if I weren't madly in love with Rick, I wouldn't marry you. Remember, I like corgis. Your sheps would eat them for breakfast!"

As she walked toward the front door, she stopped so suddenly, Dom almost ran into her. "My God!" cried the vet, pointing at the TV. "Who is that blond in the center of the row? She is the spitting image of you! Is that your niece or something?"

Dom glanced back at Serena but didn't notice much resemblance. "How do you figure?"

"Dom, open your eyes! She has your mouth, your nose, your eyes, your hair color, oh my God, even your mannerisms. Look! She's twisting the corner of her t-shirt, just like you do when you're nervous."

Dom took another look. He had noticed that Serena looked like his mother to him or, rather, like photos of his mother when she was young. Now he leaned forward and studied her every move. Just then she spoke. "Well, Vance, I have lots of interests. I love to paint, especially landscapes and trees, lots of trees. I like to play chess and swim, but mostly I love my dogs. I have three Dobies, and they go wherever I go. They even sleep in my bed."

Laura's mouth dropped and Dom whistled. "There's a few coincidences for you, although I wouldn't know a game of checkers from a game of chess. And I hate to swim."

One last time, Serena held up the photo of her birthmother, and Dom noticed something he hadn't seen before. It had been taken in front of Dallas West High, his old high school. Suddenly, he felt a little faint, and his knees were wobbly.

He explained what he had heard earlier on the show to Dr. Laura and asked her to call *High Noon, Dallas,* which she promptly did. A few minutes later, a woman called him back and identified herself as Marge Baker, Serena's birthmother.

"This is most awkward, Mr. Wallace, but for Serena's sake and since we attended the same high school at the same time, I hope you will hear me out. She was conceived as the result of a brief encounter, I guess you'd call it a one night stand, after a dance at Dallas West High. I was a new transfer student, and the boy and I had been drinking wine with a small group of friends. We were all pretty drunk there behind the—"

"Field house, right?" said Dom. "And the wine was Strawberry Hill, if I recall."

There was silence at the other end and then one last question from Marge. "Do you remember anything after we ceremonially buried the empty bottles on the fifty-yard line?"

"Nope," replied Dom, "not a thing. I had never been drunk before and I have never been drunk since, but that whole night is a blur. The last thing I recall is that the gravesite was at the five-yard line, not the fifty . . . Marge, do you have a fax machine? I'll fax you photos of myself and my mother if you will fax me more of you and Serena."

Laura stayed by his side until the faxes arrived and confirmed his suspicion. "I'm a father, Laura. Me, a birthfather. I don't know whether to whoop and holler or run and hide. I have always thought it might have been nice to have a kid, but one who is already 20 years old?"

"Dom," responded the vet, "I have two sisters who are adopted. They were born in Korea and adopted as foundlings. That means that they will probably never know who left them at the orphanage. They will never know their birthparents, and they are old enough now that they have some natural curiosity, even a longing. You and Serena are blessed. You have found each other. Start out as friends, and the dad thing will happen, slowly and sweetly . . . and by the way, Eleanor's birth is on me this time. You'll need to save your money. Daughters are expensive!" She laughed, gave him a quick hug, and was gone.

Twenty-four hours later, Marge, Serena, and Serena's adoptive mother all arrived at Dom's house and were introduced to each dog individually. Serena had a hug for her birthfather, but her attention was riveted on the animals. "I think I've died and gone to heaven!" she exclaimed as she counted Eleanor's ten fat pups. "You actually have thirty-five dogs at this moment!"

"No need for a blood test in this case," Marge said as she stared at Dom.

"Serena could not look more like you if she were your identical twin. About the only thing she got from me was her knobby knees and a passion for a good game of chess!"

They talked for hours. Marge described how she hid her pregnancy from her parents as long as she could and when it was discovered and she could not name the birthfather, her parents almost disowned her. In the end, she had to agree to an adoption to keep from being kicked out of the house. She completed her studies from home that year and relinquished Serena when the baby was 24 hours old. "It nearly killed me," she said, "but I swore that someday I would find my baby again. Then she found me!"

Serena's adoptive mother explained how Serena had been placed with them as a foster child and then was adopted. But right after their daughter's first birthday, her father died of colon cancer. With her mom's help, Serena searched for and found Marge right before turning 18. The three women had been trying to figure out how to find Dom ever since. They had even searched the high school year books for a face that resembled Serena's.

"You never saw my photo because I never showed up for photo sessions," explained Dom. "I never saw any point to it. Boy, was that a mistake!"

Dom and Serena took Dr. Laura's advice and went slow. They kept their mutual expectations at the friend level and then took it to an uncle and niece level. Slowly, Dom began to feel like a father, and Serena began to respond to him as a daughter. They hit a few bumps along the way. Serena wasn't very good with budgeting so co-signing a car loan for her created a lot of stress.

"Big mistake in general to co-sign loans," Dom told Vance when he appeared on a follow-up segment of *High Noon, Dallas*. "It's better to keep money and religion out of a new relationship while you are getting to know each other."

Of course, he never said anything about politics, at least not the canine variety. You see, eventually, Serena chose one German dog breed over another and became a shep fan. For her twenty-first birthday, Dom gave her a pup from the first litter of President and Mrs. Carter.

She hugged his neck so hard, he thought it would snap before she let go. As he watched her playing with her new "baby," he thought back to that day when he turned on the TV, and there she was. Parenting, even parenting a young adult, is always challenging, but Dom will tell you that, for him, being a visible parent is much better than being an invisible one.

ভ৽ঌ৩

Family Values on the David Swanson Show

"I knew you were going to ask me that," said Elizabeth, smiling a little warily.

"I always feel self-conscious saying this, but the word that comes to mind when I ask myself 'why' is 'calling.' At some point in my life, adoption became a calling."

"Do you mean calling in the sense of religious calling like being called to priesthood or ministry?" asked the interviewer, David Swanson.

Elizabeth looked around the cramped set and wondered what she was doing there. This guy had Nazis and people who had been abducted by aliens on his show. A couple of the broadcasts had ended with estranged family members rolling around on the floor punching each other. Swanson had once been hit over the head with a chair by a disgruntled woman with husbands in four different states. Oh, well, maybe dignity was overrated.

"I sure didn't start out with the intention of adopting seven children," laughed Elizabeth. "When I was 28, I had a good job in a public relations firm in Chicago. I'd like to say that there was a big hole in my life, because it would make the story better, but that really wasn't so. I loved my job, had a lot of friends and couldn't get enough of the city. I grew up in rural West Virginia. Chicago was so exciting.

"One day, a friend of mine and I were driving somewhere and an announcement came on the radio about becoming a foster parent." Elizabeth laughed again. "She got all enthusiastic and wouldn't quit talking about it until I promised I'd go down to the children's services agency with her. 'You'd be a great foster parent,' she kept saying. Well, as the oldest of six kids, the idea of taking care of another one didn't have a lot of appeal at the time. But I went along to a meeting for prospective foster parents the following week. On the way home, my friend was bubbling over with plans to become a foster mom, while I was thinking, 'I'm glad that's over. I'm too busy.'

"And I was busy. At odd moments over the next several weeks, though, I would picture the children the agency social worker described at the meeting. I had known a lot of children like that growing up in West Virginia. I had a dozen reasons for putting it out of my mind: My career. I was still single. It was impractical. I should wait until my life was more settled. At first, it was easy to reject the idea of becoming a foster parent. The idea never quite went away, but I wasn't haunted by it or anything like that."

"Was there some specific event that became a turning point and changed your mind?" asked Swanson.

"I can't remember any one thing. That's what I mean about a calling. Gradually, against all my logic, the idea of becoming a foster mom began to take hold."

"Was guilt a part of it?"

"Guilt may have had something to do with it, I guess. I mean, here I was so blessed, while these children were being separated from their parents because life in their homes was too dangerous. A little guilt's not such a bad thing, but guilt wasn't the biggest part of my decision to try foster parenting. I was fairly active in volunteer work at a family shelter. No, it was something more positive, a growing sense that it was something I needed to try.

"The first child the agency placed with me was a 10-year-old boy named George who's now my 23-year-old son. He'd already been in two other foster homes. George and I had quite a time the first three months. Talk about your mixed feelings. George gave me some the worst nights I have ever spent. He lied, stole, broke things, swore like a sailor, and tried just about everything he could to be rejected. And he almost succeeded. I was ready to throw in the towel just about every week. At the same time, nothing I had ever done before was so . . . I don't know . . . absorbing, so . . . important. Dealing with George required a total commitment, mind and heart. I discovered that, with all of the frustrations, I was pretty good at this parent thing.

"Somewhere along the line, George ceased to be just a responsibility and became my son. That's when I first thought of adoption. It's funny, each time I've adopted, I told myself, 'This is it; no more.' But then I would find out about some other child through one of the state listings and . . . the familiar questions would surface: Should I? Could I do it? What if no one comes forward? What about the other children? Would it work? You can see how I answered those questions. I've adopted seven children altogether. Five are currently living at home."

"What's George doing now?" asked Swanson.

Elizabeth hesitated for a moment, wondering idly if gale force winds could make Swanson's sprayed silver hairdo move.

"For awhile George went through lots of dead-end jobs. He was doing a lot of cocaine, GHB, and some other designer stuff. He moved back home a couple of times. At age 22, things didn't look good. When I confronted him with his drug use, he would just deny it. I did a lot of praying in those days.

"Then, one night after he'd moved out again, he called and said he needed to talk. That wasn't typical George, so I thought, 'What now? He owes some drug dealers money. He's sick. He's HIV positive.' He looked nervous when he walked in the door. Then he sat down and said, 'Mom, you're right. I've got a drug problem and I don't know how to handle it on my own.'

"A week later, he was in a rehab program. While he was there, he struck up a relationship with a counselor who was somewhat of a computer nerd. George always had an interest in art but no discipline to go along with it. But through this counselor, he discovered graphic design. Last fall he enrolled in a media and graphic design course at the local community college. So far, so good."

"It sounds like you live with a lot of uncertainty," said Swanson softly.

She was a little surprised by the gentle tone of the question. He usually came across with the subtlety of a sideshow barker.

"I suppose so, but in the final analysis, who doesn't? I don't know how successful George will ever be. The thing that matters is that he has a chance to lead a normal life and is becoming a decent young man. And he'll always have me."

"As an adoptive parent, what did you do that made the most difference in raising George?" asked Swanson.

"You mean the 'Seven Big Habits of Effective Adoptive Parents?' " laughed Elizabeth. "Habit 1, construct a new paradigm and define your skill set. Habit 2, offer creative alternatives to lying, stealing, and destruction of other people's property. . . . As you might expect, there's a lot of on-the-job training. Consistency is important. Most kids adopted from the foster care system didn't have much of that. You have to develop a strong resistance to being conned and, for the most part, let them take the consequences of bad judgments. If they spend all of their allowance, then it's gone. If they skip school, then they make up the work on weekends, when everyone else is going out.

"I've learned a few clever techniques for taming uncivilized children over the years, and some of them are essential, particularly if you are raising a child with a serious clinical problem like reactive attachment disorder. But sometimes I think the most important thing I do lies in convincing my children through the mundane activities of everyday life that they are loved and that we are family no matter what happens.

"A lot of young people who leave the foster care system at 18 don't do very well. They suffer from high rates of homelessness, unemployment, and incarceration. The difference in George's case was having a family that cared about him, a family to come back to while he was out there floundering around, doing dumb things. Those of you with adult children, think of what might have happened if you weren't there to help with college, or rent and furniture for a first apartment, an occasional meal. What if they had no one that they could really count on if they got scared or lonely or made some stupid mistake? Children are in the foster care system mainly because they couldn't count on their parents."

The audience gave Elizabeth a nice round of applause. She was moved but also wary, particularly after Swanson announced, "After we return from a commercial break, we will take some questions from our studio audience." This was the moment that she had been dreading since slick-talking Kevin Doolin from the Adoptive Families of Illinois had first approached her about doing the infamous *David Swanson Show*.

When Doolin first broached the idea of going on the show, she laughed; then when she saw he was serious, she responded with an earthy phrase that went way beyond "no."

"But this guy reaches millions of people!" said Kevin.

"I don't find that very comforting," Elizabeth answered.

"Look, the producer told us that they're trying to upgrade the quality of the show. I think they want to compete with Oprah and begin to move out of 'people do the most disgusting things' category. They're going to do ten straight shows on children's issues. No clowns, no lunatics. Look at the proposed guest list: The Children's Defense Fund, The Child Welfare League of America, a governor, two senators . . . and you! Your family's an inspirational story."

"Kevin, people tend to sensationalize adoption too much already. And by doing that, they trivialize it. Either it's the Mickey Rooney tear-jerker where dirty-faced little urchins find that 'all you need is love' and another place at table, or it's the movie of the week's 'Child from Hell' plot where the kid burns down the town and runs off with the mayor's trashy wife. The truth is that most adoptive parents are pretty ordinary folks. That's the real story, the day-to-day challenge of connecting with kids who, by the time they're 5 or 6, hell, even 6 months, have lost everything that most kids take for granted. It's hard work, but the best parts don't make great theater. These kids have had enough 'excitement.' Some of them have seen people killed. We're trying to make their lives a little less exciting, more predictable. Swanson's audiences are expecting family feuds and cross dressing firemen. What am I going to say to them?"

"Start with what you just said to me."

And the first time someone stands up and says: 'I notice yer not married and you live in a house with several young men. Ah think it's an abomination. You wouldn't be one a them perverts that likes kids, wouldya?' And then a brawl breaks out."

"Just pregame jitters, kid. Swanson's producer has promised to be a bit more selective in screening the audience."

"I'll bet. Nobody who's been institutionalized or fired a weapon in anger within the past week."

But in the end she reluctantly agreed, and now here she was, ten seconds away from the "audience participation" phase of the program.

"Well, we're back," said Swanson. "And it's time to go to our audience."

Elizabeth swallowed hard.

A tall, middle-aged woman stood up and spoke into a microphone poised a few inches from her face. "You spoke earlier about adoption as a calling? I'm still not sure what you meant by that."

"Well, sometimes it's easier to start with what I don't mean. It wasn't a St. Paul-on-the-road-to-Tarsus experience. I wasn't driving to work one day, when the voice of God told me to turn left and head for an adoption agency. I probably would have wrecked the car if that had happened.

"I like the word calling, but, at the same time, it conjures up images of dramatic conversion experiences and saintly deeds that make me a little uncomfortable. Most adoptive parents I know don't think of themselves as anything special, especially as saints. For most people, adoption is a journey of the heart. It starts as an idea that you explore and think about and, over time, becomes a strong conviction. Was God involved, encouraging me to consider adoption? Yes, I believe so, but his or her voice came to me in a soft whisper, rather than a shout."

"Well, do you think that most parents who adopt emotionally traumatized or physically disabled children are motivated by religious or spiritual beliefs?" the woman followed up.

"Wow, that's a hard question to answer because it has so many implications" Elizabeth said slowly. "A lot of adoptive parents I know have strong religious beliefs or spiritual values. Living with children who have experienced nothing but betrayal and pain at the hands of adults who were supposed to care for them is not easy. Restoring trust and teaching these kids to love can bring great joy, but it doesn't happen quickly or easily. There are a lot of setbacks and failures along the way, even in the stories with happy endings. My own religious faith provides me with a sense of direction, of hope when I'm feeling particularly lost and discouraged. I think that's true for a lot of adoptive parents. And some studies have shown that special needs adoption has a higher success rate when the adoptive parents do have strong religious beliefs. It doesn't matter which religion, by the way, as long as it is a part of their lives."

"When I use the word calling, I think of that voice within urging us to love one another. To me, that voice is the voice of God. The mysterious thing about adoption, like any other calling, is how we can become so drawn to activities that are not instantly rewarding, that, on the contrary, can be very trying and involve us with other people's pain. Adoption is a spiritual calling, I think, but no more so than joining the Peace Corps, teaching in Appalachia, visiting people with AIDS, working the streets as a cop, or a thousand other things. Like I said, I don't think that adoptive parents are comfortable in the role of saints."

The woman smiled and sat down amidst a warm round of applause that surprised and touched Elizabeth deeply.

The microphone was passed to a pretty, blond woman dressed in a dark suit. She smiled.

"Do you get subsidies for raising your children?" she asked. The smile was still there, but several degrees cooler.

"Here it comes," thought Elizabeth.

"Whether or not I chose to avail my family of the benefits provided by the federal Title IV-E adoption assistance program is a personal matter. However, I know many families who could not have afforded to adopt without the modest help this program provides."

"Do you think that's right, getting paid to adopt children?"

Elizabeth could hear hissing and murmurs of assent among the audience.

"I think the phrase 'getting paid to adopt' is misleading," said Elizabeth measuring her words. "The adoption assistance programs were created to enable adults to care for children who, because of physical or emotional trauma, required a great deal of attention and services that are often very expensive."

"But you're still getting paid," persisted the woman, who wasn't smiling now. More muted hissing and murmuring from the audience.

"Well, again, my personal financial matters are personal. However, I don't know anyone who gets paid a salary to care for children in their home twenty-four hours a day. Even career foster parents can only hope to recoup expenses. The IRS sees this as reimbursement and does not require W-2 forms or income taxes. You can make more money working a daily shift at a day care center in most cases. And you would eventually get some benefits, too, like vacation days, which Title IV-E makes no provision for!"

Elizabeth reached for and took a long drink from the glass of ice water that had been provided for her. She continued, "You should realize what some parents give up for this special calling. I was making a great deal of money before I quit working full time. After I adopted my second child, I sold my condominium and have used that money and savings from my PR job to get us by. I also do free lance consulting and writing to supplement our family income.

"Years ago, Richard Barth, a researcher at the University of California at Berkeley, showed that the typical adoptive parents contribute thousands of dollars of their income to their children's care, just like birthparents. In most cases, adoption assistance supplements the resources provided by the family, not the other way around.

"Don't forget, for most of these children, the alternative is state-supported foster care. Most adoption assistance is far less than what a child receives in foster care support. Today a large portion of children are being adopted by their foster parents. And in most cases, the parents voluntarily agree to large cuts in assistance in order to make the child their own."

Most of the audience cheered. A young black woman stood up. "My cousin adopted a brother and sister after their mom went to prison. She gets adoption assistance, but let me tell you, she isn't gettin' rich."

More cheers and a few hoots.

The blond woman was in tears. "Well, we never had any help when my husband got laid off and our son got leukemia. I don't see why your children are more valuable than mine."

Elizabeth hesitated. "I don't think that there is anything adequate I can say to respond to the sense of helplessness you must have felt," she said. "But adoption assistance programs were established to invest in families for children who had already lost one set of parents, to enable more adults to create families for these children. And to some parents who have watched their own flesh and blood suffer, that must seem terribly unfair. But please believe me, I never meant to suggest that one child is more worthy of love and support than any other.

"And, well, the advocate in me can't resist telling you that there *are* several wonderful programs available to help all kinds of families in your situation, programs that don't care if your kids are yours by blood, marriage, or adoption. For example, the American Cancer Society, the Ronald McDonald House Foundation, unemployment insurance, food stamps, free lunch program, temporary Medicaid, and the like. You may wish to look into some of these."

Elizabeth was rescued by another commercial and wondered how she was going to make it through the next twenty minutes.

After the break, one of the few men in the audience stood up. His shirt and tie looked a little unnatural on him, like he had spent most of his life working outside with his hands.

"I just wanted to ask you one thing," he said shyly. "My wife and I raised two boys and a girl and it wasn't easy. How do you do it by yourself with six!?"

"Well, I've learned to become a lot more organized. Scheduling doctor's appointments, teacher visits, meals—that was a real challenge for me because I'm not by nature the most organized person in the world. I think that's what surprised my mother the most. As a kid, my room looked like a riot had broken out most of the time. Everybody has their chores to do.

"But, after a time, raising four or five kids of different races or with a bunch of medical problems seems normal to us. I think that's hard for people to understand. I don't know how to program computers or build bridges. Being an adoptive parent is like anything else. People get good at what they are committed to. I got better with practice. The chaos started to subside. The tearful phone calls to family, friends, and even bureaucrats became less frequent. And one day, it all became normal. And normal is such an important concept. A big part of what I try to do is help my kids to experience the normal, everyday, even boring activities of life that most of us took for granted from our earliest memories."

Another round of applause. Maybe she should get her own show.

The rest of the segment passed uneventfully with questions about how to explore adoption, whether or not single parents could adopt, the kinds of children who were available for adoption, and what kind of assistance adoptive parents could receive. No one probed her personal life as a single parent or made any insinuations about her living with a house full of strapping young men with raging hormones.

At the very end, a woman with an odd hat gave Elizabeth a start when she stood up and said she wanted to ask a question about her alien children. The audience began to buzz. Several thoughts raced through her mind. Was this the incident that would finally set off the bench clearing brawl? If asked about her alien status, would it be better to simply admit it? Should she accuse the woman in the funny hat of being an alien or confess that she and all her children were definitely from another galaxy?

Happily, as it turned out, the woman's question was about international adoptions rather than children from outer space, and the show ended on a happy note.

A few days later Kevin called. The show had been an enormous success, receiving a record number of phone calls, faxes, and e-mails. "You're a star!" he said.

"I'm sure the offers are pouring in, but nothing for under a mil or I walk. Also, no yellow M & Ms in the dressing room."

"Actually, we did get a call from *Dateline*? Would you consider it? It would be more of a family piece. I told them you wouldn't consider it without covering the adoption assistance issue. What do you think?"

"I'll have to talk it over with the guys. They'll probably want to do it. I think the problem might be toning them down. Can we negotiate on the approach they take? It's got to be real, not the Waltons."

"We can give it a try. You don't have to agree to anything you're not comfortable with okay? Oh, by the way, there was this other offer. Your family and a foster family are flown to a deserted tropical island in the South Pacific. Viewers tune in each week to see how you are surviving, you know, building a hut, fishing, feuding with the foster family, maybe trying to adopt some of the foster family's children so you can take over control of the island . . . Elizabeth? . . . Elizabeth?"

4

ADOPTION AS PROCESS

Process (noun): continued forward movement, lapse of time, a series of actions, a method of operation, regular progress

INTRODUCTION

The adoption process from initial interest to adoption finalization is like a busy street. At certain hours, cars move quickly. At other times, traffic can snarl, collisions bring movement to a halt, and a simple left turn can cause a large back-up of cars within seconds. Frustrations build. And then home is within sight. And yet, for all its problems, there is only so much we can do to improve conditions. A middle left turn lane helps, wider lanes are always good, and improving nearby alternate routes can relieve some of the traffic. But in the end, rush hour remains with us, and the commute is never without some stress. Not everyone who starts down the adoption road will finish the trip. For some, the navigation is more than they can handle. The adoption process today is interesting, exhaustive, nerve-wracking, slow, and obtuse, but it is, for the most part, a necessary evil. The process is designed to screen out people who have no business being parents or who shouldn't be parents right now. It protects children who have already suffered so much from further suffering. It also inadvertently tests our mettle and challenges our commitment.

We can make the process better by giving families more personal help with the immense amount of paperwork, by assigning "buddy families" to offer support throughout the ordeal, by offering genuine encouragement from the first phone call, and mostly by hiring enough social workers to shorten the length of the process. But ultimately, the only good adoption homestudy process is one that's over and done with. These stories look at everything from the humor of a homestudy home visit gone awry to adoption as seen through the eyes of a judge. They take you inside the process for a close-up look at what adoptive families go through on the road to parenthood. It is an exciting and sometimes wild drive.

૭૦ન્૨

Murphy's Law and the Rileys

The myth of the white-gloved social worker running a hand across the mantle in the home of the prospective adoptive parents to look for the slightest trace of dust and, thereby, the ammunition to deny them their hearts' desire is one that continues to this day. The stern-looking old maid social worker with her hair in a bun peering over the top of her reading glasses is an American icon brought to life again and again in books, movies, and television programs. But if she ever existed, she does no more. Today's social worker is young or old, male or female, single or married, licensed or degreed, and trained to encourage and help families adopt waiting children, not to throw obstacles in their path.

But knowing this gave Lyle Riley and his wife, Susan, little comfort. Preparing for the first home visit in an adoption homestudy was, for them, a nerve-wracking experience. They had no way of knowing that for them, even with the most careful of preparations, everything that could go wrong would.

In a way, they had been preparing for this home visit for a full decade of their lives. That is how long they had lived in their home, a house bought for the sole purpose of filling it with children. Lyle and Susan were one of those unusual couples who had always wanted the exact same thing—kids! Even before their wedding, they talked about names, child-rearing philosophies, favorite kiddie adventures they wanted to recreate for their kids someday, and how having kids and pets at once was the only way to go. They didn't even want to wait a few years after getting married before starting a family. They wanted one right away! But even as the house grew cozier with a dog, furniture, rugs, toys, and a backyard garden, there was no pitter-patter of little feet. The Rileys were among those to know the excruciating agony of infertility. Year after year, they hoped and waited and hoped some more.

While some couples will pursue infertility treatments and hope for a pregnancy while applying to adopt, after ten years of waiting for a pregnancy, the Rileys had decided to go with adoption alone. Their private agency's social worker had recommended that they travel "one road or the other" but not both, so as to give the effort their full energy and attention. Lyle and Susan were both ready to work as hard at adoption as they had at trying to get and stay pregnant.

When Susan wondered aloud if following such a course would result in a surprise pregnancy, as so many people laughingly predicted, Mr. Jenkins, the MSW on their case, assured them that this was not likely. "It is a myth that trying to adopt will often result in a long-awaited pregnancy," he told them. "While it has happened, it is simply because infertility, by nature, is a temporary condition for some couples. They would have conceived with or without an adoption application."

Lyle checked out an armload of books and videos from the library, Susan found several online chat rooms and adoption support groups, and they threw themselves into the process. The first step was the homestudy, and the first step in the homestudy was deciding what kind of child to adopt— healthy baby, baby with special needs, sibling group, preschooler, teenager, and so on. They finally settled on "boy or girl, sibling group up to two members, maybe three, under age 6, and healthy to mild special needs." Deep in their hearts, they wanted a young sibling group immediately, two brothers or two sisters, a ready-made family to fill their home and their lives with love and the kind of chaos only children can create.

Once the first of the homestudy paperwork was filled out, they had two weeks to prepare for Mr. Jenkins' visit to their three-bedroom suburban home. The Rileys prepared as though they were selling the house, from reseeding the front lawn and repainting the front door, to polishing the bathroom tile until it looked new and washing every window, inside and out. One spare bedroom had been turned into an office, but the other was filled with a set of bunk beds, two dressers, and a giant plastic tub full of toys and stuffed animals. Except for the lack of clothing, this was a room waiting and ready for children, down to the cartoon character posters on the wall and the brightly colored sheets and bedspreads on the beds. A baby crib was folded up and tucked away in the closet, just in case the newest Riley was still in diapers. Twenty-four hours before the visit, Susan was so nervous, she felt ill, tired, and sick to her stomach. Lyle had a monster headache. What if Mr. Jenkins did not like their home? What if it wasn't clean enough? (Should we shampoo the carpet one more time to be sure?) What if? What if? They barely slept at all the night before.

Arriving home from work, they quickly changed into their Sunday best and greeted Mr. Jenkins together at the door when he rang the bell. He asked to see every room in the house because "it is our policy," and they gave him the tour. That's when things started to go very wrong.

The toilet in the master bath was stopped up, something neither one of them had noticed before. There was a fresh ketchup spill in the refrigerator door, discovered only when they opened the refrigerator to show Mr. Jenkins how roomy it was, and the red stuff dripped out onto the floor near his shoes. There was a dead mouse on the lowest shelf of the food pantry, not only the first dead mouse they had ever seen in their home, but the first mouse they had ever seen, living or dead.

As if this were not enough, Mr. Jenkins tripped over the model train and the train track running out from under the bunk beds in the bedroom that would hold the new child and fell into the plate glass mirror on the wall. Miraculously, the mirror did not crack, but it fell off the wall to the floor with a crash.

As they began the backyard tour, the back door stuck and wouldn't open until Lyle had tinkered with it. Their elderly Lhaso Apso, Will Rogers, so named because he had never met a man he didn't like, decided he had met one after all. He jumped up on Mr. Jenkins shoe, growled momentarily, and bit him square on the ankle through his trousers. The bite didn't break the skin, but Susan froze in horror. When Mr. Jenkins jumped back to shake off Will, he ran into Susan, knocking her back into the flower bed. As Lyle reached out to break her fall, he upset the bird bath, which cracked in two with an awful thud when it fell over and landed on top of the old stone turtle.

Later, Susan sloshed lemonade everywhere when she brought it to the living room, so violently were her hands shaking. Lyle jumped up to help her but only succeeded in knocking the sugar bowl off her tray. As they stood there, wondering whether to clean the sugar up now or after the home visit, Susan fought back tears. For some reason, Lyle felt like laughing instead. The day so far reminded him of an old Vaudeville routine he'd once seen in a black and white movie.

Mr. Jenkins smiled, reassured them that he was quite sure their lives did not normally resemble the script of a disaster readiness drill, and continued with the questions. After sipping his lemonade, he congratulated them on creating a "wonderful home for any child or sibling group." He suggested only two changes, in addition to setting out a few mouse traps: one, a more secure cabinet to place medicines out of reach than the one they were currently using, and two, the bunk beds would have to be taken apart and used as twin beds. They had a policy against bunk beds because of the potential for falls and other injuries. Easy changes, all!

Susan and Lyle were visibly relieved to have passed the home test. As Mr. Jenkins drove away, they hugged and jumped up and down. The first home visit was over and he liked them! He really liked them! Oh, joy!

The rest of the homestudy, which took about two months, was easier, and the rest of the visits went smoothly (as long as Will was on a leash). There were financial statements, a letter from their doctor stating that they were free of communicable disease, recommendations from relatives, friends, and their pastor, and a couple more home visits.

Seven months to the day after walking into the agency and filling out an application to adopt, they were officially in the "search and match stage" with a completed, typed, and approved homestudy. Susan was already online at the web site run by the National Adoption Center (www.adopt.org) looking at photolistings of waiting children and contacting their social workers. She was especially taken with two brothers, Jermaine and Christopher, ages

6 and 7. Jermaine, biracial, loved trains and computers. Christopher, Caucasian, who had recently undergone successful surgery to correct a moderate heart birth defect, was quieter and more shy than his half brother, but he was also a train enthusiast. And he loved dogs. Plural. More than one dog. Lyle liked that. He had been after Susan for a long time to consider a second dog, a friend for Will. If they were chosen for these kids, how could she continue to say no?

Lyle's nervous headaches had long subsided, but Susan continued to feel tired and queasy. Finally, she went to see her doctor without telling Lyle so as not to worry him, and there she received the shock of her life. "Pregnant?! Three months pregnant already?! Are you sure?!"

Susan was sure she floated home. She certainly didn't remember driving. She fell into her husband's arms laughing and crying tears of joy. She couldn't speak but waved at her middle and showed him a doctor's visit receipt. Lyle caught on. They laughed and cried and hugged and cried well into the night. A baby! At long last. They had completely given up on the idea of ever giving birth to a baby. And here it was going to happen—and in only six months. They couldn't go to sleep before taking the crib out of the closet, setting it up, and attaching the colorful vinyl butterfly mobile to the headboard. A baby!

Susan's first thought upon waking was one of horror, however, not joy. What about the adoption? It hadn't occurred to her before that a pregnancy might stop an adoption. Could it? What about the sibling group they had looked so long for and had prepared for so carefully? Lyle's thoughts were the same. As thrilled as they were about the pregnancy, they were not ready to give up on the adoption. They already felt an emotional bond to their unknown but living children, somewhere out there in foster care.

Their parents thought them insane. "Do you know how much work a baby is?" asked Susan's mother. "You won't get much sleep, son, for months," added Lyle's dad.

But what no one but Susan and Lyle could truly understand was that they knew all of this, and it didn't matter. When you have longed for something year after year after year and have seen all of your friends, neighbors, and co-workers get that something before you, you are more than ready for it. You are past ready. Their children—born, unborn, almost adopted—were all very real to them. They already had three children in their hearts. At this stage, losing the adoption would have felt no less painful than a miscarriage. Lyle searched the fine print of all of the agency's literature looking for a rule or policy that had to do with their situation but found nothing specific. If they told the agency, would Mr. Jenkins stop the adoption? After all, he had encouraged them to follow one path to parenthood, not two. If they lied, would their eventual adoption be undone?

The couple sought help online at their adoption support group chat room. Susan logged in anonymously and described their situation. "Please tell us what to do," she begged. "We are ready and able to do both. How can we be sure they will agree?"

The chat room moderator told them, "In my opinion, no one should ever lie to their adoption agency, no matter what, about anything. Technically, if you do not offer information you have not been asked for or have not been required to disclose, you are not lying. But it does seem less than honest. My suggestion is to consider sharing your news and your feelings and hopes with your worker. At worst, your pregnancy will only delay your adoption by a year or so. At best, your worker will agree with you that you can handle both. I know several families who adopted children with special needs soon after giving birth."

The Rileys discussed it some more but eventually decided on silence as the best course of action. However, the whole issue became academic when they were told that Jermaine and Christopher had entered a "kinship" adoptive placement with a birth uncle. More tears. More grieving the children that were and weren't. They toyed with the idea of stopping the adoption process and asking the agency to stop searching, but something told them not to.

At this point, the Rileys believed they were meant to adopt, and soon. They couldn't explain it, but they knew that two kids needed them, so they went back to the photolistings even as they prepared for a new baby.

Ninety long days passed with little contact between Mr. Jenkins and the Rileys. None of the listings they inquired about worked out. Then one day, Mr. Jenkins called with a voice full of excitement and anticipation.

"Do you remember Jermaine and Christopher? As you know, they had been adopted at the last minute by Christopher's uncle. But the adoption fell through. The uncle decided that he did not want to adopt two children, and, well, the state is determined to keep the brothers together, so they want to know if you are still interested! Are you?"

This was a side of calm, collected Mr. Jenkins they had never heard before So, he was an old softie who loves kids, after all. It was obvious that Mr. Jenkins dearly loved this part of his job. This was likely what kept him in the field of social work. And who could blame him? Social workers in adoption get to be the stork. What happier job could there be? Except, well, their obstetrician liked her stork duties, too. Susan's eyes were already filled with tears of happiness. Lyle, grinning from ear to ear, spoke for both of them. "Please tell them *yes* from us. We can be at your office in an hour to hear more about the boys. Is that okay?"

This was the best way they knew to tell Mr. Jenkins that Susan was now going into her third trimester—to simply go in and see him. They said a prayer that their unborn daughter would come into the world with two big brothers waiting to greet her, and then they set off for the agency.

Lyle walked in first and shook hands with a delighted Mr. Jenkins, who was holding a thick file full of information on Jermaine and Christopher.

Susan greeted him next, extending a hand and smiling weakly. Mr. Jenkins reached out to shake her hand, glanced at her round middle, and his face fell. He slumped down in his chair as though someone had just knocked the air out of him. He couldn't have looked more disappointed if he had just lost Wimbledon in the final round. Looking up at the Rileys, he said, "I don't understand. Is this it? Are you here to back out?"

Susan's eyes nearly popped out of her head. This was not the reaction she had expected. Did he really think that she and Lyle did not want to complete the adoption? "No! No, Mr. Jenkins! We're here to tell you that we desperately want to *continue* this adoption. Honest! Our daughter is due in three months, but we have an excellent support network. We *can* parent three kids. You must believe us."

At this, Mr. Jenkins smiled, first a little, then broadly. Finally, he leaned forward and laughed out loud. "Thank heavens!" he cried. When something like this happened last year at this agency, the couple backed out, and they had already had their adopted infant in their home for a whole week. They didn't feel they could do both. So I just, well, I just assumed that you might feel overwhelmed, too!"

The relief in the room was absolutely palpable. Susan and Lyle had worried for the last three months for nothing. All was well and everything was back on track. And that was the last bump in the road on their long and difficult journey to parenthood.

After two visits, their new sons were home a month later, greeted by Will's new sibling, Murphy, the Labrador puppy, and baby Catherine was born on her due date, two months after that (just ten-plus years late!).

Jermaine showed a keen talent for making babies laugh. And Christopher, Will, and Murphy were inseparable. The family loved their new busy lifestyle, and the adoptions were finalized the following year. The Rileys went from a family of three to a family of seven, including four-legged family members, in a matter of months, and they haven't had a moment's regret since.

୧ംൟ

Black Robes and Ribbon Candy

Finalization day is a family event unique to adoption. Judges will tell you that finalizing adoptions is one of the few activities they look forward to in their job, because everyone in the courtroom is happy. There is no crime, no punishment, no heartbreaking divorce, no decision—just a swearing in, a little paperwork, and happy photographs all around.

Judge Denise Woodward was looking forward to the finalization scheduled in her court today and not only because it was likely to be one of her final duties before she retired. Her clerk had told her it was a very unique step-parent adoption. A family consisting of a widower with seven children, recently remarried to a widow with three children, would presently be descending on her quiet corner of the world so that each parent could adopt their step-children.

The goal was not to erase the memory of the beloved deceased parents but to unite the family through a legal ceremony that would give them one familial identity. After today, no one would be introduced using the term "step." It would be simply, "This is my brother," or "Oh, that's my dad," or "Meet my little sis." Judge Woodward had been on the bench for thirty-five years, and she had never seen an adoption like this. She'd finalized adoptions of children who came from the same county and from across the nation, kids from Korea, China, Guatemala, a sibling group from India, and children ranging in age from a few months to 17 years old. She had even presided over two adult adoptions whereby foster parents had formally adopted their grown-up foster children. Those were particularly emotional. And she had enjoyed signing adoption papers for many step-turned adoptive families. Step-parent adoptions were not at all uncommon, but a family this size and both parents widowed instead of divorced? What were the odds?

As she ate breakfast that morning, she described the upcoming case to Fred, her spouse of thirty-one years. He laughed out loud trying to imagine her tiny chambers full of so many people. "Oh, no," the judge cried, "we'll stay in the courtroom. No private chambers this time. We'll protect privacy by simply closing off the courtroom with a sign taped outside the door. I'll not have ten children running around my office!"

Fred just grinned. His stern, disciplined wife was a pushover when it came to kids, and everyone in the world knew it except her. They had lived childless quite happily their entire married lives and had no regrets to this day, but where Fred lavished his parental love on their two elderly beagles, Denise played momma to the children who occasionally appeared in her courtroom. She even kept a huge dish of old-fashioned, brightly colored hard candy shaped like wavy ribbons—just for the kids. "Keeps them quiet," was her excuse, but Fred knew better. She traded candy for little smiles, and she loved it.

"Better take this, honey," Fred said as he reached into a kitchen drawer and pulled out a disposable camera. "I bought this thing for my last fishing trip so that if I dropped my camera into the lake taking a shot of 'The Big One,' it wouldn't matter much. But that was the trip where all I caught was a cold. So there's twenty-four shots here and a built-in flash, too. Get me a photo of this family right after you pass out the ribbon candy!"

"Oh, Fred," admonished Denise, "you know I can't take photos of people who come into my courtroom. It's not professional."

"But your honor," argued Fred, "you're retiring in a matter of days. So how could it hurt? I want to see this huge family, so just take the camera in case you change your mind."

Denise stuffed the cardboard-wrapped camera into her briefcase along with some papers she needed to review concerning her retirement. With the refill bag of ribbon candy already inside the case, there was barely enough room.

Three hours later, the adoption case was upon her, and she knew it before she ever saw a member of the family. Seated behind the bench, gavel at hand, she could hear them coming down the hallway looking for her name among those on the wooden doors of the various courtrooms.

A child's voice, a little girl, probably the lead scout of the party, squealed with delight, "Here it is, Dad! Right here! Judge Woodward! We found it!" Moments later, the door swung open slightly and a 40-something man with graying temples poked his head into the courtroom. Judge Woodward's clerk motioned them to come in, and Denise counted silently as the parade commenced. Dad, holding a satchel of papers, came in followed by three teenaged sons, all taller than him, and each holding the hand of a younger brother or sister. The scout was apparently a precocious little girl, no older than 9, pulling her older brother after her. She tried to march right up to the judge but was yanked back. Five-year-old twin girls appeared next, identical in every way except their clothing. One wore a frilly dress, and the other, jeans and a new t-shirt. A woman looking to be about 35 came in next, holding a diaper bag and a toddler in her arms. The tenth child, a shy little boy about age 7, clung to her side and looked nervously at the judge. His lower lip quivered as if he were about to cry.

Their lawyer popped in seconds later, a bit out of breath and checking his watch to decide if he was tardy or not. He introduced himself as Mr. de la Vega and handed the clerk a bundle of papers to give to the judge.

The family stood about 10 feet away from the Judge's bench, all of them looking extremely well groomed and clean. The children were quiet, except for a whisper here and there, and obviously knew their manners. But Judge Woodward was concerned about the little boy now cowering behind his mother. He was more than intimidated. He was downright frightened.

Her clerk spoke. "Judge, this is the Ramon family. Mr. and Mrs. Ramon are here today to adopt their respective step-children. Here are the legal documents. Should I swear them in now?"

"Just a moment," said the judge softly. "I want to ask Mrs. Ramon a question."

She stood up and asked Mrs. Ramon for the name of the little boy who was standing behind her. The mother smiled and stepped forward a little. "Your honor, this is our son, Carlos. He is 7 and a half years old and loves to watch courtroom dramas on TV. He wants to be a judge someday, but he is a little shy this morning. Perhaps his imagination is running away from him, verdad?"

"Yes, I see. A future judge, eh?" said the woman in the long black robe. "Carlos, it is a pleasure to meet a future jurist. Would you like to step up here and see what a gavel really looks like?"

A hush fell over the family as all eyes turned toward the little boy. He stepped out from behind his mother and silently shook his head "yes." Judge Woodward leaned forward and held the gavel out. He pushed through the small swinging carved wood doors, ran up to the judge's bench, stood on tiptoe, took the wooden mallet from her, and turned it over and over in his hands. Then he smiled and handed it back.

"Oh, no, Carlos," the judge said with mock somberness, "you must bang the gavel on that wooden witness chair next to you before you give it back to me."

Carlos grinned broadly as he gave the chair's seat a good whack and then a second one for good measure, handed back the gavel, and raced to return to his family. But now he stood in front of them all proudly. All signs of fear had vanished.

The clerk stood up and said, "Raise your right hands please, everyone. Do you all swear and or affirm to tell the truth and nothing but the truth?"

Various answers filled the air in English and Spanish ranging from "I do" to "okay" to "yes," and a nervous Mrs. Ramon blurted out, "Si, señora, I mean, yes!"

Judge Woodward reassured the adopting mother that she knew a bit of Spanish herself and that this was not an English-only courtroom. "Comprende?" Mrs. Ramon flashed a grateful smile and nodded.

The judge checked each adoption petition to see that they were filled out properly, and then she instructed the clerk to have everyone step up to the bench.

"Now, children, adoption is a serious matter. Once done, it cannot be undone. I want you to know this. Adoption is a lovely way to bring a family closer together that has been brought together through remarriage, but adoption won't eradicate sibling rivalry. It won't make everything perfect. Do you understand that?" All but the toddler nodded their heads in affirmation.

She continued, "Now, I always ask this question. It is routine. Is there anyone here who can give me a good reason for not signing these papers?"

The little girl whose voice had filled the hallway earlier put her hand high up in the air. Several of her siblings gasped. The parents stared in disbelief.

"Yes? What is your name?" asked the judge with just a hint of sternness in her voice.

"Margarita, your honor ma'am," she answered sharply while stepping forward.

"And what do you want to tell me, Margarita?"

"Do you know where the bathroom is, please, your honor?"

Giggles were closely followed by sighs of relief as the clerk pointed down the hallway to the restroom. When Margarita returned, the judge again asked if there were any objections. There were not. "Very well," she said. "I am now going to sign the paper that makes Mom the mom of ten children, and Dad the dad of ten children and all of you will have the last name of Ramon. There. It is signed. Congratulations!"

The dozen people standing before her cheered and hugged. Mr. and Mrs. Ramon embraced and kissed around the toddler still in Mrs. Ramon's arms and sound asleep. Margarita pulled on her mother's dress and said, "Now can we go home and have the big party? I want to break the piñata and grab the most candy!"

"Well, almost," replied Mrs. Ramon. She turned to the judge and said, "May we take a photo of you and our family together before we leave? This is such a happy day for us!"

"Of course," said the judge. "I always expect that. It comes with the robes." She stepped down onto the floor of the courtroom, and Carlos hurried quickly to her side and took her hand. Margarita had her other hand in hers in a flash, and the rest of the family lined up. Mr. de la Vega offered to snap the photos. It was then that Mr. and Mrs. Ramon began speaking in hushed tones in Spanish, and they sounded upset. Mr. Ramon explained, "Your honor, in all the confusion this morning of getting the children ready, we forgot to pack the camera in the diaper bag. I am sorry to have bothered you, but there will be no photos today."

Instantly, the euphoria in the room faded. Mrs. Ramon looked like she was about to burst into tears and Carlos' lower lip began to tremble again.

Then the judge remembered Fred's disposable camera. "Wait, don't move!" she commanded and flew into her chambers to retrieve it. She came back out moments later, waving the cardboard camera in triumph. "You may have this camera—my gift to you!"

Again the room exploded into jubilation, and amid cries of "thank you" and "gracias," everyone lined up again. Mr. de la Vega snapped several poses and then joined the group, and the clerk took several more. And when they were finished, there was plenty of film left to take photos of the kids at the big statue of the soldier and the horse in front of the courthouse.

Only after the courtroom photos were taken did the judge remember the ribbon candy. The children had been so well-mannered, she hadn't thought to give it out before as a pacifier. So she brought out the large candy bowl now and encouraged each child to take several pieces. "Judge Woodward," said Mrs. Ramon, "it is a sign from heaven that you should have this kind of candy. In my family, Santa Claus always brings ribbon candy on Christmas morning. This makes today our second Christmas!"

Later that evening, as Denise returned home, Fred and the beagles were waiting on the front porch swing. They scooted to make room for the judge to sit down and swing, too. "So what happened?" asked her spouse. "Did you take any photos of this supersized family?"

"Fred, my love," responded a tired but happy judge, "your little camera saved the day. The parents had left their camera behind. You will never see those photos, but you can be sure that many other people will see them and enjoy them for generations to come."

Fred was all right with that idea. "Well, it looks like my camera caught sight of "The Big One" after all. Only it was a 12-member family, not one of my 12-pound fishes!"

ᔑᵒ⋞ᒷ

Elliot's Uneven Dozen

"Well, Mrs. Greene, I know of one child on the exchange that might be a good match for you, but this one is neither school-age nor a boy. Her name is Elliot, and she's 5 months old. Would you like to know more?"

Ahhhh. A baby. And a great age, probably sleeping through the night. But how odd that when they had looked for babies, they were offered older children. And now that they wanted an older boy. . . . Morgan Greene suppressed a laugh. This might be the adoption that made her finally believe in "adoption signs." Was this child meant for their family? Or perhaps it was simply a coincidence that she and Elliot shared the feminine gender and masculine first names.

She glanced over at her three young daughters, ages 1, 2, and 3, playing with the new puppy on the dining room floor and, to her great surprise, said into the telephone, "Tell me more, please, Mr. Yellow Knife."

The man from the Waiting Indian Child Adoption Exchange continued, enthusiasm building in his voice. "Elliot is half black and half Indian. I have her photo here. What a doll! The name of the tribe is not on this form, but she was born on a small reservation not too far from the Canadian border. Her birthfather is unknown, possibly a military man passing through, and her birthmother is an unemployed waitress who has relinquished three other children, all boys, due to chronic alcoholism. All of them are half siblings with different fathers. One is permanently placed with a paternal uncle and his wife, and the other two are in foster care but unavailable for adoption at this time."

"Why not?" Morgan's first instinct has always been to keep siblings together, when possible.

The sound of shuffling papers was followed by an explanation. "Well," said Mr. Yellow Knife, "it looks like the birthmother, Jane, intends to go back for the other two kids as soon as she can stop drinking. But she wants Elliot to be adopted because . . . oh . . . because she is black instead of full-blood. I'm sorry."

The social worker was embarrassed by the birthmother's racism, but Morgan was relieved. "Well, at least this precious baby won't be going home to that kind of sad attitude," she commented. "Can you tell me if the baby is having health problems?"

"Not yet. On target in all developmental areas and even a little bit ahead. This baby rolled over in the hospital bassinet on the day she was born! Seems the nurses nearly fainted."

Precocious little girl, thought Morgan. She could feel it happening. Her heart was pounding; her eyes were filling with wet emotion. She was falling in love. "Would you please send in our homestudy on Elliot and mail me the photo?"

Mr. Yellow Knife sounded pleased. "Sure will, Morgan. It's good to be working with you again. Tell George that the baby is considered a high risk for alcohol-related problems, but as you know from the research you did on your last adoption, a good home can minimize those problems, too."

George. Oh, no, George! Morgan couldn't believe she had actually put their study in on a baby before her husband heard about the child! What would he say?

He wasn't a bit angry, to her relief. George Greene loved being a daddy. He said it was the only job in the world where you are guaranteed at least one decade of hero worship. His daughters' love for him was exceeded only by his love for them. And why shouldn't he put his advanced baby changing and baby rocking skills to good use one more time? There would be opportunities later to adopt a son.

Elliot's photo arrived three days later, along with a brief description. She was indeed beautiful. Thick, small, blacks curls surrounding a delicate oval face and Indian eyes accented perfect medium brown skin. Morgan did not see any of the facial characteristics that are associated with Fetal Alcohol Syndrome (FAS), but she knew that severe disabilities remained a possibility with or without the facial characteristics. Under the federal law, the Indian Child Welfare Act (ICWA), the tribe had final say over the family chosen for Elliot but waived its right to review the decision, something this particular tribe usually did with mixed-race children. The state had preferred an adoptive family with black and Indian parents or a black family, but when one was not to be found among the hopeful applicants, they settled on the Greenes as the next best thing. George is one-sixteenth Cherokee, not Elliot's tribe, but American Indian. And their oldest daughter, Cora, an African American child, would be delighted to have a sister who looked like her racially.

Ever since Morgan had left her sales job to stay home, money had been extremely tight. The family was overjoyed that the state covered all placement expenses, including the homestudy update, and the plane tickets that brought Elliot and her social worker, Mrs. St. Michael, to the Greene's house.

What a joyous day that was! Morgan had heard about airport adoptions, but this was the first time she had heard of this happening with an American-born baby instead of an international adoption. Elliot deplaned sitting upright in the worker's arms, looking around intently. She was surrounded by so much attention and love that no one heard the sound of her cry, even for a moment, until she had been home for three days.

On day two, Mrs. St. Michael prepared to leave, having satisfied herself that the Greenes were a good match for the child and that the bonding process was off to a good start. As she prepared to go, she gave Morgan and George a subsidy contract and a Medicaid card transfer application, two documents they had never heard of before. As the worker explained what an adoption subsidy was, Morgan fought back tears of joy. Financial help? What a blessing! The contract called for the parents to receive $380 per month, no matter their personal income, until Elliot's eighteenth birthday to help with the costs of raising her. And the Medicaid would transfer to the medical assistance program of her new home state and also remain in effect, regardless of the Greene's income, until adulthood. "You can renegotiate the contract amount upward, later on, if the baby's needs change," she added.

Elliot thrived in her new home and the "adoption subsidy" check meant no immediate or drastic change in the family's standard of living in order to accommodate another person.

One year later, as the family ate lunch together in the dining room, Elliot's adoption was finalized. Under tribal rules, Elliot's adoption had to be finalized in tribal court, not state or county court. Elliot, however, did not have to be present as long as the social worker was present in the courtroom to stand in for the family. Mrs. St. Michael called when the simple legal proceeding was over, and everyone cheered. They had cake and ice cream for the celebration. Elliot's adoption was irrevocable now.

Just a week later, Mrs. St. Michael was calling again. "How's Elliot?"

It sounded like a polite query, but Morgan took the opportunity to describe an ongoing concern. "She still isn't talking or even babbling, except to say Da-Da and Ma-Ma. The other girls all had growing vocabularies by 18 months of age."

"Yes, but Morgan, don't forget. Elliot was walking by 9 months of age. That's early. Maybe she is concentrating on physical development and the language will come later."

Morgan smiled. "That's what our doctor says. But I have this feeling that there's a problem. I guess it's just mommy worry."

The phone call was about to take a surprising turn with the next question. "Have you and George ever thought about adopting again? Perhaps a little boy or two?" Mrs. St. Michael's voice sounded conspiratorial. She knew something!

"You know we have, Mrs. St. Michael!" Morgan blurted out. "We've always wanted a son. Why do you ask?"

"It's Beau and Bradley, ages 3 and 4 and a half, Elliot's half siblings. The courts have determined that they cannot be returned to their birthmother—ever. We'd like to see the siblings reunited. The uncle who adopted Shane, the oldest of Jane's children, does not want to adopt again. How do you feel about two more?"

Morgan gasped for air. For a moment she thought the joy inside of her would cause an explosion. She and George had discussed this possibility many times. How they had prayed for it! A son at last, with a built-in brother. And their precious Elliot can grow up with biological relatives, as well. What could be better? George was just as excited with the news as his wife had been. The Greenes scraped together enough money to drive to the reservation to meet the children while the paperwork was started. The foster mother, Mrs. Duvall, an elderly widow, spoke glowingly of the boys. She had been caring for them since they were each a few weeks old. She was not being considered as an adoptive mother for the children because of both her age and her lack of Indian ancestry. The tribe wanted an Indian family or a blood relative. Elliot's adoptive family was the state's choice.

Brad and Beau, as they liked to be called, did not resemble Elliot much physically, but they shared her quiet, shy temperament. Brad showed off his "warrior hair," a long braid that ran down his back. Beau, the more out-going sibling, preferred to wear his straight black hair short. They were dressed in shorts and t-shirts, perfect outfits for a day spent at the park.

Both children spoke little but smiled often and seemed happy to meet and play with their little sister. The day-long visit ended much too soon, but before the Greenes left, Mrs. St. Michael gave them reason to believe that the next time they saw the children, they would be taking them home for good. "The tribe will make the final decision," she explained, "but they almost always follow our recommendation, and we are recommending you."

Saying good-bye to Brad and Beau was difficult, but Morgan and George managed to hug them without tears. Beau was a little upset that he could not take Elliot home with him, but when told he would see her again soon, he agreed to let go of her hand. All that remained now was to go home, finish the homestudy update for this final adoption, and wait for the tribe to officially approve the match.

Within a few days, a disturbing call arrived from Mrs. St. Michael. She reported that Mrs. Duvall had suddenly hired an attorney and was asking to be allowed to adopt the two children. She had decided that she could not bear to see them go. She had cited a state law that gives foster parents precedence over other applicants in the adoptions of the children they have cared for longer than six months. Morgan's heart jumped into her throat. Mrs. Duvall had said nothing to her at the park about wanting to adopt the children. Indeed, she had seemed happy that they would be reunited with their sister in adoption.

Mrs. St. Michael was not concerned, because ICWA was a federal act that had to be considered before the state law, and ICWA strongly encouraged the adoption of Indian children by Indian families and by kin. Morgan and George were concerned, but they were also relieved that Mrs. St. Michael was still confident. They waited some more, all the while sending cards and photos to Brad and Beau by way of Mrs. St. Michael.

Morgan readied a small bedroom for them. They had recently moved to a larger home, a fixer-upper, with five bedrooms. She planned to put the brothers in the same room to help them feel more secure. She decorated it with Indian print bedspreads, bright colorful stenciling, and a shelf full of books about the history and folklore of their tribe. When the waiting made her feel blue, she went to their room and decorated some more, and she felt better.

Another month passed. The homestudy update was long finished, and the wait was becoming unbearable. Finally, the tribe made a decision and sent the family a letter. George brought it into the house and tore it open excitedly. Morgan had been so busy all day with the four girls, she hadn't even noticed that the mail had arrived.

But their joy quickly turned to shock, disbelief, grief, and then anger. Since no families from the tribe had applied, the tribal adoption committee had decided to allow Mrs. Duvall to adopt the children for reasons that the Greenes saw as tinged with nothing less than racism. The letter read:

The tribal committee feels that it is important for the children, Bradley and Beau, who are not of mixed race, to be geographically closer to the reservation, even if that means being raised by a white family. The mixed-race family of their black half-sister, Elliot, was also considered. However, they live hundreds of miles from the reservation boundary and theirs appears to us to be a black family, not an American Indian family. . . . The decision of this committee is final. . . . Mrs. Duvall may finalize the adoption of these two children immediately, and her adult son and daughter have agreed to finish raising the children should Mrs. Duvall not survive until their adulthood.

Morgan and George read and reread the letter several times. Was this not blatant racism by the tribal committee? How could they decide to ignore the Indian ancestry of Elliot and of George? If they had read the homestudy at all, they would have known that the Greene's were equally proud of all of the cultures and races within the family. How could the tribe decide against them when they had already adopted a biological relative of the children—their own sister?

"The prior relationship of the children to their foster mother is an important factor," explained Mrs. St. Michael when they reached her by phone, "and we would have hoped for ongoing contact with Mrs. Duvall should the tribe have ruled in your favor. However, the prior relationship does not seem to have been the main reason why Mrs. Duvall was chosen to adopt the boys. Rather, it was genes and geography."

"What?" queried an exasperated Morgan. "What does 'genes and geography' mean?"

"Some tribes, Morgan, have seen many of their adoptable infants spirited away by white adoptive couples and their lawyers for decades. This is why the Indian Child Welfare Act was written back in 1978—to help keep Indian children on or near the reservations. Every child is important, especially to small tribes like this one. They strive to keep the tribal genes nearby and to keep the children in the general area so that, hopefully, they will live among their tribe for all time. That's the geography."

"But, Mrs. St. Michael," argued George, trying to keep the anger out of his voice, "how can they ignore the sibling relationship or our ties as a family to our Indian heritage? It's as if they can ignore accepted social work practice—and what's best for the individual child—for any reason they choose."

"George, I understand your feelings. Remember, I voted for you. But the tribe, in this case, decided in the best interest of the whole tribe instead of individual children. And ICWA gives them the right to make that decision. There's no way around the law, I'm afraid."

And so the grieving began. Elliot was too young to understand what she had just lost. But she saw her mother go into the newly decorated empty bedroom and cry. And she saw her father work for hours on a long letter to the committee begging them to reconsider, a letter which the tribe never answered.

It took many months, but in time, the sadness passed like a slow-moving storm and life returned to normal. Mrs. Duvall finalized the adoptions of her former foster sons and eventually agreed to allow them to exchange birthday cards and holiday gifts with Elliot.

At age 3, Elliot was officially diagnosed with fetal alcohol exposure (FAE). Tests revealed her to be physically healthy and coordinated but mildly mentally retarded. They also suspected attention deficit hyperactivity disorder, which is common among alcohol-exposed children. She needed oral surgery to pull badly malformed teeth and to have artificial replacements screwed into her jawbone. The Greenes were once again grateful to have an adoption assistance contract with Medicaid for their daughter that helped with the many new expenses.

When Elliot was 4 years old, the Greenes had their homestudy updated and started looking at photolistings again for a son or two. They were only days into this process when a familiar name greeted them by phone. It was Mrs. St. Michael, and her voice was breathless with excitement.

"You won't believe it, Morgan," she said, "but the court just terminated the birthmother's rights to Elliot's baby brother, and the tribe has waived their right to consent to our choice because this sibling—his name is Kevin—is half African American! Not the same birthfather as Elliot, but a man who is not interested in raising Kevin because of his FAS diagnosis. We're quite sure that alcohol exposure has caused some degree of mental retardation in Kevin, but no one can say how much. This baby is free for adoption now. Are you interested?!"

Morgan's mind was a whirlwind of reactions to what she had just heard and its implications—that there was yet another sibling in the picture, that the tribe would not be involved this time, that Elliot and Kevin had so much in common besides genetics, that Kevin was also disabled, that FAE was more challenging and debilitating than they had expected, and that they might at last be adopting a son and a sibling of Elliot's. Never before had she been so full of questions, emotions, joy, hope, and fear. Her mouth would not cooperate when she tried to speak. A long silence followed.

"Morgan? Morgan, are you there?"

"Yes, Mrs. St. Michael. I'm here, and we remain committed to sibling reunification. We've always wanted a big family. We're very open-minded about more children—but—well, let me talk to George, okay? You're asking us to take another big emotional risk, to get attached to a child . . . and we are still grieving Beau and Bradley."

Mrs. St. Michael understood perfectly. "Once burned, twice shy."

Slowly, the fears of George and Morgan turned to hope, and the hope, to excitement. This did seem to be more of a sure thing. And another baby, and a son!

But their happiness was not to last. Less than two weeks after they had asked to be considered for Kevin, the foster family, a married couple with two biological teens, fostering only Kevin, hired a lawyer and filed suit to stop the adoption on grounds that it violated state law. The baby was almost 6 months old, said the brief, and when he reached that age, they could adopt him based on their "prior relationship." Once again, Mrs. St. Michael was not too concerned. "The courts take the sibling bond very seriously," she said. "Kevin is a baby who can easily bond to you if removed from his white foster family now and placed with his sister's family. We believe the court will side with us."

But for reasons that were never to become clear to the Greenes (they suspected a seriously overworked legal department), the state dragged its feet about trying to get the case to court before Kevin was 6 months old. And when it was finally scheduled, the foster family's attorney asked for and was granted several extensions of time. The state lawyer did nothing despite pleas from the Greene family. By the time the case reached state court, Kevin was 8 and a half months old.

The district court judge awarded adoptive custody to the foster family based on a lengthy prior relationship. Morgan and George, who had not had the money to appear in court personally, were represented by the state's attorney. Mrs. St. Michael was a powerful witness for their family, but it wasn't enough. Worse, the state decided against appealing the decision, because there would be more delays and less of a chance of getting the child removed. The foster family finalized the adoption quickly and refused, for the time being at least, to allow any contact between Kevin and Elliot.

The Greenes were speechless with grief. Again, they had failed to give Elliot the greatest gift, the chance to grow up with one of her four birth-brothers. First, the tribe failed them, and then the state's attorney. Money had kept them from participating more actively in the process or from hiring their own attorney, and now all they had left was their sorrow.

But they could not stay sad for long. Their own county department of human services called about twin brothers, African American, age 2, who needed to be placed together. The boys were emotionally healthy and bright with IQs well above average. Fremont and Edward both had sickle cell disease (SCD), but it was well controlled with medication. They had been in the same foster home since birth and were now free for adoption. The experienced foster parents, an African American couple by the name of Mr. and Mrs. Biltmore, wanted very much to stay in contact with them after adoption. The Greenes readily agreed, and placement quickly followed several day-long visits.

Eddie and Fremont also qualified for an adoption assistance contract, and this eased the money worries. With their contract in place, the Greenes were able to trade in the battered four-door sedan for a slightly used minivan. They started work on their home to enlarge the family room.

The Biltmores became a third set of grandparents to all of the Greene children. It was every bit as wonderful an adoption experience as the last two failed attempts had been nightmares. From one extreme to the other. Morgan and George had never been happier or more proud of their family—six kids!

Three and a half months after finalizing the adoptions of Eddie and Fremont, Morgan was sprawled out in the living room, leaning on pillows, and reading a story to her children when the phone rang. The man identified himself as the social worker who had taken over Mrs. St. Michael's caseload when she retired recently. His name was Alfonso Lenzini. He asked about Elliot's progress, and Morgan explained that Elliot had been diagnosed with FAE, speech delays, speech impairment, and permanent developmental disabilities.

"However," added Morgan, lest he think she was unhappy with her daughter, "these are not conditions that are uncommon to children exposed to alcohol. We are committed to helping Elliot achieve her potential, and we are hopeful she will live independently some day, with just a little more help than usual."

Alfonso was glad to hear it and suggested that the Greenes apply for an increase in Elliot's adoption subsidy based on the new, more detailed medical diagnosis and prognosis. Morgan was happy to hear that her daughter might qualify for an increase and promised to send in a doctor's letter as soon as she could acquire one.

It was then that Alfonso dropped the bombshell when he asked if they might be interested in adopting Elliot's half brother, born about four months ago and recently relinquished by Jane. "The birthfather is unknown.

We believe him to be African American, although not the same man who fathered either Kevin or Elliot. The foster parent wants very much to adopt Baby Carl, but we believe in putting siblings together whenever possible—"

Morgan jumped up from the floor in one motion. "Jane's had *another* baby?!" she asked incredulously. "Why, why does she keep having babies when she has no intention to stop drinking or to raise her children? Why do you allow her to? This is unbelievable!"

"It is not as uncommon as you may think," he replied. "I have known several birthmothers in my caseload who have had more than three children, never intending to raise any of them. And in a free nation, there is not much we can do about it. However, Jane finally agreed to have and did receive a tubal ligation recently, at state expense. She won't be having any more children. And the department would like to see this last baby, Carl, adopted by a family who has adopted one of the other siblings. We're asking you first."

Morgan never paused, never thought about what she would say. The response was automatic and instantaneous, having been suggested by George long ago just in case this very situation ever arose again.

"Then, Mr. Lenzini, you should have placed this baby with us or with Kevin's family at birth, either as a foster child or in a 'legal risk' adoption." Morgan was surprised at the stern tone of her voice. "In a situation like this, you don't need to involve another foster family, but now that you have, we couldn't even consider taking another chance on having our hearts broken."

Morgan wasn't the slightest bit tempted to jump at the chance to adopt Carl, and George, who had walked in and picked up the phone extension, was also shaking his head "no." Morgan and George spent the next fifteen minutes telling Alfonso the long sad story of their failed attempts to adopt Brad, Beau, and Kevin and of their success in adopting Fremont and Eddie. The social worker had not known any of it.

"It's not just that our family is complete, Mr. Lenzini," explained George. "We would add a seventh child in a minute who is the sibling of any of our kids—if we thought the match was a good one and if we believed that we had a fair chance of completing the adoption. But we must decline in this case because we have no faith in your department to fight, really fight, for Elliot's right to be raised with one or more of her biological siblings. We simply can't risk another cycle of loss and grief, even though we very much want to stay in contact with the families of all of her biological brothers. I hope you understand."

The social worker replied, "I understand completely, and I consider myself fortunate that you didn't hang up on me when I asked, considering what you've been through. I had not read your file and did not understand your feelings. But please understand, we couldn't have placed Carl with you at birth anyway, because out-of-state foster care is against our regulations, and Kevin's adoptive family is no longer licensed as a foster home either.

We had no choice but to place Carl temporarily in one of our licensed foster homes."

"Then, sir, I would suggest you look into changing your rules and policies," concluded George in a voice that barely contained his anger and frustration. "When rules and policies keep brothers and sisters apart, the rules need to be thrown out or modified. It's just that simple."

As they hung up, Morgan and George embraced each other for a long time. And then they took turns hugging their children. They felt at peace with their decision to say no. They still had regrets, but the sons they had now were a great solace. And unlike Elliot and all but the oldest of her biological siblings, Fremont and Eddie did not suffer from FAE or FAS. Raising more than one child with the severe learning problems typical of FAS would have been very difficult. This was a slender silver lining in their black cloud of loss.

In time, the Greenes would tell their story many times to various state adoption authorities in Elliot's home state. To date, the state has not modified any of its policies to accommodate similar situations that might arise with other sibling groups that come into care one child at a time in the future.

Carl's foster family and Kevin's adoptive family went to court, both seeking adoptive custody, but Carl's foster mother was able to adopt him using the same legal strategies that Kevin's family had once used in fighting the Greenes.

Years passed. By the time Elliot was 10 years old and old enough to be curious about and want some contact with her biological brothers, all of the families were reconciled. They even had a big reunion where all six children met and were photographed together for the first time. Several biological aunts, uncles, and cousins came, too. Jane was unable to attend because she was in a rehab program for the time being. Elliot counted all of her siblings again and again, and with just a little help, was able to ascertain that she had a total of seven brothers and three sisters between her birth and adoptive families. She spent the whole day playing with all of them. Counting her, it was eleven or, as Elliot put it, "heaven eleven."

5

ADOPTION AS CAREER

Career (noun): profession, conduct in life, or progress through life

INTRODUCTION

When adults decide to pursue adoption, they often find themselves hopelessly lost in a bureaucratic wilderness, a strange land where common sense assumptions do not apply. Buried beneath lurid tales of mindless procedures, inexplicable delays, and Kafkaesque suspicion, however, is a more inspiring picture. Not only do most adoptive parents manage to hack their way through the paperwork jungle, but they often find dedicated professionals who are willing to serve as their guides. Here are a few of their stories.

Give Me Your Tired, Your Poor, Your Orphans . . .

If you had told Mack Petersen, M.D., several years ago that he would someday become an advocate for orphaned children around the world, he would have laughed at such a thought. There was no room in his life for anything but his long-held ambition to someday become America's Surgeon General, a post his great uncle had once held. Toward this goal, he spent all of his energies on his twin passions, medicine and politics. He was an active and dedicated member of the Republican party in his home state of South Dakota and, at age 35, was climbing the ranks of medicine at the largest hospital in his state, located in the capital, Pierre. He was currently being considered for a promotion to head of the pediatrics department.

Mack had even put off marriage and parenthood to single-mindedly pursue his goal.

His education in adoption began innocently enough. A family had approached him asking for his help to adopt internationally. They had a videotape of a toddler living in a Russian orphanage. They asked if he would review the tape for any signs of medical problems in the tow-headed child. He agreed to do so as a volunteer, because he did not want to risk any legal liability if he proclaimed the child to have the appearance of good health and then disabilities surfaced later. Besides, these people had put a second mortgage on their home to adopt from overseas. They couldn't afford his fee anyway.

The ten-minute video was bleak. It showed a well-lit and fairly clean orphanage "playroom" with scant furniture and almost no toys. Seven or eight older babies and toddlers lay on the tile floor in diapers and t-shirts, playing with worn out dolls and building blocks covered in chipped and faded paint. Ivan, the 20-month-old in question, had lots of white hair, a quiet temperament, and a sadness in his hazel eyes that was almost haunting. But, physically, he appeared healthy, if a bit thin. Emotionally, Dr. Petersen noticed a surprising lack of affect, or facial expressions, and a lethargy about his reactions that said this child was simply not interested in interacting with his caregivers or his environment.

Since the last child he had seen in his practice who was like Ivan had been an abuse survivor living in a foster home, Mack set about to research what might make Ivan look and act in such a manner. One article or book led him to new questions and new research until he noticed that he was immersed in research about the effects of neglect, abuse, multiple caregivers, and institutionalization on babies. Research had always been Mack's first choice when dealing with any new challenge. He worked feverishly to learn everything he could about a topic, and then he went forward with the confidence gained from his newfound knowledge. He never bought an automobile, for example, until he knew more about the model than the salesperson selling it to him.

After giving the family the devastating news that Ivan might, just might, be suffering from an emotional disorder that is not uncommon among babies in overcrowded and understaffed orphanages, he determined to learn even more. The family expressed an interest in proceeding with the adoption anyway, in spite of the risk, and Mack wanted to know what to tell them about finding real help for Ivan if they brought him to South Dakota.

More research, reading, and several medical journals later, Mack had a good grasp of the causes of disorders like fetal alcohol exposure and reactive attachment disorder and the various treatments and therapies available. And just in time, too. He was getting calls daily from a five-state area, from couples wanting his opinion of their photos and videos and descriptions. Apparently, someone had mentioned his name and phone number in an online adoption chat room, and he was suddenly very popular. Mack followed up on each family to see how many adoptions resulted and what the outcomes were. He wanted to know how many adoptions were considered successful placements and how many disrupted or became chronically and seriously problematic. Happily, he noted that most of the adoptions had wonderful outcomes.

When asked to participate in an expert panel at an adoption conference, Mack agreed. He wanted to hear what other people were saying about international adoption. Since more and more of his patients were children adopted from overseas (children he had once viewed on videotape), he was anxious to meet other doctors who might have a similar clientele. Unfortunately, he was the only pediatrician on the panel. The rest of the experts included a mother of fifteen adopted children, a speech therapist, a psychologist, and an agency director.

At lunch time, he was approached by the support group president who had put the conference together and asked if he would substitute at the last minute in one more workshop. Apparently, a scheduled speaker had been unable to show up. The name of the workshop was, "Which kind of adoption is right for you?" Mack would describe the pros and cons of international adoption.

When he walked into the workshop, he immediately regretted agreeing to do it. Whereas he had spoken to only a dozen people earlier, this room held four times that many people. Most of them were thinking about adoption and knew very little about the process. Mack couldn't help but think that his nonparent experience might be lacking in some way. Still, he was very well read on the topic, and he was a great admirer of the families in his practice. He decided to simply try and do his best.

Four people were on this panel, representing four major types of adoption. There was a woman affiliated with a national organization of adoption attorneys, a director of an association that represented private adoption agencies, a former director of adoption from a neighboring state, and Mack. Once the attorney-facilitated and private agency adoptions were discussed, the former state official rose and began speaking. Her name was Cordelia Jefferson.

Dr. Jefferson spoke eloquently about the thousands of children in foster care who needed families. Her commitment to finding adoption homes for those children reverberated in every sentence of her presentation.

"I know this might sound a bit harsh," she said, "but it is discouraging to see so many people adopting children from other countries when our foster care systems are bursting at the seams with homeless children. I know a few people who have avoided the children in foster care because of racism, plain and simple. They wanted light skin, eyes, and hair. They wanted babies that they can pretend they gave birth to, babies who won't remember their homeland or be raised with any of the beauty in their own culture. They had to have a 'tabula rasa,' a blank slate, on which to project their own religious and moral values without the complication of a preformed personality. And they didn't want the messiness of a disability, not even the risk of one.

"If their children do develop unexpected problems, they want federal adoption assistance. But the purpose of adoption assistance is to enable single parents and families with modest incomes to adopt special needs kids in the child welfare system. If couples are able to spend thousands of dollars adopting infants from Russia or China, that's their business. But then they ought to expect to assume full financial responsibility for their care. Couples who adopt internationally are relatively affluent compared with families who adopt our foster children. Adoption assistance does not provide adequate support for our own special needs children. We should not encourage childless couples to strain those resources even further by ensuring them financial support and services will be available if things go wrong."

When Dr. Jefferson concluded her talk, some clapped, while others carried on animated conversations. She had certainly gotten the attention of the audience. Now it was Mack's turn. All nervousness had left him as he approached the podium. He decided to speak from the heart, and his heart supplied all the words he needed.

"My name is Mack Petersen. I'm a pediatrician right here in Pierre. I work with a lot of people who adopt internationally both as a volunteer and in my practice. I'm also proud to tell you that I am a Republican. I've even been a delegate at a national Republican convention. I tell you this because Republicans are known for wanting to control the flow of immigration, for wanting tighter borders, and I agree with that idea. The land of promise does not have unlimited resources. But allow me, please, to tell about my experiences with international adoptions.

"The United States of America still has a love-hate relationship with her immigrants, doesn't she, even the very youngest immigrants. Never mind that this is a nation built by and through immigration or the fact that immigrants and their labor historically have been two of America's greatest strengths. And I won't even go on about individual foreigners who made their homes here and made important contributions, immigrants like Albert Einstein.

"I've gotten to know dozens of couples who have adopted children from overseas orphanages. Some of them just fell in love with a photo or a story or a letter from a missionary and wanted to help a particular kid who was doomed to a short, miserable life without adoption. Some of them have been burned trying to adopt domestically or turned away by an overworked social worker with a caseload three times larger than it should be. Some have experienced a painful adoption disruption here before going to another country. Some simply don't know that we have many U.S. kids waiting, because no one ever told them.

"Quite a few simply want a baby, and waiting babies here are scarce. But many who start out seeking the healthy child of their dreams come home with little ones bearing the scars of emotional and physical malnourishment. Some of these wounds will heal; some will mark them for life. To these parents, geography is meaningless. To them, all homeless children are 'our children.' "

He paused for only a moment as he tried to remember his next point. "Should we offer financial assistance to families who adopt disabled kids from other nations? Would doing so discourage the adoption of children in our foster care system or deprive them of needed assistance? Maybe. It's worth studying. On the other hand, once a child has been adopted from another country, they are here to stay. They are Americans. Isn't it in our best interest to help them become happy and productive citizens?"

He had everyone's attention now, including that of Dr. Jefferson.

"I certainly don't have all the answers. These are difficult issues that arouse strong feelings. If today's session tells us anything, it's that the different ways of adopting children have given rise to different communities that spend far too little time trying to understand one another. Instead of engaging in dialogue to discuss the difficult policy issues facing a rich nation in a poor world, we content ourselves with easy stereotyping that questions the motives of people we don't know. We could do so much more if we stopped complaining and ignoring one another and started looking at adoption through new eyes, through the eyes of children."

"In closing, I want to quote a poem by Emma Lazarus that I was required to memorize in sixth grade. If it sounds familiar to you, it's because this poem is engraved on the Statue of Liberty. The quote goes like this:

> A mighty woman with a torch, whose flame
> Is the imprisoned lightning, and her name
> Mother of Exiles. From her beacon-hand
> Glows world-wide welcome; her mild eyes command
> The air-bridged harbor that twin cities frame.
> "Keep ancient lands, your storied pomp!" cries she
> With silent lips. "Give me your tired, your poor,
> Your huddled masses yearning to breathe free,
> The wretched refuse of your teeming shore.
> Send these, the homeless, tempest-tost to me,
> I lift my lamp beside the golden door!

As Mack thanked the room and moved toward his seat to sit down, one person started clapping, then two, and in a few moments, the entire audience was on its feet giving him a standing ovation. He blushed deep red and smiled to the people who were smiling at him. Suddenly, he couldn't remember why he had always wanted to be the Surgeon General. But he had a very good idea about why he would continue helping families who want to help kids, no matter how or where the kids are adopted.

✎

Natural Born Advocate

The morning sun streamed into the corner office. From the thirty-sixth floor of the state office tower, Tom Burke could see the gentrified "Gas Light Village" and the curves of the Shawnee River beyond. He had been summoned to Arnie Phillips' office again. Burke glanced at his watch, a fashionable twenty minutes late. If there was going to be a lynch mob in attendance, he wanted to be the one closest to the door.

But it was just Arnie. Arnie smiled a little nervously. He was basically a good guy, but twenty years in the military had taught Arnie all about following orders and the chain of command. As assistant deputy director for children and family services, it was Arnie's job to deal with difficult employees. Tom Burke was every bit of that and more.

"We've had some complaints from county directors."

"Anybody I know?"

"Brown, Richfield, Washington, and Highland, just to name a few of the more ticked off ones. Adoptive parents are telling them that Tom Burke says the agencies are misinterpreting state law."

"That's not exactly the way I put it, although in a lot of cases, they're probably right." He paused, trying to keep his sharp tongue in second gear. "Look, many of these families are so stressed out it's a wonder that they retain anything I tell them. They think that invoking the name of a state guy will make someone at the county agency take them seriously. Sometimes they exaggerate a little bit. They feel desperate, and they're grasping at straws. Maybe these agency directors should spend a little more time talking to them."

Arnie gave Burke the more in sadness than in anger headshake, the one employed by generations of teachers when dealing with a particularly obdurate child. "I looked at your job description. It says policy analyst; I didn't see anything about an ombudsman or advocate or defender of the oppressed. The county director's association wants you transferred or suspended. You're causing all kinds of dissension between the agencies and adoptive parents. If the parents don't hear what they like, they just call you and you tell them that the county is wrong."

Burke wrestled with his temper and lost. "Oh, I get it! It's the outside agitator theory. 'Our adoptive families are simple folks. We've pretty much ignored their requests for help with services for their children and most of them are generally content with going broke. In fact, they had no idea they were even havin' iny problems with their kids until that slick talkin' agitator from the state come ta town and stirred 'em all up.' Don't you think that's a little patronizing Arnie? I mean we investigate and study these people down to their choice in underwear. Then, we help them assume complete responsibility for little human beings who have been abandoned and neglected. But somehow these same people are too dim-witted to know they need help for their children. That is until Black Bart rides into town."

"The department was already working with the county agencies on improving service. When you go outside the system, you just delay things. You haven't made the agencies more responsive; you've made them more resistant."

Burke always hated that charge because there was no way to know if more families would have been helped if he had gone through channels. He didn't think so but could never quite rid himself of some nagging doubt. What if his less than subtle attempts to work with a few adoptive families made things worse for the majority?

"Director Haywood wanted you suspended. Instead, Ellen drafted this memo to you."

Ellen Marshall was Arnie's boss. The gist of the memo was that Burke was to refrain from dealing directly with adoptive parents and to refer any calls to the district office. The "or else" was unstated but clear. Disobey and he was subject to the dreaded insubordination rap and the resulting two step: a three-day suspension and reassignment to the paper clip division.

"Is that it?" asked Tom casually. He wondered if Arnie could hear his heart pounding out a drum solo and if his face registered the nausea in his stomach.

"Yeah. Look Tom, I know you mean well, but what if everyone in the agency did everything they wanted?"

Tom started to say something but instead got up and slowly walked out of Arnie's cheerful office and back to his cubicle without saying another word. Ironically, Burke had gotten involved in adoption entirely by accident. A history major, he had gotten a job with the state department of human services after knocking around in a series of adjunct teaching appointments at a half dozen colleges. Tom was originally hired to work on a child welfare evaluation project, but after a new governor, the arrival of the governor's political appointees, and the inevitable reorganization, he found himself in the adoption and foster care unit, analyzing rules.

On a whim, Burke volunteered to take the section on the federal Title IV-E adoption assistance program. When he phoned county agencies to ask technical questions about time frames and eligibility, he was greeted with an earful about the obstacles parents faced when they applied for adoption assistance. At that time, the families who finalized an adoption without an adoption assistance agreement in place were completely shut out of the program. Pretty soon he was meeting once a month with a small band of adoption workers who were trying to make adoption assistance programs more responsive to the children they were intended to serve.

Burke soon discovered that the federal IV-E foster care program had gotten most of the attention because of the complicated mechanisms through which states claimed federal reimbursement for various expenditures. As weeks went by, he realized that by comparison the adoption assistance program had received little attention from the State Department of Family and Children Services.

Burke couldn't remember how he had gotten involved with the families themselves. Direct services were provided by county children's services agencies. The state department generally set regulations and oversaw the disbursement of federal and state funds. Maybe it was at the annual state adoption conference or a local support group. Or maybe one of the adoption reform groups Burke worked with had referred a family to him.

Before long, he was spending at least a couple hours on the phone each day with adoptive families on issues pertaining to adoption subsidy. Pretty soon after that, someone at a county agency complained. The growing disparity between his role as advocate for adoptive families and what his superiors expected him to do bothered Burke more than he let on. After all, he was advising adoptive families on the most effective ways of obtaining adoption assistance, often over the outright opposition of the county agencies. Was it somehow dishonest to take money from the state and then spend a good chunk of every week doing what the agency clearly did not want you to do? On the other hand, families were citizens and they were being denied information that could help their children. Wasn't that the duty of the state agency charged with administering the federal adoption assistance program? Wasn't the purpose of the program to support the adoption of special needs children? The stories of adoptive families around the state clearly indicated that they were being ill-served. Somebody needed to provide them with a more supportive system. But who appointed Tom Burke?

Burke's familiar reverie was broken by the arrival of Ed Miller at his cube.

"I heard you had a meeting with Arnie. Did he tell you that it hurt him more than it did you? Did he salute? Order you to drop and do fifty?"

"Arnie's not so bad. I could have gotten hauled in by 'Yellin' Ellen,' the Marshall. Yew gonna arrest me, Marshall?"

"Yeah, Arnie's not bad for an invertebrate. 'I could work with more precision. Maybe even make a decision if I only had a spine.' "

"They've ordered me to quit taking calls from adoptive parents. Even put it writing." He handed Ed the memo.

"I strongly urge you to barge into Yellin' Ellen's office and start screaming at the top of your lungs, 'It'll take more of man than you to shut me down,' " advised Ed. "Just get right up in her face, veins bulging in your neck, beet red. Maybe knock a few things off the desk. Then walk out. I strongly urge you to do that."

Whenever Burke started whining about what the bureaucracy had done to his tender sensibilities, Ed was always available to strongly advise some course of action usually involving a lot of screaming and the underlying threat of violence. Ed's preferred method of dealing with organizational stress, on the other hand, was scheduling himself out of the office at least four days a week.

"I can have Yellin' Ellen silenced if you like," he offered. "One of my buddies with the Road Kill would be glad to do the job for a couple hundred bucks. He's always had a thing for bureaucrats after they rejected his disability claim. I won't say he's being very reasonable about it, you understand. He was driving on the wrong side of the road with more drugs in him than the local Rite-Aid when he collided with the tour bus. Logic is not Billy Ray's long suit, yah know?"

"Thanks anyway, Ed, but at this point it might be an overreaction."

Ed shrugged. Tom always figured he was kidding. Tom hoped real hard that he was kidding, but sometimes he wondered.

A few minutes after Ed left, the phone rang.

"Mr. Burke?"

"How did you manage to break through our crack citizen defense system?"

She hesitated briefly, probably trying to guess if she had fallen into the clutches of a dangerous lunatic. Then she laughed uneasily and decided to forge ahead.

"My name is Kelley Sebastian. I'm an adoptive parent and I heard that you know a lot about adoption subsidy. We really need some advice."

There it was. The thought of advising Ms. Sebastian to call the district office flashed through Burke's mind. Lying low for awhile couldn't hurt, could it? With the heat off, he could be more effective couldn't he?

"What's happening?" he asked.

"We adopted our son Barry in 1997 at the age of 3 and a half. We know his birthmother used cocaine regularly and had a minimum of prenatal care. She was married to Barry's father, but he took off a couple of months before the children's services agency removed Barry for neglect. We don't know much about the father but heard he used drugs too.

"Barry was 6 months old when he was removed. Several attempts at reconciliation failed. The court terminated the mother's and father's parental rights, and eventually Barry was placed with us."

"How's Barry doing now?"

"He has a problem controlling his impulses. He's very aggressive toward the other kids in his class and destructive at home. Barry may also have some learning problems. My husband and I are working with a counselor and having some testing done. We still don't have a clear diagnosis. We're trying to see if there is more information about Barry's background and the family history. The psychologist suspects that there may have been instances of abuse either in his parent's home or while he was in foster care."

"And Barry was placed in your home by a county agency, right?"

"Yes, Grant County."

"Ah yes, Grant County, a living monument to the nineteenth century. Oh, did I say that out loud?"

That brought a small laugh, but Burke wondered if he ought to lay off the flippant remarks. He sometimes thought they helped to disarm the parents, but maybe they were simply self-serving. "Look at me. I'm different. I'm not like them."

"Did the agency discuss adoption assistance with you?" he asked.

"Only a little. The caseworker said that he probably wasn't eligible and we never really pursued it. Barry was prone to temper tantrums but seemed healthy at the time. My husband had a good job as an engineer, and we figured that I could quit mine to take care of him."

"Did they tell you why he wasn't eligible?"

"The caseworker said he wasn't really a special needs child. She also told us that adoption assistance was for families who couldn't afford to raise additional children, and it didn't look like we needed any help. When we contacted the agency to tell them about Barry's problems and ask about counseling or other services, the adoption supervisor told us that Barry wasn't eligible for any adoption assistance because the adoption had been finalized."

"Well, happily, that statement is not entirely true." Burke was into it now, his doubts gone. "You can apply for adoption assistance after finalization. You have to go through an appeal process."

"I don't want you to think we're trying to be greedy, Mr. Burke. Jim's company is merging with a firm based in Chicago, and there are rumors of layoffs. The psychologist is using terms like reactive attachment disorder and wants to send us to the attachment center for an assessment."

Her voice was starting to break a little. "We've been so worried that Jim would lose his job and, if Barry's problems are really serious, how we will be able to afford the treatment. If we could get some help through an adoption subsidy, we thought it might provide a backup in case the worst happens and we lose our health insurance. I'm not even sure how much of the testing and treatment our current insurance will cover. Barry needs help now!"

As many times as Burke had heard such stories, he could never get over the irony of the dialogue that was taking place. Here was a parent, usually, but not always, a mother who was desperate enough to call a bureaucrat of all things, not the normal first option when one was seeking support and consolation. How much did it cost these strong, self-sufficient people to pick up the phone and bare their souls to a stranger in a culture where asking for help is considered a character flaw? And how does the system respond? It usually reinforces the parents' sense of failure by treating them with the clinical detachment reserved for society's needy. These people were actively recruited to become adoptive parents, but inevitably, they found it necessary to apologize for appearing greedy if they inquired about a program that was established to help families like them raise special needs children.

"You're not being greedy," said Burke. "Try to get that out of your head. The adoption assistance programs were created to help to raise children like Barry. Like any good responsible parent, you are trying to get your son the services he needs. Let me ask you one question before we move forward. It may not make a lot of sense now, but I'll explain why it's significant. You say that the birthfather and birthmother were married, but the birthfather took off a few months before the agency moved in and placed Barry in foster care?"

"Yes."

"Was it less than six months?"

"I'm sure it was."

"Okay, was the birthmother working before Barry was taken out of the home?"

"I don't see how she could have been."

"I'm asking because if Barry was removed from a home in which he would have been eligible for welfare benefits, which used to be called AFDC (Aid to Families with Dependent Children), then he meets one of the major eligibility requirements for adoption assistance. He has to have been poten-tially eligible in the month the agency filed the action to remove him from his birthmother's home or in any of the preceding six months. It looks like that's going to work. The other eligibility requirements also look pretty good."

"What should we do now?"

"The first step is to submit an application as if the adoption had not been finalized. Expect a letter of denial, but that will kick in your appeal rights. Then you request an administrative hearing, and we'll go from there."

"Do we need to hire an attorney?"

"At this point, I would say no. Get the application in. Give it a few weeks and then get back in touch. I'll give you my home number and e-mail. According to federal regulations, the agency cannot ignore your application. If they do, you can request a hearing on grounds of unresponsiveness."

"Is there anything we need to do to prepare?"

"Start documenting Barry's special needs and any links that you can make about the relationship between his current problems and his background. If there is any information that you didn't find out until after the adoption, that also might be helpful. What you basically will be trying to establish is that Barry had sufficient risk factors in his background to be considered a special needs child due to his parents' drug use and any other trauma you can identify. His current problems are a logical outgrowth of those early experiences.

"Pull the information together as best you can, but don't think of this as a science contest. It's not. You already know much more about Barry's special needs than the agency ever will, and you can get written and oral testimony from psychologists and other professionals to provide all the documentation that you will need. I don't think that the special needs are going to be a problem. Pull the information together, but don't kill yourself."

"So the first thing I do is apply for adoption assistance?"

"Yeah, I would call them and ask for an application for Title IV-E adoption assistance and follow up with a formal request in writing. Mention that extenuating circumstances prevented you from receiving assistance prior to finalization. Then we'll take it from there. I'll tell you what. Why don't you draft a letter and e-mail me a copy. I'll take a look at it and throw in some law references and genuine policy gibberish."

"I don't know how to thank you. We didn't know where to go," she said, her voice breaking again.

"Well, I haven't really done anything yet," Burke said laughing. "Let's wait and see if all this hot air is of any use to you."

Maybe it was the cheap thrills that made adoption assistance so compelling for him; such gratitude for so little effort. Here was a person who had taken on a challenge that he didn't think he could handle. She quit her job to try and make a family for a deeply troubled child who probably had little capacity to respond to her love. And here she was thanking him. For what? For listening. Some days it felt like stealing, but it was the one area of Burke's bureaucratic existence where he felt he was making a useful contribution.

Within an hour after the latest heart to heart with Arnie, he had already violated the ultimatum, thought Burke ruefully. But the day's excitement wasn't over. He could hear some laughter a few cubicles over but didn't think much about it at the time. Pretty soon, he would find out.

Burke usually had lunch on Tuesdays with his friend, Steve Ford, another loose wire in the bureaucratic machinery. Steve was in the research and evaluation division and waged a constant losing battle with the number crunching faction over the question of concepts and definitions. As they walked down the block toward the state office tower, Steve stopped to pick up a copy of *The News*, a free weekly containing a mix of muckraking journalism, arts, and entertainment.

"Hey did you see this?!! You're famous!!"

Burke looked puzzled. "What?"

Steve picked up another paper and handed it to Burke.

"Tom Burke recalls one of the 'Great Moments in Bureaucratic History' on page 13," he read.

He'd forgotten about it. Two months ago, on a whim, he had contacted *The News* and asked them if they ever published any satire. They seemed pretty indifferent but said they'd take a look at it. Burke e-mailed it to *The News*, heard nothing, and wrote if off. Now here it was.

He and Steve retired to a bench in a little park across the street and both turned to page 13.

"Great Moments in Bureaucratic History"
By
Tom Burke

Few people are aware that the proud history of bureaucrats and their noble deeds stretches back into the very dawn of history. It is not an exaggeration to say that the universal ability to arouse murderous impulses in the mildest of souls would be impossible today without the unsung efforts of that long gray line of bureaucrats who paved the way over the centuries. The following is just one of their inspiring stories.

1200—England

Sherwood Forest rings with laughter as Robin Hood and his Merry Men launch their campaign to rob from the rich and give to the poor. Soon the evil Sheriff of Nottingham is sore beset with apoplectic rage and Robin is a hero to all the oppressed throughout the English countryside.

But alas, the merry band, while marvelously cunning at separating fat merchants from their purses, cannot redistribute the wealth fast enough to the widows, orphans, and other plain folk, and soon their simple yeoman's camp is awash in treasure. Grumblings and murmurings are heard that some of the poor are receiving more than their fair share and are, in fact, poor no more. Merriment comes to a grinding halt when Edgar the Pollster arrives in camp with the depressing news that Robin's approval rating has slipped twenty percentage points among the peasantry.

The next day, a stranger appears in Sherwood forest and finds Robin sitting on a large mound of gold coins, brow furrowed in thought. The stranger introduces himself as Wilfred the Spinmeister and informs Robin that his "Take From the Rich and Give to the Poor" policy has only succeeded in creating a class of lazy, freeloading rabble. He tells Robin that what the peasants need are jobs, not handouts. They must be made to work for the booty extracted by Robin's Merry Men, thereby acquiring a greater sense of dignity and self-esteem.

In exchange for a hearty percentage of the swag, Wilfred creates "Sherwood Works," the shire's very first welfare reform program. Soon an assortment of ale houses, witch burning services, ox cart repair shoppes, and mutton-on-a-stick emporia are springing up all over Greater Nottingham.

At first things go well. The peasants are unable to acquire the work ethic, of course, because it hasn't been invented yet, but Robin soon observes some definite changes in their behavior. In keeping with the strict new work requirements, the first grog break is postponed until 9A.M. and the percentage of shire residents who are falling down drunk by noon drops precipitously from 85 percent to 70 percent among the adults and to 50 percent among children under the age of 8. At the same time, literacy rates sky rocket to 1 percent of the population.

But alas, soon new problems begin to arise. Working peasants arrive in Robin's camp complaining that they have no one to care for their twenty-seven children while they sling gruel or string crossbows in one of the many enterprises that have materialized along the Kings Highway. Others demand a reliable system of public transportation, pointing to the difficulty of traversing bogs and eluding the colorful brigands and cutthroats that infest the byways of the forest. If that weren't enough, villagers in a burst of entrepreneurial fervor gleefully burn local midwives at the stake and hang everyone else with a passing knowledge of herbal remedies, thereby creating a full-blown health care crisis. Providing medical coverage for a population whose life expectancy has risen to the ripe old age of 23 is no laughing matter, and Robin grows less merry with each passing day.

Instead of spending their days engaged in spirited archery contests and taunting the evil Sheriff of Nottingham, Robin and his men are forced to go on longer and longer sorties to pay for the Whistling Yeoman Child Care Center, the Sherwood Light Coach Transit Authority, and the Al Shabaz Moorish Managed Health Care System.

Revenues continue to shrink, but when Robin sends for Wilfred the Spinmeister, he discovers that Wilfred has hired on as a consultant to manage the Sheriff of Nottingham's reelection campaign. Running on the slogan, "Give to the Rich By Oppressing the Poor," affectionately dubbed the "Tinkle Down Strategy," the sheriff successfully characterizes Robin Hood as an old-fashioned rob-and-spend liberal and is reelected in a landslide. Robin, merry no more, retires to write his memoirs and await the arrival of Richard, the Lionhearted from a tour promoting his latest book, *Let's Go! A Pillager's Guide to the Holy Land.*

Upon taking office, the evil Sheriff of Nottingham invents the first adoption subsidy program in response to the orphan problem created by his brutally efficient army. Agents from the sheriff's Department of Oppressive Services place dirty-faced street urchins with hearty peasant families. In exchange, the agents collect a monthly subsidy of wheat and mead from the families and promise not to burn down their quaint thatched cottages.

Steve thought it was funny. That was a plus. The timing posed a bit of problem, particularly on the heels of the recently issued ultimatum delivered by "Yellin' Ellen" that very morning.

"Maybe they'll take it in the playful spirit in which it was written," Steve said without any conviction.

"It gets worse," said Burke. "I took a personal day off tomorrow to make a presentation on adoption assistance to the continuing education section of the State Bar Association."

"Does the department know about it?"

"Yep."

"Well, they can't do anything. You're on your own time as a private citizen, freedom of speech and all that."

"Yeah, that's true, but it's not a good time to draw a lot of attention from the upper ranges of the bureau food chain, ya' know?"

Burke had taken Wednesday off for several reasons. He had agreed to testify via teleconference at an administrative hearing on behalf of an adoptive family's petition for adoption assistance. Burke figured that it would have been imprudent to participate in the hearing at his desk in the office tower. The hearing was scheduled for 9 A.M., which gave him plenty of time to make the ninety-minute presentation to the Bar Association at 3:30 in the afternoon.

It was unusual to have so many things going on the same day. He had also agreed to sit in on a roundtable discussion on adoption assistance at the monthly meeting of New Beginnings, a local foster and adoptive families support group.

One of several issues at the hearing was the state's contention that the child's eligibility for adoption assistance could not be reconsidered because the extenuating circumstances claimed by the adoptive parent were not specifically listed in the primary federal policy document, Policy Announcement (P.A.) 01–01. In this case, the adoptive mother, Lynn Hill, was aware of adoption assistance but had adopted her daughter, Marissa, in infancy when she seemed to be in normal health. Even though she was adopting the child as a single parent, Lynn felt that her job provided sufficient support, so she did not apply for assistance.

Unfortunately, Marissa's tender age masked a number of medical and emotional problems that she was too young to express at the time of her adoption. As these problems mounted, Lynn was forced to devote less and less time to her business, so she turned to the state for help. The state turned her down, citing several reasons for the denial.

The first hurdle was the issue of extenuating circumstances, which provided the grounds for revisiting a child's eligibility after finalization. Lynn's basic argument was that she was unaware of the extent of Marissa's special needs. The state countered that since no one knew about Marissa's problems, the state could not be held accountable for failing to implement adoption assistance. To substantiate this argument the state pointed to a situation cited in P.A. 01–01 as grounds for reveiwing a child's eligibility after finalization. According to the P.A. a child's eligibility could be considered if "relevant facts regarding the child were known by the State agency or child-placing agency and not presented to the adoptive parents prior to the finalization of the adoption."

By prior agreement with Lynn, Burke focused particular attention on the issue of extenuating circumstances in his statement. He argued that the situation cited by P.A. 01–01 was intended to serve as example. Quoting from the Commonwealth Court of Pennsylvania in the 1999 case of *Barczynski v. Department of Public Welfare*, he noted that "the essential question in determining extenuating circumstances is whether a family has had a reasonable opportunity to be determined eligible for adoption assistance." Obviously, he added "if the child was too young to clearly express a serious emotional problem, then Lynn Hill did not have sufficient information at her disposal to be held accountable for not pursuing adoption assistance. A policy that would deny adoption assistance to families because the true severity of a medical or emotional problem is not discovered until after finalization, clearly discriminates against infants and young children."

Burke also managed to introduce some regulations from other states that listed discovery of special needs after an adoption as grounds for reviewing ility for adoption subsidy.

so much more at stake for the adoptive parents than for the

state. That's what made the hearings so intense. His admiration for Lynn Hill had grown immensely since their first e-mail contact four months before. The state had decided to throw a list of objections at her. While coping with Marissa's severe allergies and bonding problems, she had developed a remarkable grasp of Title IV-E eligibility issues and managed to run a small Internet business at the same time. Her presentation of the case was both articulate and passionate.

The details of hearings were always different, but certain patterns were remarkably common. The adoptive parent desperately tried to remind the parties about the human consequences of what was taking place while addressing the required policy questions. The state, on the other hand, assuming the gatekeeper's mantle, often tried to reduce the hearing to a literal interpretation of a few phrases in the administrative regulations.

The state agency didn't always try this hard. Sometimes the agency really wanted to help and was merely looking to the hearing as a means of granting it permission. When the hearing was fiercely contested, as this one was, Burke always wondered about the gulf that must separate a lot of children's services agencies from their primary customers. He had no doubt that the agency representatives and the attorneys who represented them sincerely believed that they were doing their duty as civil servants. He even had some sympathy, realizing that it must often be an unpleasant duty. Burke sometimes wondered about his own motives in playing the role of self-appointed advocate. In the process he avoided much of the pain of saying no.

Still, the more he was involved in the laws and policies governing the adoption assistance program, the more he saw opportunity for flexibility and creativity. At some point in hearings like this, he always became angry at the time and resources the state devoted to denying adoption assistance to one special needs child. How much misery could they have saved Lynn Hill and her child if they had spent even a portion of that energy searching for ways to help them?

When Lynn called Burke after the hearing, both felt it went well. The administrative law judge seemed on top of things and had asked the state some tough, insightful questions, always a good sign. They agreed to talk in a few days.

The Continuing Legal Education Forum had drawn a full house, and when Burke arrived, he noticed some Family and Children Services people sitting together on the left side, about halfway down the aisle. He suddenly had an image of one of them, Sally Jennings, leaping to her feet in the middle of his presentation, screaming, "Liar! Traitor!" and rushing the stage with some sort of antique pistol. At the moment, however, she looked pretty calm.

Contrary to some rumors, Burke didn't live for the opportunity to voice his twisted hatred of the Department of Family and Children Services before appalled captive audiences. He wondered what they imagined him doing: A fist pounding Fidel Castro-style diatribe? A bad lounge act filled with hilarious references to how many bureaucrats it took to lose your check? An aggressive white boy version of the dozens' "The director is so fat . . . ?

On the other hand, he frequently did yield to temptation and sprinkle a few snide remarks into his presentations. Today, he thought, might be a good day to leave those out. And so, at a little after 3:30, Burke introduced himself and began a presentation entitled, "Adoption Assistance and Advocacy for Special Needs Children." One of the parts that always amused him was the standard disclaimer. Although he worked for the Department of Family and Children Services, he, Tom Burke, was not representing the agency but speaking as a private citizen whose views were entirely his own. Burke presented the disclaimer to protect himself but found it oddly funny that the agency also seemed to prefer the arrangement, or at least that was his impression.

Since he was there presenting himself as the friend of adoptive families and not representing the views of the agency, he often wondered what that implied about the Department of Family and Children Services in the minds of the audience. The agency was on the other side? Although he delivered the disclaimer with a sober expression on his face, it occurred to Burke that he couldn't have insulted the agency any more if he'd stayed up all night thinking about how to do it.

Burke tried to keep his tone fairly detached and scholarly in describing the various programs and services, but there were turgid waters ahead. It was hard to draw a happy face around the problem of the state's low adoption assistance rates. "While foster care rates have continued to rise steadily in recent years, adoption assistance rates have remained the same," he said. "Given the high percentage of children who are being adopted by their foster parents, this poses a serious policy issue. As of July 2000, the state's adoption assistance rates had fallen into the bottom 20 percent."

That brought frowns from the department's contingent and some furious scribbling on note pads. Sally Jennings didn't show any signs of jumping out of her seat, but she did turn to a colleague and nod as if to say, "See I told you!!! There he goes again."

The frowns deepened when Burke recommended that adoptive parents and their representatives challenge the adoption assistance rates offered them through the state hearing system and cited some policy arguments that might be put forth on behalf of an appeal. Then he offered to share some hearing and court decisions in which parents had either won higher amounts of adoption assistance outright or the agency was ordered to reopen negotiations. More scribbling in notebooks followed.

Finally, Burke offered to help attorneys in the audience with some of the policy arguments if they represented families who needed additional support to care for their children. He tried to wrap his offer in the mantle of due process and the need for families to know their legal rights, but the department contingent wasn't buying it.

Representing adoptive families in subsidy cases is not exactly a major area of legal practice, but after the talk, Burke did talk to a couple of attorneys who had received inquiries from families and offered to work with them. Sally Jennings and her crew left immediately without saying good-bye.

The strange thing that Burke would later discover is that much of the tension with Family and Children's Services was situational rather than personal. As it turned out, most of the conflict didn't involve different beliefs about adoption assistance but how you behaved as an employee of the department. If you made someone's life more difficult by flaunting the rules, then you were by definition an enemy. On the other hand, if the person you were bothering changed jobs and you were no longer a problem for her, then all was pretty much forgiven. In the coming years, it became common for former antagonists, even Sally Jennings, to refer parents to him after they left the agency.

Burke was a little down as he drove to the support group meeting that evening. He was tired of the tension with the department, of wondering what unpleasant surprise lay around the next corner. The idea of spending the next decade as the resident dissident wasn't very appealing at the moment. He had deliberately created his situation one step at a time, but at the moment he felt like indulging in some good old-fashioned self-pity.

The support group provided a solid dose of reality. Once again, Burke was filled with a sense of awe by these ordinary people and their extraordinary commitments. As a group, they were notably unsentimental about their children, discussing bouts of stealing, school suspensions, and brushes with juvenile authorities with dark humor that undoubtedly helped them to cope with the pain. While they had few illusions about their troubled sons and daughters, they were completely dedicated to them at the same time. And these people were grateful to him! Amazing. All he did was listen and offer to share a little knowledge about the system and its laws. The parents were putting it all on the line—jobs, houses, financial security—all for children who only recently had been strangers. He tried to remind them from time to time, but because they didn't think of themselves as anything special, they would never really see themselves through Burke's eyes. They were a gift, a very precious one.

৩৯৹৵৶

True Masters of Social Work

Sheryl Miller was so tired of people asking her what her college major was, she took to saying, "Um, um, um . . . UM. That's short for undeclared major!"

She was the only junior in the off-campus apartment housing complex where she lived who had not yet declared something—anything—at least once. And she was teased for it. "Hey, Miller! How about Procrastination for a major?"

It was time to commit. She had no more core curriculum courses to take. For the hundredth time, she made a list of all the courses she'd liked best and all the jobs she'd ever had that she enjoyed most. What most of these things had in common was kids, helping kids, and striving to make things better for kids. Her mother had always said she'd make a great social worker. Maybe Mom was right, just this once.

Sheryl wandered down to the Social Work (SW) Department and asked a good-looking young man sitting outside the department head's office if he was a SW major.

"Damn straight," he replied, extending his hand in a friendly greeting, "and I do mean straight. I'm a SW major—Darren Miller—and I'm not gay. Believe it or not, straight guys go into this field all the time. Are you busy this evening, by the way?"

And that, in a nutshell, is how Sheryl Miller found a major and a husband all in the same day. Two years later, she graduated with a bachelor's degree in SW and became Mrs. Sheryl Miller Miller, later shortened to Miller. Three years later, she and Darren both had their MSWs, Masters of Social Work degrees, and were both employed full time by the Department of Human Services (DHS) in their county. Darren was assigned to foster care, and Sheryl, to adoption.

They liked their jobs right away, thanks to a dynamic young unit supervisor who had boundless energy and a matching amount of enthusiasm. However, six months into their careers, the supervisor was diagnosed with a stress-related malady and replaced by Mrs. Brim-Thatch, a career bureaucrat ten years short of retirement with a tough as nails reputation and a nononsense attitude about social work. "Sentiment has no place in this office," she liked to say. "It's inefficient."

She increased caseloads and tightened budgets to the point that Sheryl had to go without mileage reimbursement on some of her postplacement home visits, and to stay caught up, she had to make a few of them on her own time. She was forever falling behind on homestudies, home visits, or filing.

Darren was even more miserable. The one thing he loved best about his job, spending time with kids, was the one thing he no longer had time for. Saving time and money was the rule of the day. Kids simply got in the way.

In spite of Mrs. Brim-Thatch (or "Brier Patch" as she was nicknamed), the Millers managed to find ways to plan ahead for the kids. Darren would tell his wife about kids new to foster care who were not likely to be reunited with birthfamily members, and Sheryl would begin looking in earnest for the perfect family weeks before one was actually needed. This resulted in well-prepared and well-chosen matches, a higher number of adoptions for the unit, a lower disruption rate, and federal dollar bonuses for the state.

Mrs. Brim-Thatch was not bashful about taking all of the credit for her unit's statistics. "Efficiency is the key," she sermonized.

After four and a half years of despotic rule, Darren and Sheryl had had enough. They were ready to work somewhere else, where the pace would allow them to actually help people. A dream became a plan and then a reality when they opened their own adoption agency. They called it "Family Builders" and specialized in the placement of sibling groups and teenagers. They contracted with their old state adoption unit to find families for waiting children in state custody in exchange for a finder's fee from the state called Purchase of Service (POS). With POS, the state, not the adopting families, paid their expenses, kids received more personalized attention in the private agency, and adoptions were made more stable by the strong postadoption support services system developed by the Millers.

Two years into their venture, they had placed almost one hundred children and were still in business, a great accomplishment when it comes to private special needs adoption agencies. The vast majority go out of business within two years for lack of adequate funding. But Sheryl, who knew a thing or two about grant applications, and Darren, who negotiated POS contracts with every surrounding state, were flourishing. During their third year of operation, Mrs. Brier Patch called to tell them about an unusually large sibling group that had recently come into foster care. Parental rights would be terminated very soon due to the chronic alcoholism and life-threatening liver disease of the birthfather and the long-term incarceration of the birthmother on drug dealing charges. This left ten children, yes ten, six girls and four boys, with no home and no parents. Worse, no relatives were interested in adopting any of the children, much less all of them together. Darren and Sheryl both went to see the children, who were together, for the moment at least, in a local children's shelter, awaiting assignment to two or three different foster homes.

They were amazed at the cohesiveness of the group. The children were "parented" by 17-year-old Joseph and, to a lesser extent, by 16-year-old Daniel. Right down to the twin toddlers, Rose and Daisy, each child listened to Joseph and obeyed his every command. Almost unconsciously, they helped each other. Daniel always had one of the little ones in his lap, rebraiding hair or tying a shoelace. The group watched out for each other and viewed every person who approached with a cautious attitude.

Joseph and Daniel made it clear that they had to, they must, they would stay together no matter what. They explained that throughout their tumultuous lives, through their dad's drinking binges and their mother's long periods of absence when she was "using or dealing," the one steady factor was their togetherness. Sarah, 15, who loved to cook, was self-taught and talented. She could make a feast from nothing more than the simple foods purchased with the Women, Infants, and Children (WIC) vouchers Daisy and Rose still received. Brian and Delores, 14, the other set of twins, knew how to find money to buy ingredients for Sarah's kitchen. They had "jobs" washing cars for tips at the local self-serve car wash. The last three middle kids, Michael, 10, Marie, 9, and Jean, 8, were in charge of cleaning up and laundry when there were enough quarters for the laundromat. They also scavenged. They could tell you how much one hundred aluminum cans, or a bundle of newspaper, or six glass cola bottles would fetch. Joseph also brought in money delivering phone books and newspapers. When things got really tight, Joseph and Daniel used fake IDs to sell their blood plasma.

The greatest area of neglect in the children's lives, besides their cavity-riddled teeth, was in their education. The three oldest had dropped out of school before high school, and the rest of the kids had extremely poor attendance. Little was known about their academic abilities. They needed a foster home immediately so they could be enrolled in and remain, for a while at least, in the same schools for evaluation and Individualized Education Plans (IEPs). Sheryl's heart broke for the middle kids, who had to work so hard so young, and Darren felt strongly that Joseph, Daniel, and Sarah needed to be liberated from their roles as pseudo parents and be allowed to be and act like normal teenagers.

After interviewing the children and ordering full-scale evaluations for all of them, they looked high and low for a foster family that could take them all or two foster families that lived on the same block in the same town, or even in the same school district. No luck.

Joseph was unimpressed with Darren's assurances that they would be separated only for awhile and continued to insist that they *must* stay together no matter what. Darren was sure Joseph would try to run away with the kids if separation seemed imminent. Sheryl was not as sure but agreed to his plan anyway. For the time being, just for a short time, the ten children would have to move in with them. It wasn't something social workers did routinely, but the nature of social work is that every child's needs are unique. Flexibility and creativity are the parents of good social work.

Mrs. Brim-Thatch saw it another way, calling the plan "dangerous," "unprofessional," and "inefficient." Taking care of so many children would practically shut down their agency, and she needed their agency to keep her placement statistics strong. But in spite of her protestations, the Millers took the children home and immediately called on old friends from the department to certify them as a foster home on an emergency basis. The paperwork was started, and basic level financial assistance was provided. The children had meager possessions slung over their shoulders in blue and pink plastic trash bags: a few worn items of clothing, the shoes on their feet, some dirty dolls and toys, and an assortment of snapshots and books. It took weeks just to get them all haircuts, dental appointments, school supplies, and new clothes! The biggest challenge was not the sheer number of children living in their modest three-bedroom home but in convincing the three teens to relinquish some of the parenting responsibilities to Sheryl and Darren.

Joseph had no desire to go to high school, and saw no point in college. He'd never learned that a college education offered any kind of advantage. To him, making money was a matter of hustling, a little here, a little there, just making do for the day. They had to help him learn a whole new philosophy. Concepts like planning, career goals, budgeting, and saving were all new to the very bright and resourceful young man, who could barely read on an eighth grade level.

Daniel adjusted a bit more easily. He immediately became attached to Darren's video gaming system and Sheryl's computer games. He showed a talent for free cell solitaire on the computer and strategy and war video games. Because of this, he more readily relinquished his role as caretaker. The younger children learned pretty quickly to go to their foster parents to meet their needs like food and medicine, but they still ran to Daniel or Joseph when they were upset or angry.

Sarah stubbornly refused to even try school. She had a full-size kitchen and real pots and pans to cook with, and she was determined to stay right there and cook, bake, and fry.

Testing showed the eight oldest to be of above average intelligence. Only Rose and Daisy appeared to have learning disabilities, but it was thought these might be correctable developmental lags due to a lack of exposure to the outside world. The five middle children adjusted well to school in a short period of time, because they could see their new friends every single day. Peers! Daisy and Rose were enrolled in a special day care program where they could receive speech and occupational therapy.

Finally, since they refused high school, it was decided to place the three oldest teens into GED preparation class so they could catch up on their academics and take the General Equivalency Diploma exam. All of them learned quickly with the one-on-one tutoring and passed their GEDs on the first attempt. Joseph reluctantly agreed to try junior college, found that he liked it, and eventually decided to major in business. Daniel went to vocational-technical college to learn computer repair, and Sarah took her GED and went right to work as an apprentice in one of the city's top restaurants. The manager had wanted to start her off as a dishwasher, but after he saw how quickly she learned, he put a chef's hat on her head. Slowly, the three teenagers mastered the brand new routine of school, job, chores, homework, and regular bedtimes. Alone, the Millers discussed the kids' futures on many occasions. They loved the children, but they had never envisioned a large family for themselves. They were sure that a perfect home was nearby, but it would not be their home.

Three months flew by, the birthparent relinquishments were complete, and it was time to redouble the effort to find the large sibling group an adoptive family. Darren updated the listing and photos of the children in the state's photolisting book. He also arranged for them to participate in an adoption "picnic," a large gathering of waiting children and adoptive parents, meant to be a party for the kids and a way of helping prospective parents see the real youngsters behind the paper or electronic photolistings.

At the picnic, Daniel was surprised to run into his favorite vo-tech instructor from modem repair class. Alton Steinman and his wife, Shirley, had just seen their only child, a son, off to college and were trying to adopt a sibling group to fill their large country home. Daniel, no stranger to a bit of the hustle, immediately introduced them to his adorable toddler sisters. Shirley Steinman was delighted with the beautiful twins and exchanged misty-eyed glances with her husband more than once. Then Daniel introduced them to the other younger kids. "Daniel," said Alton, "dare I ask you how many siblings you have altogether?"

"Only nine, Mr. S!" Daniel said cheerfully, "and one of them is about to turn 18, so he hardly counts, and three of us already have our GEDs, and you already know how wonderful I am . . . and all ten of us are almost as special as me!"

The adoption equivalent of Cupid's arrow hit home that day, and the match was made. Over the next few months, the Steinmans and the Millers worked out an arrangement. The Steinmans actually adopted the ten children, but the Millers personally provided emergency babysitting and weekend respite care, not to mention a quiet retreat when the older ones wanted to get away.

The last anyone heard, Sarah had just turned 18 and was leaving for Quebec, Canada, to go to cooking school, and Daniel was working in a computer store upgrading systems. He was thinking about going into vo-tech teaching, like his dad. Joseph was still in college, majoring in business and keeping close tabs on all the kids. The younger ones were catching up verbally, developmentally, socially, and academically. Rose and Daisy were a big hit with their kindergarten teacher, Mrs. Orchid, and not just because of their names. The Family Builders agency is going strong even with the birth of a baby girl in the Miller household right around the time of the Steinman children's adoption finalizations.

The Millers are still working hard to help kids. They showed up for Brier Patch's retirement party just to make sure she really did retire. And they like her replacement, Mr. Harold Arms, a lot. He is a retired Navy officer with a new doctorate in social work and a lot of innovative ideas for shortening foster care stays. Department morale is way up. And no one has given this supervisor a nickname, not yet anyway, as much as his name happens to lend itself to one.

❧

Changing the Tide's Direction

"I've had sex with five different men, all of them related to me. You should know that, Ms. Dawson, since I am going to be in your math class this year."

Ashley Dawson, a first-year teacher, stopped filling out her new roll book and looked up to see which fifth grader had just said that and to check that she had heard it correctly. In front of her stood a well-groomed young girl, no older than 10 or 11, pretty, long auburn hair tied up in a ribbon, lace-trimmed dress, old-fashioned black patent leather shoes, a Pollyanna with a lovely smile and straight white teeth.

"Ex-excuse m-me?" she said, hoping she had not heard the self-introduction correctly.

Ladawna Moreland just smiled and repeated herself, almost word for word. Then she added, "I'm the newest McGuire, straight from the shelter, arrived just in time for the first day of school." Then she bounced off to her desk, ponytail swinging side to side, and sat down.

"McGuires" was the name everyone in town had for the steady stream of foster children who came and went from the McGuire home, a rambling old three-story farmhouse on the edge of town kept in tip-top shape by Mr. McGuire, aged 61, and scrubbed till it shone by Mrs. McGuire, aged 58. They had been career foster parents for as long as anyone could remember. Mrs. McGuire had stopped counting years ago when foster child number three hundred moved in. At any given time, there were five to eight children in the house, one dog, one cat, and a number of chickens in the backyard.

Some stayed for days, some for a year, but the average was shorter all the time as the system got better about making decisions on kids more quickly. Some of the children went to live with relatives within three months of becoming McGuires, and others went to nonrelative adoptive homes almost as soon. But no matter how long they stayed, the McGuires saw to it that the children were well dressed, learned their manners, went to school, and knew how to feed chickens.

Everyone in town admired their hard work and dedication, and the merchants went out of their way to help the McGuires with all of their kids. The pharmacist never charged a delivery fee to take medications right to their door. The local pizza place gave them a standing 10 percent discount on all orders, as did the movie theater, and the bank kept plenty of candy on hand to pass out whenever Mr. or Mrs. McGuire brought a car full of kids to the drive-through.

Apparently, Ladawna was now in foster care due to sexual abuse. Ashley saw the school counselor walk by and rushed out into the hall to grab her elbow.

"Elaine," the teacher whispered, "one of my students just announced her sexual history to me. She's a new McGuire. Can you talk to her please?"

"Ladawna Moreland, right?" asked Elaine Lestrade. "You're the third teacher to report this. I've already spoken to her and to Mrs. McGuire. This child goes up to strangers in the market and tells them her abuse history. Don't know why. Her therapist is working on this. We'll need to be patient."

Days became weeks, and the cool late September breezes finally arrived to chase away the summer heat. Ladawna, true to her testing, was a bright, straight A student, but the complaints were starting up again. Students were telling their parents about a little girl who liked to describe sex acts in great detail on the playground.

A conference was called. The participants included the McGuires, Ladawna's therapist, Ashley, Elaine, and the principal. Mrs. McGuire began by explaining that she and her husband had tried everything they knew to get Ladawna to stop talking about sex to the other children. But she only wanted to talk to children. She did not like going to counseling, she never asked Mrs. McGuire for her ear, and she refused to speak to her social worker at all. After discussing all options, the committee decided to place her into a special smaller lab class for children with emotional problems—until Ladawna was in better control of her conversational ability.

No sooner was Ladawna transferred to the lab class than a new McGuire was placed in Ashley Dawson's classroom. Shane Gregg was a very confused 11-year-old. Fully Caucasian, he was convinced he was an African American hip-hop musician, and he rapped nearly everything he said, liberally laced with inappropriate words and phrases. He twisted his straight blond hair into dozens of tiny braids, pulled his shorts down as low as he could without them falling off, and flashed gang signs to every student who came near him.

He was also extremely hyperactive and impulsive and completely resistant to typical medications used to treat that disorder. His hobby was threatening to "slice" kids after school. He claimed to have a razor blade under his tongue, although nothing was there. After three long months of trying to deal with his near constant disruptions and two more conferences with school officials, Shane left to join Ladawna in the special lab class. Sadly, the behaviors and acting out of both children became more and more serious. Within a year, both were living at a residential treatment facility for children with severe emotional disabilities. The hope was that, once stable, they could go back into the McGuire home and then into an adoptive placement.

In her second year of teaching, Ashley's class gained one more McGuire, but this time, it would be two months before Ms. Dawson even knew she was a McGuire. Alanna Smithers was quiet, studious, painfully shy, and sad-faced. Some days, she looked like she was about to burst into tears over nothing. On other days, she seemed to seethe with anger, like a smoking volcano. Ms. Dawson often ate lunch with her in order to encourage her to eat. Alanna was quite thin and seemed uninterested in food. She also didn't care much for conversation over lunch, whereas the typical fifth grader is a chatterbox. To Ms. Dawson, she was a mystery.

One Monday morning in October, Alanna did not come to class. Elaine took Ashley aside during third period to tell her horrible news. Alanna had killed herself Friday evening after walking home from school. She announced her intention to take a nap after dinner, drank a small bottle of rat poison, and then went to bed. When Mrs. McGuire found her, she was under the blankets and had been dead for over an hour. The funeral would be held at 5:00 that afternoon.

Ashley was stunned. A ten-year-old? Since when do elementary school kids commit suicide? She attended the funeral with several other teachers but remembered little of what was said. Her mind was occupied with a list of questions, mainly, how could this have happened? How could this have been prevented? Alanna, explained Elaine later, suffered from severe depression and had been hospitalized several times in treatment centers after previous suicide attempts. She had gone into foster care after her birth-mother's attempted suicide. A new combination of medications, coupled with group therapy, seemed to be helping, so she had been moved to a foster home. The McGuires, the social worker, and the psychiatrist were all surprised and extremely upset by her death.

But Ashley Dawson was just as upset by something else, the lack of communication between the DHS and her desk. At yet another meeting, she demanded to know why the histories of these three deeply troubled kids, one after another, had been kept from her until they had either greatly disrupted her classroom or tragedy had resulted.

"I am with these kids seven hours a day, five days a week. Don't you think I need to know about their conditions and backgrounds?!" asked the frustrated educator.

The McGuires instantly agreed. "We have begged the department to let us share what information we have with the schools, but our hands are tied. With few exceptions, we are told to keep our mouths shut and let the kids have a 'fresh start.' And sometimes we ourselves are not even given important information about the children and must discover the truth by living with the child!"

All eyes silently turned to the DHS social worker in attendance, who defended his office by saying, "Well, it's true that we used to discourage the exchange of information, mostly because of strict confidentiality laws designed to protect the children's privacy. But in recent years, policy has shifted more toward the 'full disclosure' model, wherein the foster parents and schools are supposed to get social, psychological, and medical histories on the kids in their care."

"Well, this teacher got nothing," said Ashley. "And you never discussed the new model with the McGuires. Maybe I couldn't have prevented Alanna's death, but then again, maybe I could have. I never had a clue as to why she seemed so sad and moody. I never suspected an illness. What's more, I graduated from the state's finest teaching college just two years ago, but never, in four years of education, did anyone teach me anything about what to expect when dealing with foster children, abuse survivors, children suffering from mental illness, or older children who are newly adopted. Now I want to know why!"

"As to the first issue," interjected the principal, "we will institute an immediate policy, subject to the school board's approval, of providing files on all foster children to the appropriate teachers and to the counselors in those buildings. But as for the second issue, this is something you might wish to bring up with the teacher's union. The statewide teacher's convention is coming up. You could present a workshop, training for teachers who find themselves teaching foster and newly adopted older children."

Ashley liked that idea. She immediately contacted the union and was introduced to Jay Brawner, a high school history teacher and coach in the same school district. He and his wife had adopted an older sibling group several years earlier, and Jay was active in adoptive parent support groups. The two teachers put together a training course for teachers and sent their proposal to the union. To their delight, their idea was accepted and scheduled.

"What Teachers Should Know About Foster Children and Newly Adopted Students" would be one of fifty different workshops the state's teachers could choose to attend at the upcoming two-day convention. Ashley and Jay were told to prepare for twenty-five to fifty participants.

They scanned a dozen books on adoption and foster care issues, parenting, treatment methods for emotional disorders like RAD and ODD, and what to expect with children diagnosed with conditions like FAE, ADHD, and learning disabilities. They interviewed the McGuires for several hours about school adjustment and how foster parents and teachers can work together more effectively.

Mr. McGuire asked them to also list ideas on encouraging foster children to do homework. "Many of these kids," he explained, "have never done homework in their whole lives when they come to us. Their educational training has been completely ignored. It takes a lot of communication between our home and the school to get these kids to do their homework!"

Jay and Ashley wrote up fact sheets on how children handle loss and grieving, how they adjust after adoption, and what teachers can do to make the transition easier. They assembled information about the adjustment process of older children arriving from other countries, including English as a Second Language (ESL) issues. They photocopied their handouts, prepared transparencies for the overhead projector, and had everything ready just in time.

But no one came. Or almost no one. To their surprise, only four teachers, all women, chose their workshop. Ashley began the presentation by speaking about how confusing the world of the adopted child can be—new home, new family, new school, new diet, and so on. As she watched her small audience, she tried not to notice how they were folding their arms in disapproval, shaking their heads slightly from left to right, and even giving her hostile looks. Finally, one of the teachers raised her hand.

"Do you have a question?" asked Ashley.

"More like a comment," replied the forty-something teacher. "I teach seventh grade, and these other teachers are in my building. We came here today because all of us have adopted children. Our babies are older now, but we are amazed that you can say these things about adopted children. We have never experienced any of this. Our children are just like any other children. They have no 'issues.' And when you talk about such, well, such nonsense, you make them feel different, and the last thing you want an adopted child to feel is out of place. We are trying to give them a sense of security, not tell them that they are somehow not normal!"

The other three teachers nodded their heads in agreement, and their spokesperson sat down, a triumphant look upon her face.

Ashley, who had not expected such a reaction in her wildest dreams, turned to Jay, who was already approaching the lectern and reaching for the microphone.

"We're teachers, too," he said, "and we have experienced something very different. You are talking about infant adoptions. It's true that children who are never told they are adopted may not share these feelings and experiences, but this workshop is not geared for these children. We are talking about abuse survivors, kids who know they have been adopted, kids adopted at older ages—"

"C'mon," argued the spokesman in the audience, once again on her feet, "we have several decades of teaching experience between us and have had only one or two such children in our classes—and they were just fine!"

"But," said a desperate sounding Jay Brawner, "maybe the next child will need specialized help from you, a little more understanding . . ."

His voice trailed off because his audience was trailing off. All four teachers had picked up their workshop folders and walked out of the room without another word. Jay and Ashley were left staring at an empty room. "You'd think," said a stunned Ashley to her partner, "that we were trying to change the direction of the ocean's tides."

"That might be an easier task," muttered a discouraged Jay. "Who could have predicted that educators would resist becoming educated?"

Hoping the workshop's failure had been a fluke, they next took their research and materials to the teaching college where Ashley had graduated and asked the dean of the education department to consider creating a class or a section of a class to prepare teachers to teach foster and newly adopted students.

The response they received was lukewarm at best. The dean finally agreed to review the materials they left behind, but he never returned their calls, and the curriculum was not modified.

Five years later, both teachers are still in the classroom. They now present an annual ninety-minute in-service workshop each fall on teaching foster and adopted children to the new teachers of their school district. They are thinking of writing a pamphlet to distribute at their own expense to new teachers being certified in the state. The state's Department of Education has agreed to review the pamphlet for possible inclusion in "new teacher certification packets." They are still hoping to modify curriculum at the teacher colleges but realize it will take time.

They continue the struggle to teach teachers about foster care and adoption issues. Sometimes they feel like "voices in the wilderness," but Ashley Dawson and Jay Brawner won't give up. Their cause, they will tell you, is just too important.

6

ADOPTION AS JUSTICE

Justice (noun): equity, merited reward or punishment, administration of the law

INTRODUCTION

In an ideal world, the state would regard adoptive parents as valuable resources and adoption assistance as a sound investment in permanent families for homeless children. Thanks to the tireless efforts of parents and adoption advocates, considerable progress has been made and adoption assistance has become more accessible. Nonetheless, parents who feel called to adopt special needs children soon learn that the role of advocate often arrives with the responsibilities of parenthood.

Applicants and participants in federal programs have the right to appeal agency decisions that adversely affect adoption assistance subsidy benefits. Federal regulations at 45 CFR (Code of Federal Regulations) CH.II 205.10, (a) (5) provide that "an opportunity for a hearing shall be granted to any applicant who requests a hearing because his or her claim for financial assistance . . . is denied, or is not acted upon with reasonable promptness, and to any recipient who is aggrieved by any agency action resulting in suspension, reduction, discontinuance or termination of assistance." In most cases, the right to an administrative hearing also extends to adoption assistance programs that are supported entirely with state funds.

The stories in this chapter attempt to capture the experiences of adoptive parents as they exercise their hearing rights to advocate for their children. The issues and events are based on actual cases.

❧

Extenuating Circumstances

Linda Cozza was worried. "I wonder if we should have tried to get a lawyer."

Sam Cozza paced the living room nervously and turned to his wife. "With Anthony's bills, we can't afford a lawyer," he sighed. "Besides, I thought NACAC told you we didn't really need one at the initial hearing."

"I'm just nervous, I guess," said Linda. "There's so much riding on this hearing, and I don't know what to expect. I wish there was someone we could talk to. We never got in touch with that woman that NACAC recommended—what was her name?"

"Ann Shane. Do we even have her number?"

"I think I put it in my billfold," muttered Linda, rummaging through her purse. "Here it is. Do you think I should call her?"

"I don't know what she could do for us at this late hour, Linda. On the other hand, I guess we don't have anything to lose. The worst thing that can happen is she'll tell us there's nothing she can do and hang up on us," he chuckled. "We ought to be used to that by now after dealing with the Department of Family and Children Services. If it'll make you feel better, let's do it. Do you want me to call?"

"I'll call. At least, I'll feel like I'm doing something besides worrying about the Department of Family and Children Services hitting us with a bunch of questions that we won't be able to answer."

Linda felt foolish as she dialed Ann Shane's number. Then it occurred to her that until recently she would never have made such a call. Since their strange odyssey to obtain adoption assistance for Toni began, she was becoming used to baring her soul to strangers. She wondered if the bureaucrats at the Department of Family and Children Services had any idea how hard that was?

In spite of her newly acquired talent for sharing family problems, Linda began the conversation with the traditional adoptive parent gesture of apology, sometimes known as the kowtow. "I'm sorry to bother you at home, but the North American Council on Adoptable Children gave me your name and number. We have an administrative hearing tomorrow and I was wondering if we could ask . . ."

Forty minutes later, she was glad she called. Shane acknowledged that because administrative hearings were more informal than regular court proceedings, they were harder to predict. But to finally talk with someone who recognized and supported what they going through for their son was terrific. There wasn't enough time to add much to the substance of the Cozzas' presentation, but Shane's obvious expertise boosted Linda's confidence. No matter how many times the Cozzas read the state and federal regulations, there was always an element of uncertainty in confronting the intimidating world of state government. Did the words they read really mean what they appeared to say? And if so, why did the agency appear to give them a different construction?

"Trust your instincts," Shane told her before she hung up. Linda tried to cling to that advice as she fell off to sleep.

The next day the Cozzas were ushered into a windowless conference room on the fourth floor of the state Department of Family and Children Services. Across the long conference table sat the supervisor of adoption assistance from the state's regional office and a young woman who turned out to be from the state attorney general's office. At five minutes after nine, a thirtyish man entered dressed in a gray pin stripe suit. He called the hearing to order and introduced himself as Perry Smart, the administrative law judge (ALJ).

The Cozzas realized that, in spite of the imposing title, administrative law judges were typically young attorneys under contract with the state to serve as administrative hearing officers. That knowledge didn't keep them from feeling a little intimidated. After more introductions, the ALJ called the hearing to order and asked each party to make a brief opening statement.

Margaret Finch, the young lawyer from the attorney general's office, rose to her feet. "The state's case is quite simple," she intoned. "The Cozza family has applied for federal adoption assistance on behalf of their son Anthony, but unfortunately, he does not meet the eligibility requirements. First, we maintain that Toni was not a special needs child at the time that the adoption was finalized. Second, the Cozzas were aware of adoption assistance programs but chose not to apply. There is no provision in state regulations that allows adoption assistance to be given to a child who develops special needs after the final decree of adoption. State and federal policy both stipulate clearly that a child must be determined to have a special needs condition prior to finalization."

Linda Cozza fought back waves of resentment as Ms. Finch concluded her statement. Toni's problems, his progress, his future were never mentioned! Her son had become an abstraction, a case! Why did they think that their job was to come up with reasons for denying Toni any assistance? How could that kind of attitude be in a child's best interest?

Sam found it hard to concentrate on Ms. Finch's argument. They were again forced to plead their case to a bunch of kids dressed up in expensive suits. He had worked to support himself since he was 18, but here he was, hat in hand, asking for help, while bureaucrats fifteen or even twenty years younger than him questioned his motives and commitment. This reverie was suddenly interrupted when he realized that the children's services attorney had finished her statement. The judge asked the Cozzas to make their opening remarks. Linda took a deep breath and began.

Her voice quavered at first but grew steadier as she proceeded. She pointed out that federal Policy Announcement (P.A. 01–01 authorized families to apply for adoption assistance after a final decree of adoption. "Toni was eligible for adoption assistance at the time he was placed for adoption with us," she argued. "We would have applied had we known the full extent of Toni's problems, but we didn't really learn about Toni's family background until about three years after we adopted him. We feel that this qualifies as extenuating circumstances and, should allow Toni to receive adoption assistance." She paused. "Furthermore, we believe that Toni should be entitled to retroactive placements back to the date of his placement for adoption." She sat down. Sam squeezed her hand and gave a thumbs up.

The ALJ suggested that each side could make a more detailed presentation of its position. At the end of each statement there would be an opportunity for questions from all participants. The agency's attorney agreed, and the Cozzas looked at one another, then nodded their assent.

Ms. Finch asked Karen Simmons, the state adoption assistance supervisor, to explain the reasons why Anthony Cozza was not eligible for federal adoption assistance. Ms. Simmons conceded that the boy met some of the requirements. He had been eligible for public welfare or AFDC due to his birthmother's lack of income, and the court of jurisdiction had determined that placement in foster care was in Toni's "best interest." The problem, in the state's view, was the special needs requirement and the fact that the Cozzas had voluntarily adopted Toni without assistance.

"At the time Toni was placed with the Cozzas," she argued, "he was considered a normal, healthy child with no special needs. The information packet sent to Mr. and Mrs. Cozza included a section on adoption assistance, but they declined to apply. We are not authorized to establish adoption assistance agreements after an adoption is finalized unless there were some extenuating circumstances. We don't see any extenuating circumstances here."

Ms. Finch rose. "Do you recognize the document labeled as Exhibit F?"

"Yes," answered Simmons. "It is a copy of the state's special needs definition."

"Would you read section (b)?"

"All right." The regulations, like those of most states, paraphrased the federal statute. "Children who cannot be placed without assistance because of such factors as medical conditions, emotional problems, physical or mental disabilities, age, or membership in a sibling or minority group . . ."

"Did Anthony Cozza fall into any of these categories before he was adopted?" asked Ms. Finch.

"No, he did not."

"Would you read section (c)?"

"Certainly," said Ms. Simmons, gaining confidence.

"Unless it is the child's best interest because of factors such as the emotional attachment to a foster parent, a reasonable but unsuccessful effort must be made to place the child without assistance."

Even though she suspected this was coming, Linda Cozza could feel her stomach tightening into an angry knot.

"Was that standard met?"

"Well, certainly," said Simmons with a smile.

"In short, by placing Anthony, who was a normal healthy child, without an adoption subsidy, you were carrying out the requirements of the state regulations."

"Yes."

"Nothing further at this time, your honor." Finch sat down.

"Are there any questions you would like to ask at this time?" asked the ALJ, looking at the Cozzas.

"Oh yes. More than you can imagine," muttered Sam sarcastically.

"Ms. Simmons," he asked, "did we receive all of the available information about Toni's family history when he was placed with us?"

Simmons hesitated. "Well . . . I wasn't . . . I assume so. It's normal policy to provide the adopting parents with a summary of the child's social, medical, and family history. But . . . I . . . wasn't the caseworker, so I can only assume that . . ."

"Your honor, I'm going to have to object," snapped Finch. "Ms. Simmons was not the caseworker and cannot verify that all of the information was shared. She can only state that existing regulations required the agency to provide a summary of the child's social and medical history."

The ALJ paused. "I'm going to sustain that objection. Is there anyone on the list of witnesses who can testify on the question of what information was disclosed?"

"Toni's caseworker left the agency, and we have not been able to locate her," said Sam. "This is a very important point. The information, or actually the lack of information, influenced our decision to adopt and, later, not to apply for adoption assistance."

"Well, you can present whatever evidence you have in your statement. The objection is sustained. Do you have any other questions for Ms. Simmons?"

"Yes." Sam knew what he wanted to get at, but he couldn't quite figure out how to put it in the form of a question. Finally, he asked, "What does the statement in paragraph (c) of the special needs definition mean? Why was it in Toni's best interest to adopt him without any assistance?"

Warning bells went off even before he finished the question. Somewhere, maybe from an old *Perry Mason* or *L.A. Law* episode, some pearl of wisdom about the risk of asking questions without knowing the answer flashed through his consciousness.

And sure enough, veteran Simmons recognized a hanging curve when she saw one. "Paragraph (c) is to ensure that families actually need the subsidy to proceed with the adoption. You obviously didn't feel that you needed a subsidy, because you adopted Anthony without applying for assistance. I assume that you felt that your income and resources were sufficient to meet Anthony's needs. We have an obligation to provide adoption assistance only in cases where it is needed to complete the adoption."

Sam desperately wanted to say something that would wipe the officious look off of Ms. Simmons' face. If parents adopted without agreement for a subsidy, then that was proof that they didn't need a subsidy to complete the adoption even if all hell broke loose. Ms. Simmons was doing lines right out of Joseph Heller's *Catch 22*, but he didn't know how to respond.

"Do you have any further questions?"

Linda tapped his arm and pointed to something in her hand. "Can we save a response for our presentation?" she asked.

"That would be acceptable. Would you like to proceed?"

"Could we take a ten-minute break?" asked Linda.

"Yes, let's take a five-minute recess."

During the break, Linda showed Sam a passage from the federal policy announcement that seemed to address Simmons' point. "What's it mean?" he asked, trying to digest the wording.

"I think it means that the agency is supposed to discuss the child's need for a subsidy with the parents. Take a look at this. I think we can use it."

The hearing reconvened, and Linda Cozza began to describe the events leading to their application for adoption assistance four years after the adoption was final. Toni had come to them at the age of 2. The court had terminated the parental rights of Toni's birthmother when she was 18 months old, after three out-of-home placements and failed attempts at reconciliation. Efforts to locate the child's birthfather had been unsuccessful. Linda testified that the agency had presented Toni to them as a physically healthy child who had experienced some neglect at the hands of his birthmother. The Cozzas had married young. They had two biological children, a daughter in college and a son who was a senior in high school. Linda said that they felt blessed in their lives and began to think about adopting a foster child when they heard a series of spots on local radio. After numerous discussions, they decided to go ahead.

Toni was a beautiful child. Linda said that she and Sam were so committed to making a home for Toni that they overlooked his frequent temper tantrums and his aversion to being cuddled. When she asked the social worker, she was assured that Toni was just acting out his insecurity from being moved in and out of foster homes. In a short time, he would begin to feel comfortable.

Linda acknowledged that they had been told about adoption assistance programs by the head of a local adoption support group. At one point, she mentioned adoption subsidies to Toni's social worker but was told that Toni probably wouldn't qualify because he didn't have any special needs.

Sam took up the story at that point. "The placement supervisor, Mrs. Patricia Alberts, told us that we didn't seem to need a subsidy. I made decent money as an electrician. Linda had been substitute teaching since the kids were older. We had good insurance through the union. She made us feel that were being greedy for asking about adoption assistance. I'll never forget what she said to us: 'Are you having any second thoughts about the adoption? If you have doubts about your ability to care for Anthony, we can always consider another family. We want you to feel fully committed to Anthony. It's a big step and not everyone is ready.'

"She made us feel that if we brought up the subsidy issue anymore, then we were not really committed to Toni. I felt guilty for even mentioning it. I mean, we could get along all right, couldn't we? I began to wonder about my own motives. If we were going to be Toni's parents, we had to be responsible for him, right? So we dropped the subsidy issue. They told us he wasn't eligible anyway, and we were afraid they might doubt our commitment to him and place Toni with another family. I'll let Linda continue. She has handled most of the therapy issues."

Linda told the ALJ that the couple had proceeded with the adoption when Toni was 2 years old. The temper tantrums, however, did not go away. As he grew older, he seemed to turn on the charm with total strangers while resisting affection from his parents, especially Linda. Friends told the Cozzas what a delightful little boy they had at the same time he was wreaking havoc at home. Toni was especially cruel to the family pets. Max, the family cat, learned to stay away from him. They had to watch Katy, their affectionate yellow lab, after Toni poked her in the eye and tried to hit her with a bat. At day camp, Toni tried to set a shed on fire and attacked a fellow 4-year-old with a rock after the boy refused to give him his candy. When confronted, Toni looked his accusers straight in the eye and denied everything. The Cozzas finally took Toni to a child psychologist. After interviewing the child and parents, the psychologist referred them to Dr. Alice Wheeler, a therapist who had treated a number of adopted children with behavioral problems. Wheeler requested records pertaining to Toni's family and social history, and when they arrived the Cozzas received quite a surprise.

"There were records that we had not seen before," noted Linda. "Toni's birthmother had left him alone for hours at a time when he was an infant. A medical history form indicated that his birthmother received little or no prenatal care and, although the tests were inconclusive, that Toni was considered to be at risk for exposure to drugs and alcohol. The records came from the state Department of Family and Children Services. We don't know exactly which case worker knew about them or who was responsible for providing the information to us, but certainly the agency had them in its possession and the information was witheld.

"Toni began therapy with Dr. Wheeler when he was 4 and a half. The therapy seemed to work for awhile. The tantrums didn't cease altogether, but they diminished. Toni became less destructive and seemed a little more eager to please. At any rate, he was making progress until he entered the first grade. Then, his behavior took a turn for the worst. He began to steal things from the other students. When confronted by the teacher and us, he denied everything and blamed it on another kid. When frustrated, he attacked other students with rocks, scissors, or any weapon he could find. He seemed to have no control over his impulses. He always blamed the attacks on other children.

"After one particularly violent incident last March, Toni was hospitalized. The school doesn't know how to handle him, and we are exploring alternate placements including a private school. I quit substitute teaching three years ago because he was such a handful. Our insurance does not cover all of his treatment now and will max out within the next year or so. And we are looking at years of therapy. Next year, we will have two children in college, and at this point, we don't know how we can cover their expenses and Toni's treatment. Exhibits 8 through 15 contain information about Toni's treatment.

"I would also like to respond to Ms. Simmons' point about the language in the special needs definition that says, 'unless it is the child's best interest because of factors such as the emotional attachment to a foster parent, a reasonable but unsuccessful effort must be made to place the child without assistance.' P.A. 01–01 explains this requirement. It notes that 'once the agency has determined that placement with a certain family would be the most suitable for the child, then full disclosure should be made of the child's background as well as known and potential problems. If the child meets the state's definition of special needs with regard to specific factors or conditions, *then* the agency can pose the question as to whether the prospective adoptive parents are willing to adopt without a subsidy.' The policy announcement is saying that the decision about the need for adoption assistance is essentially up to the adopting parents. The agency should ask, 'As the chosen parents, having considered the child's background, do you need federal adoption assistance to incorporate the child into your family and to meet the child's future needs?' If the parents say yes, then the requirement is met.

"We never received complete information about Toni's background. We never had an informed discussion of his potential problems and whether adoption assistance might be needed. The regulation quoted by the state says that an effort to place the child without assistance should be made 'unless it is contrary to the child's best interest.' We never had sufficient opportunity to consider if providing adoption assistance was in Toni's best interest. Can there be any doubt that it was in his best interest, given all that we have been through?

"Congress created the adoption assistance program to enable parents to provide new, permanent families for children in foster care. As P.A. 01–01 indicates, 'it is not necessary to leave a child hanging in foster care, while the agency shops for a family who is willing to adopt without assistance.' "

"Do you have that document listed as an exhibit, Ms. Cozza?" asked the ALJ.

"No, we just received it last night."

"Then let's mark it as Exhibit N."

"Questions for the Cozzas, Ms. Finch?"

"You said that the tests for drug and alcohol exposure were inconclusive?"

Linda knew where this was going and found her voice rising as she spoke. "The tests could not confirm exposure to drugs, but the hospital didn't rule it out because Toni's birthmother didn't receive much in the way of prenatal care and was suspected of using drugs. So the hospital described Toni as 'at risk.' "

"But there was no documentary evidence of prenatal drug exposure?"

"May I ask what point you are trying to make?" Linda couldn't contain the exasperation in her voice.

"Well, I'm trying to establish whether Anthony was a special needs child prior to the adoption. You testified that tests for drug and alcohol exposure were inconclusive. Toni's behavior problems seemed to start well after the adoption."

"May I respond, your honor?"

"Go ahead, Mr. Cozza."

"Ms. Finch seems to be suggesting that Toni's problems didn't exist until after we adopted him. Is she trying to suggest that he was fine until he came to live with us and that somehow we caused his impulsive and destructive behavior?"

"No, I certainly did not say that. I—"

"Please let me finish, Ms. Finch." The ALJ nodded at him. "No, you didn't say it exactly, but what other interpretation is there? Toni either came to us with these problems and we inherited them, or we somehow caused them. Now, you've heard my wife's testimony and you've seen the psychologists' statements. Do you really think that life in the Cozza family could have somehow encouraged Toni to torment animals and to attack other children with scissors or a baseball bat? What kind of people do you think we are, Ms. Finch? I find your questions extremely insulting!"

"I apologize if I offended you, Mr. Cozza. That was certainly not my intention. I was merely trying to make the point that there is little evidence that Toni had special needs at the time you adopted him. Unfortunately, that is the eligibility requirement. The state can't be held responsible for what can't be foreseen. Every family takes a risk when they have children.

Biological children also develop medical and psychological problems, and their parents are responsible for dealing with them."

Sam was speechless. There it was. You people don't want to accept responsibility for your child. As if all of the long hours in therapy, the worrying, the bills, the strain on other family members were signs of irresponsibility. Hell, when was the last time he and Linda had been out to a movie or to dinner? He wanted to ask Ms. Finch to take Toni for a week and see if her views on being a responsible parent stayed the same. What did she think they wanted the adoption assistance for? Why did she think they were putting themselves through this kind of demeaning process? So they could get rich?

They had changed their lives for Toni at a time when they could have been planning vacations after Mike went off to college. It wasn't as if they were trying to dump Toni back on the state. All they wanted was enough support to give him a fighting chance of growing up to be a normal person, to have a life. Wasn't that the purpose of adoption assistance, for God's sake!? Sam wanted to say all of those things, but knew he couldn't. So he sat, trying to compose himself. Finally, he turned to Linda. "Do you want to say anything?"

Linda had been looking at P.A. 01–01 and other federal documents and scribbling notes. "Your honor, I would like to add one further point."

"Perhaps you should save it for a closing statement, Mrs. Cozza."

"Its important, your honor. I would prefer to include it now."

"Very well," he said a little impatiently. "Go ahead"

Linda was momentarily deflated by the tone of the AlJ's ruling. She tried to get her voice under control as she began speak. "We feel strongly that extenuating circumstances existed in our case and that our contention is supported by current federal policy. The Federal Policy Announcement 01–01, explicitly says that grounds for a review of adoption assistance exist if 'relevant facts regarding the child were known by the State agency or child-placing agency and not presented to the adoptive parents prior to the finalization of the adoption.' Crucial information indicating that Toni was severely neglected and received little in the way of prenatal care was in the department's possession, but was not disclosed to us for more than two years after the adoption. Even then, the agency only sent the information after receiving a request from Dr. Wheeler, Toni's therapist. We don't know if the facts about Toni's family history were withheld deliberately or as the result of some bureaucratic screw up. It doesn't matter; the results would have been the same. Our situation is just the kind that P.A. 01–01 refers to."

"Anything else, Mrs. Cozza?"

"Do we get to make closing statements?"

"Yes."

"Then I'll save the rest."

"Okay, Ms. Finch, do have any further questions for the Cozzas?"

"No, your honor.

"Well, then let's take a fifteen-minute recess."

Linda and Sam stepped out in the hall. It was 10:30 and the adrenaline was wearing off. They looked wearily at one another.

"How do you think we're doing?" she asked.

"I don't know. I can't get a read on the hearing guy. Sometimes he seems sympathetic, and then the next minute, he looks bored, like he wishes we would go away."

They spent the rest of the break going over their statement and trying to anticipate what the state was going to say.

When the hearing reconvened, Ms. Finch rose to present the state's closing argument. "The Cozzas' reference to the discussion of extenuating circumstances does not apply in this case. First of all, Anthony Cozza did not meet the criteria of a special needs child prior to the adoption, regardless of whether or not his parents had complete information about his background. It has not been established that the information was readily available to the agency. Second, the Cozzas were aware of the existence of adoption assistance programs, yet they never submitted an application. The agency followed state regulations by making a reasonable effort to place Anthony without assistance. It is unfortunate that Anthony has developed behavior problems. Our hearts go out to the Cozza family. But life is not without risks. The state should not be held accountable for unforeseen circumstances."

"Mr. and Mrs. Cozza?"

Linda Cozza decided to remain seated. She felt too drained to be nervous. "Here goes," she thought. Sam said a silent prayer that Linda would do her best.

"We dispute the claim that Toni was not a special needs child prior to his adoption. The doctors' and psychologists' statements that we have submitted clearly show that he has serious emotional and behavioral problems. The letters from Dr. Wheeler and Dr. Morgan from Memorial Hospital both point to early neglect and possible exposure to drugs and alcohol as the probable sources of his rage. The information we received after the adoption supports this view. The only alternative explanation is that our poor parenting caused Toni's problems. He either came to us a traumatized child or became traumatized after he came to live with us. There are no other possibilities." Linda's voice rose as months of repressed feelings bubbled to the surface. "We are absolutely certain that we did nothing to cause him such pain. How could the state think otherwise? After all, they placed Toni in our home and approved us as adoptive parents after subjecting us to weeks of investigation.

"The state should know that infants and young children often do not exhibit medical, psychological, or learning problems until they mature.

ADHD, dyslexia, and a host of other disabilities may not be discovered until a child begins school. The fact that the symptoms fully manifest themselves at the age of 4, 5, 6, or even older does not mean that the disease originated at that time. It's not like a person being crippled in a traffic accident. The medical or emotional conditions of most special needs adopted children have their roots in the family's genetic or medical history or trauma resulting from severe abuse or neglect.

"By not taking this factor into account, the state's adoption assistance program discriminates against families who adopt very young children. A number of states consider children who are at risk for medical or emotional problems to be special needs children. Even though it is not specifically listed in the federal law, federal officials approve of this definition of special needs, because they recognize how many families have adopted children without assistance only to encounter large and unexpected treatment costs."

Linda paused to pick up a sheet of paper. "This letter from the NACAC, the North American Council on Adoptable Children, agrees that the use of 'at risk' as a special needs category is accepted by the federal Children's Bureau and lists several states that have the 'at risk' classification in their regulations. I believe the letter is marked as Exhibit H.

"You know' " Linda's voice broke, "I promised . . . I promised myself . . . that I would not become . . . emotional, but I can't seem to help it." She struggled to stop crying as Sam grasped her hands.

"Would you like a brief recess?" asked the ALJ.

"No, I'm all right now. I'd like to continue."

The ALJ nodded.

"I'm sorry." Linda began. "I was thinking of all we have been through since we applied for adoption assistance, all of the nights we have stayed up worrying how we were going to afford help for Toni and make sure that our other children got enough support to get through college and start their adult lives. Isn't that the whole purpose of adoption assistance, to enable parents like us to raise children like Toni? Well, I've said enough personal things. Once again, I'm sorry for getting carried away. I would like to continue now."

She picked up another piece of paper. "Paragraph (F) of federal regulations on Title IV-E adoption assistance states that 'the State must make an active effort to promote the adoption assistance program.' There was more than enough reason for the agency to classify Toni as a special needs child based on his family history. Children with Toni's background usually have emotional or learning problems. A responsible agency would have explored the possibility of an adoption subsidy. In our case, the agency never encouraged us to apply. If anything, they discouraged us. The whole purpose of the adoption assistance program is not just to place children like Toni for adoption, but to invest in the success of those adoptions. It should work like an insurance policy. In our case, the agency did not make an active effort to promote the adoption assistance program, even though there was more than sufficient reason to do so. By failing in this responsibility, the agency violated federal regulations.

"In closing, I will simply repeat that extenuating circumstances exist that should entitle us to a review of Toni's eligibility for adoption assistance. Since Toni clearly was a special needs child before the adoption was finalized, he met all of the requirements for adoption assistance. Finally, in addition to future adoption assistance, we are also asking for retroactive payments from the date that Toni was placed in our home for adoption."

With that, the hearing ended. A week went by, and then the weeks became a month. Ann Shane assured them that the absence of a decision did not have any particular significance. Still, they worried. Toni was scheduled to begin therapy with a psychologist recommended by Dr. Wheeler. They needed the subsidy to help pay the cost of the treatment not covered by their health insurance. Linda went over her testimony again and again, wondering if she had made the case forcibly enough or if letting her feelings show had somehow hurt their cause. Sam tried to convince her that she had done a fine job while his own mood swung back and forth from anger to cautious optimism.

Finally, five weeks after the hearing, a letter arrived bearing the state seal. Linda called Sam and began to scan sections while he waited tensely on the other end of the line. She waded through the summary of facts and the reference to the legal and policy issues before arriving at the decision.

"The agency bases its denial of eligibility on the fact that Anthony Cozza did not exhibit symptoms sufficient to classify him as a special needs child. Because the agency did not consider the child to have special needs, the agency maintains that it had no obligation to encourage the Cozzas to apply for adoption assistance.

"The Cozzas, quoting federal Policy Announcement (P.A. 01–01) contend that relevant facts regarding Anthony's background were known but not presented to them prior to finalization of the adoption. The family submitted reports detailing instances of neglect and suspected alcohol and drug use by the birthmother to support their argument.

"It is understandable why the agency may have felt that Anthony was not a special needs child and, therefore, not eligible for assistance."

Linda's heart sank and Sam swore softly under his breath.

"It is also difficult to determine what information about the child's background may have been accessible to the agency yet not disclosed to the Cozzas. Nevertheless, the family succeeded in establishing that extenuating circumstances exist and warrant a review of Anthony's eligibility for adoption assistance."

Linda was so surprised that she read the last sentence slowly over again. Then she let out a whoop of pure joy! Sam continued to hold his breath. Linda resumed with the hearing decision.

"Prospective adoptive parents are entirely dependent on agencies for information about the children that are placed in their homes. Given Anthony's young age and the trauma of his early years, the agency should have explored the case for special needs and adoption assistance more carefully. Children with Anthony's history often experience emotional problems as they grow older. Unfortunately, time has demonstrated this pattern all too well in this case.

"State regulations do not explicitly include 'a significant risk of medical or psychological conditions' as a special needs category. Nevertheless, Anthony Cozza's current problems almost certainly had their origins in his preadoptive experiences. The most reasonable conclusion to be drawn from the existing evidence is that Anthony had special needs prior to his adoption, but his parents did not fully discover them until they manifested themselves during the months and years following the adoption.

"To deny a special needs child access to adoption assistance because a congenital disorder has not yet been diagnosed or the symptoms of early trauma have not begun to appear is to discriminate against infants and young children who may not be mature enough to register the full effects of a preexisting condition. Even though Anthony Cozza may not have displayed all of the characteristics of a special needs child, time has revealed that he was a special needs child. As a special needs child, he meets all of the eligibility requirements for federal adoption assistance. The agency is hereby ordered to negotiate an adoption assistance agreement at a specialized rate that is consistent with the child's needs and circumstances of the family.

"Regarding the Cozza family's request for retroactive payments, there is no provision in state regulations for the payment of such benefits. Accordingly, the request for such payments is denied."

That night, after a small celebration, the Cozzas called Anne Shane to tell her the news and discuss next steps. Shane agreed that Toni should qualify for a specialized rate based on the extent of his needs. According to the subsidy "profiles" compiled by NACAC, the specialized payment rate for a child of his age in their state was $600 per month.

"I would request a specialized, 'difficulty of care' foster home rate to start with," she suggested. "The foster care rates are usually higher than the typical adoption assistance payments. You can see how the agency responds. If they offer an amount you think will cover Anthony's needs, you can accept it. If you don't think it's enough, you can appeal."

The Cozzas dreaded going through another hearing process but agreed that going after a payment rate equivalent to what a trained foster parent would receive in caring for a child with Toni's behavior problems offered the most promising strategy. They were not sure if $600 a month would be enough to supplement their insurance. The Medicaid card, which came with federal adoption assistance, was a good backup for a host of medical services, but many psychotherapists who were competent to treat Toni were not Medicaid providers.

Ann promised to serve as a long distance consultant during the negotiations.

"Do you think we ought to go after the retroactive payments?" asked Sam. "Do you think we have a chance?"

"I honestly don't know," answered Shane. "Every state is so different. Retro payments might be tough to get, but you have nothing to lose by appealing the decision, except a little time."

Linda and Sam were relieved to learn that the next level of appeal would involve not another hearing but a review of the hearing record by the legal section of the state Department of Family and Children Services.

"You will probably want to submit a brief. I can help you with that," said Shane. "In some states you appeal directly to a local court, but here there is an interim step. If you lose there, then you have to decide if you want to ask the court for a judicial review."

As the long day ended, Linda and Sam realized that they still faced a lot of uncertainty. But now they didn't feel so helpless. The long weeks of dealing with the agency had shaken their confidence, which was already eroded from years of coping with Toni's anger. Today, though, they had taken on the system and won adoption assistance for their son! The victory, though not yet final, gave them a new sense of hope.

৩৯৩৫

Fighting the Good Fight

Things were not going well. The attorney representing the state apparently had confused the concept of "evidentiary hearing" with a death penalty case. The administrative law judge was also getting into the act, admonishing Nancy and the advocate she had asked to testify on her behalf.

All of this after the state had floored Nancy by conceding that her daughter Sara was eligible for federal adoption assistance. When Nancy had first learned about the program the previous May and sent in an application, the state issued a prompt denial. The only reason given was the obvious fact that the adoption had been finalized some six years ago.

Matt Collins, the advocate she located through the North American Council on Adoptable Children, had explained that the state's action was to be expected. Federal policy required that appeals for adoption assistance filed after a final decree of an adoption had to be decided by an administrative hearing. The denial letter triggered her right to such a hearing.

Sara suffered from a rare congenital ailment that produced severe joint pains, fatigue, and a respiratory condition exacerbated by numerous allergies. She had been in and out of hospitals since infancy. When Sara wasn't battling episodes of crippling pain or asthma-like symptoms, she was an outstanding student. Not only did she read and do math five years above grade level, but on her good days she was the best soccer player in the fourth grade. Most of the time, she bore the attacks on her small body with a quiet dignity that Nancy found inspiring and heartbreaking.

After discussing Sara's background further and learning that her birth-mother had been a poor teenager from a family on public assistance, the advocate concluded that Sara almost certainly met the eligibility requirements for federal adoption assistance. Nancy felt encouraged by this news, but based on prior struggles with schools and agencies, she figured she had a battle on her hands.

That's why she almost fell out of her chair when Alice Thieboux, the state adoption subsidy official, began her remarks by acknowledging that Sara qualified for adoption assistance. The state had no regulations or written policy that addressed an application for assistance after finalization.

Matt had assembled various federal documents and a letter written by the former deputy commissioner of the U.S. Department of Health and Human Services in order to establish that the children adopted through private agencies had the same access to adoption assistance as those who were placed by the state. The federal documents were backed up by a 1991 federal district court decision in *Ferdinand v. Department for Children and Their Families*. The judge in that case ruled that "the adoption assistance program was not adequately explained to the Ferdinands. Such lack of explanation, he wrote, "was a violation by the defendants of their affirmative duty to inform the clients of the program and provided the extenuating circumstances necessary to allow the reopening of the plaintiff's case and, finally, the grant of adoption assistance."

Nancy's elation, however, was short-lived. "The state firmly opposes Ms. Gant's request for retroactive payments."This salvo was launched by the state's attorney, a wholesome-looking young man not too far removed from the frat house at State U. "Federal Policy Announcement 01–01, which Ms. Gant introduced as Exhibit C, does not require states to make retroactive payments." He was on his feet now, starting to pace back and forth as he read, "In situations where the final fair hearing decision is favorable to the adoptive parents, the State agency can reverse the earlier decision to deny benefits under title IV-E. If the child meets all the eligibility criteria, Federal Financial Participation [FFP] is available, beginning with the earliest date of the child's eligibility (e.g., the date of the child's placement in the adoptive home or finalization of the adoption) in accordance with Federal and State statutes, regulations and policies." The paragraph does not say that retroactive payments must be made. The policy announcement essentially leaves that decision up to the individual states. In this state, the department has adopted the policy that retroactive payments will not be made beyond the most recent date of application."

As it turned out, attorney Robert Caldwell was just warming up. "Not too long ago, many adoptive families were unfairly deprived of adoption assistance. But now a few aggressive adoptive families and their advocates are threatening the stability of the program by demanding thousands of dollars in back payments. I would like to read from a recent article by Theodora Staley of the Interstate Council on Adoption Subsidy . . ."

Matt Collins broke in. "I'm not an attorney and naturally lack Mr. Caldwell's profound understanding of the law, but I have to question the relevance of his last statement. What is your point, Mr. Caldwell?" he asked angrily. "The issue under consideration is whether Nancy Gant's daughter should receive retroactive payments. Mr. Caldwell's personal views that adoptive families are too aggressive and greedy and his touching concern for the integrity of the adoption assistance program—"

"Mr. Collins!" warned the ALJ.

"The Interstate Council on Adoption Subsidy is funded by the American Association of State Human Services Agencies Theodora Staley works—"

"Mr. Collins, enough!" shouted the ALJ. "If you interrupt again, I am going to dismiss you from this proceeding! Do you understand?"

Collins bit back a sarcastic reply. Suddenly, he saw the whole case going down the drain because he indulged his ego and alienated the hearing officer. He knew what he had to do. Reluctantly, but with as much counterfeit humility as he could muster, he took a healthy bite of crow. "I apologize, your honor. There is so much at stake here. I got carried away. But, of course, that is no excuse." Collins busied himself with a stack of papers to keep himself from gagging.

"Continue, Mr. Caldwell."

"Thank you, your honor," said Caldwell unctuously. Nancy wondered what his reaction would be if she walked up and casually clipped off his regimental striped tie right below the knot. She smiled at the thought.

"Theodora Staley is an attorney and an expert in federal adoption assistance. In a recent article, she writes, 'After spending the past ten years educating states about the importance of adoption assistance for families, I am now alarmed by some current trends. Aggressive advocates have found ways to take advantage of particular sections of federal law and to advance interpretations never intended by Congress when it established the program in 1980. Families who obtain adoption assistance after finalization are winning thousands of dollars in retroactive payments. At this rate, where will it end? Will children adopted from overseas be eligible someday for federal adoption subsidies? It's not a question of whether these children have special needs. My fear is that federal and state policy makers will react to the demands placed on the program, by cutting back on adoption assistance just when it is needed most."

Caldwell paused dramatically. "State funds are not unlimited. If we begin awarding retroactive benefits to every eligible child, then we limit our ability to help families adopt the children that are currently languishing in foster care."

"May we respond to that, your honor?"

"You will have your chance, Mr. Collins. Right now, we are going to take a twenty-minute recess."

"My God, that was frustrating," said Collins with a heavy sigh as they walked down the corridor adjacent to the hearing room. "I hope I didn't turn the hangin' judge against you with my big mouth, ma'am."

"I didn't get the impression that she was on our side before," said Nancy. "She was looking at Assistant Attorney General Robert Caldwell like he was Perry Mason. For a minute, I thought she was going to ask for his autograph."

"Well, I hate to admit it, but that bit about greedy people like you taking adoption assistance away from the poor urchins 'languishing,' not waiting, not hoping, but actually languishing, was a clever touch. Distorted, misleading, and largely beside the point, but clever. Hearing officers are often reluctant to make a decision that might set a new state policy, especially if it's going to cost money. Our former frat boy was playing to that fear."

"What can we do?"

"We'll just have to do our best to poke holes in his argument and the views of the redoubtable Ms. Staley. Staley works for the National Association of State Human Services Agencies. She's been scolding us for our 'irresponsible attempt to circumvent eligibility requirements' for years."

When the hearing resumed, another surprise was in store.

"Mr. Caldwell has requested a continuance because his presence is required on another matter. I will grant the request. The hearing will resume three weeks from today on September 15 at 9 A.M."

"I have three adopted children and one is only 2 years old," Nancy responded. "I would like to see if I can arrange child care on that day before the hearing is rescheduled."

"Child care is your responsibility, Ms. Gant. I would think that you could come up with some arrangement within the next three weeks. The hearing will resume on September 15 at 9 A.M. Until then we are dismissed."

Later, over coffee, Nancy and Matt licked their wounds and concluded that the continuation, though frustrating, was not all bad. "It'll give me some time to look for cases where retroactive payments have been awarded," he said.

"Yeah, if we ever get a chance to speak. I thought hearings were supposed to be accessible. What if I couldn't arrange child care? Isn't she supposed to make sure that the time is reasonably convenient for me?"

"Well, according to federal hearing regulations, which I coincidentally happen to have right here on my person," said Collins thumping a piece of paper, "the hearing shall be conducted at a reasonable time, date, and place, and adequate preliminary written notice shall be given. I'd say that the two seconds of notice she gave you probably strains the definitions of adequate. On the other hand, we really don't know if the time, date, and place are reasonable because she never bothered to ask. She probably figured that since you're not an important person with a busy schedule like Mr. Caldwell that you've got a lot of time on your hands. Hell, you don't even have a beeper or one of those electronic organizers that take your temperature and tell you what meeting you've got to go to. I bet you don't even go to meetings. No wonder she was suspicious."

On the Monday afternoon during the week the hearing was to resume, the phone rang in Collins' office. When he picked it up, he was greeted by a muffled voice with the trace of a Kentucky accent.

"Crazy Dan!" answered Collins. "How's my favorite disgruntled bureaucrat?"

Dan Kent had achieved an uneasy stasis in his fifteen-year guerilla war against the state Department of Human Services by cultivating an air of menace and refining it to the level of an art form. No one knew how or when he became known as "Crazy Dan," but he was very proud of the nickname and of the unsubstantiated rumors that followed in its wake. Dan had never actually threatened a fellow employee, much less done time for maiming a supervisor as some alleged. In fact, Collins found him to be a rather kindhearted soul who just happened to have an unusual talent for terrifying superiors with the slightest look or gesture. The fact that he was 6 feet, 6 inches tall and had an extensive gun collection didn't do much to alleviate their fears either. Not surprisingly, Dan was left pretty much alone, which was generally fine with him. At the moment, he was working his way through the complete works of Shakespeare and didn't like to be disturbed.

"Have you seen the new policy statement on adoption assistance?" Crazy Dan never wasted much time with small talk.

"No, but I'll bet it's as wise as it is compassionate."

"Think again, pal. The adoption subsidy supervisor sent a letter out to all of the county agencies that said paying retroactive payments is against department policy. I heard they tried to get an emergency rule passed first but couldn't get the legal section to go along."

"You wouldn't happen to have acquired a copy of that letter, would you Dan?"

"No, of course not. I . . . oh wait . . . here's a copy on my desk!!! I wonder where that came from? I warned my superiors about letting important public information fall into the hands of the public. But they never listen to us little people, do they? What's your fax number?"

An hour later, Collins was on the phone with Nancy Gant, reading the letter. "Because of the increasing number of requests for retroactive adoption assistance benefits, we have decided to issue the following policy clarification. Effective immediately, if a child qualifies for adoption assistance after a final decree of adoption, retroactive payments may extend back to the most recent date of application for adoption assistance received by the county agency and no farther. Blah . . . blah . . . blah . . . blah . . ."

"Can they get away with that!? In the middle of a hearing?!?" Nancy sputtered.

"I don't know. I don't think the letter has any legal force. We can bring it up. Maybe we can make them look bad. Wow, trying to run through a rule change in the middle of hearing. This is a new low, even for the Department of Inhuman Services."

Later that evening, as she prepared her testimony, Nancy reflected back over the strange turns her life had taken since those wild days back in the late 1960s: nursing school, antiwar protests, getting arrested, and volunteer work at the free clinic in Harlem. That's where she met Josh. His foster parents brought him to the clinic, an undersized 11-year-old well on the way to delinquency. Josh's birthmother was a heroin addict. His foster parents were well-meaning but had difficulty controlling him. He was not a violent child, but he devoted a large chunk of his time to compiling a record with the juvenile authorities for theft and truancy.

Nancy recognized a sweetness and intelligence lurking under Josh's tough, smart-ass demeanor. Something like a friendship developed between the white Jewish student activist and the street-wise black kid. She couldn't remember how the idea of adoption came up, but three years later she became one of the first single parents to adopt a foster child in the state of New York. Life with Josh was no picnic, but after years of painful academic progress followed by school suspensions, lost jobs, and recurring problems with drugs, he began to straighten himself out. He was still working marginal, low-paying jobs, but during their weekly phone calls, he talked enthusiastically about his interest in art and graphic design and his plans to go back to school. Nancy didn't know if he would actually follow through this time, but whether or not he was ever successful in a conventional sense, or ever returned from California, she knew how much he counted on her being there. She was, after all, his mother.

After Josh dropped out of college and began his wanderings, Nancy enrolled in a Ph.D. program in public health at a university in the Midwest. She had no intention of adopting another child. In her second year of the program, however, she made a series of presentations to local adoption support groups. The idea of adopting began to intrude again, quietly at first, then with increasing persistence. A year later, she became the parent of Mark, a three-year-old African American boy from Alabama. Mark turned out to be a cheerful, loving child in spite of daily struggles with an array of developmental and learning problems stemming from his premature birth. Sara became a member of the family three years later. By the time she adopted Amy, an infant with cerebral palsy, Nancy had lost interest in her dissertation. Applying her health care knowledge as a parent had become her calling. She left the university and eked out a living as a day care provider and freelance writer.

The crazy thing was that she was happy, in spite of turning her back on an income in the high five figures. Nancy only learned about adoption subsidy programs when the agency told her that Amy was eligible for federal adoption assistance. She had known that Mark and Sara had special needs, of course, but they seemed manageable and neither of the placing agencies ever brought up the topic of adoption assistance. The children's problems became more severe as they grew older. In the course of treating the children, doctors requested medical histories that revealed that Sara's mother and maternal grandmother both suffered from genetically transmitted illnesses that had never been disclosed to Nancy before the adoptions were finalized. Until Amy's placement, she didn't think there was anything that could be done about it. A local adoption support group steered her to NACAC, which in turn referred her to Matt Collins. Now here she was with appeals underway in two different states. Sara's hearing had come up first.

On the appointed Thursday, she sat nervously as the ALJ convened the hearing.

"I trust that you managed to arrange child care, Ms. Gant."

"No, I dropped them off on the freeway on the way in this morning. Didn't even stop the car, just shoved them out the door," she thought. Not trusting herself to actually respond, she just nodded.

"Would you like to make your statement now?"

"Yes," Nancy replied quietly.

For the next twenty minutes, Nancy walked the people in the hearing room through a tour of her family's daily life. She explained Sara's medical conditions, listed the prescriptions and therapies and recounted how far the child had exceeded everyone's expectations, except perhaps her own. Reluctantly but eloquently, Nancy told the state and county officials how she had forfeited a substantial income in becoming the adoptive parent of three special needs children. She told them that her only regret was the limited resources she now had to pay for the services her daughter would need to reach her enormous potential. Retroactive payments would enable both her and the state to invest in Sara's future.

"To me, the issue is simple," Nancy concluded. "The basic purpose of adoption assistance is to enable parents to provide families for special needs children like Sara. Had I known about the adoption assistance program, Sara would have been receiving payments since her placement in my home. Through no fault of her own, she has been deprived of the assistance to which she was entitled. The only fair resolution to this situation is to restore the benefits she would have received."

"Are there any questions for Ms. Gant?"

Caldwell tossed up a few softballs, but Nancy batted them away harmlessly and he gave up.

"Mr. Collins?"

"Our argument for retroactive payments is based on two logical propositions: One, in finding Sara Gant eligible for adoption assistance after finalization, it is necessary to determine that she actually *met* the requirements for adoption assistance prior to finalization of her adoption. In other words, the state, by conceding that she is eligible for adoption assistance, is also acknowledging that she met the eligibility standards ten years ago, when she went to live with Nancy Gant.

"Two, once it is determined that Sara was eligible prior to the adoption, one is led to the inescapable conclusion that some form of adoption assistance payment would have been negotiated and put into effect. Federal law does not permit a state to put adoption assistance into effect after finalization based on current eligibility. Federal Policy Interpretation Question 92–02 established a procedure whereby parents who apply for adoption assistance after finalization must show that extenuating circumstances prevented them from obtaining assistance prior to finalization. Policy Announcement 01–01, rescinded PIQ 92–02, but endorsed the process for obtaining adoption assistance after finalization. It even lists "failure by the State agency to advise potential adoptive parents about the availability of adoption assistance for children in the State foster care system" as grounds for reviewing a child's eligibility for adoption assistance after finalization. And that is exactly what has happened in this case.

"In his statement, Mr. Caldwell, quoted from a section of P.A. 01–01 to argue that the state is not required to make retroactive payments. But, if states had complete discretion about whether or not to award retroactive payments, then appeals panels would not be awarding retroactive benefits back to the period of initial eligibility prior to the final decree of adoption, would they? Let me offer some examples where the judges apparently interpreted federal policy a little differently than Mr. Caldwell."

Collins' first case was *Gruzinski v. Pennsylvania Department of Public Welfare.* The Gruzinski family won its initial hearing only to see it reversed by the Pennsylvania Department of Public Welfare. The Commonwealth Court of Pennsylvania found that the state's position had little merit and ruled in favor of the family. Not only did the court determine that the child was eligible for adoption assistance, but it also awarded retroactive payments to the Gruzinski family.

"Here is the significant part," said Collins.

This case meets the federal criteria for extenuating circumstances cited in DHHS PIQ 92–02 and this Commonwealth and the local agency should be bound by the federal guidelines and should welcome the opportunity to provide this much needed and deserved entitlement. Most importantly, however, CYS and DPW are bound by the determination of the Fair Hearing officer, who found Laura eligible.

PIQ 92–02 further outlines the earliest date from which adoption assistance may be provided after the finalization of an adoption. In this instance, because the adoption was finalized after October 1, 1986, adoption assistance payments may be granted when the child is placed in the adoptive home, even prior to a final decree of adoption. This is true in this instance even for retroactive payments.

"Based on the court's understanding of PIQ 92–02, it concluded that the Gruzinski child 'is eligible for Title IV-E adoption assistance retroactive to the first instance where [the child] was residing with the adoptive mother *and* the Birth Mother's parental rights were terminated, which date is December 10, 1989.' In the Gruzinski case, both eligibility and retroactive benefits were awarded over the active opposition of county agency."

"I thought that federal PIQ 92–02 has been withdrawn by P.A. 01–01, Mr. Collins?" noted the ALJ.

"I'm glad you brought that up, Your Honor. The Gruzinski case, along with other decisions we will cite displayed remarkable consistency in awarding retroactive payments. Court and hearing decisions in Pennsylvania, Washington, Arizona, and Indiana:

a. Interpreted PIQ 92–02 as enabling language, which made retroactive payments available to otherwise eligible children who had been deprived of assistance by extenuating circumstances.
b. Linked retroactive eligibility and retroactive payments by awarding benefits to the earliest date of eligibility.

P.A. 01–01 did in fact rescind PIQ 92–02, but it retains the same enabling language as PIQ 92–02. In each case, the reference to PIQ 92–02 could be changed to P.A. 01–01 with no change in meaning. The decisions we are citing, therefore, are as valid today as they were before P.A. 01–01 was issued. Thank you, Your Honor, for the chance to clarify that point."

The *Gruzinski* case was marked as Exhibit N. The next case was a 1998 decision in an Arizona administrative appeal.

"A state appeals panel," said Collins, "determined that the child was eligible for adoption assistance and then awarded retroactive payments. Citing state regulations that required the state to inform adoptive families about adoption subsidy programs, the panel determined that 'if the department had properly followed its responsibilities in November 1992, this case would not be before the panel six years later.'

"The appeals panel recognized that the family had suffered significant financial hardship that adoption assistance payments could have helped to alleviate," continued Collins. "Awarding the payments that the family should have been receiving all along could assist the parents in their continuing struggle to meet their adopted children's special needs. Based on 'the interpretation policy letters' [PIQ 92–02], the panel awarded retroactive payments back to November 7, 1992, the date the children were placed with the family for adoption."

Caldwell rose to his feet and moved that the Arizona case be struck from the hearing record, essentially because it was an administrative proceeding from another state and had no force in the present case or "in this state."

"Federal adoption assistance is a national program with the same basic eligibility requirements," argued Collins in rebuttal. "The issue of retroactive payments is relatively new. I would think rulings in other states would be relevant. Pennsylvania and Arizona regulations, like those of this state, do not address the issue of retroactive payments."

"I'm inclined to agree with Mr. Caldwell, but I'll rule on the relevance of this document in rendering my decision. For the moment, it can be marked Exhibit O. Does that conclude your testimony, Mr. Collins?"

"Yes . . . no wait. There is just one more thing," said Collins in his best Columbo. "Federal hearing regulations state, 'when the hearing decision is favorable to the claimant or when the agency decides in favor of the claimant prior to the hearing, the agency shall promptly make corrective payments retroactively to the date the incorrect action was taken.' The incorrect action in this case took place at the time Sara was placed for adoption with Nancy Gant. That is when her eligibility for Title IV-E should have been established and she should have received a subsidy. The section of the hearing regulations I'm citing may be found at 45 CFR 205.10 (18). That concludes my testimony."

Caldwell saved the recently minted policy letter to the counties announcing limits on retroactive payments for his closing statement. "This letter represents the official position of the state Department of Human Services," he contended.

Collins thought that the ALJ looked impressed, maybe seeing a way to avoid a tough decision. Nancy pointed out that the letter was issued after the hearing had started. If it represented a changed or new policy, it should have no effect on a proceeding that was already underway. The ALJ didn't look very convinced to Collins.

Nancy said that the letter not only had no force as a law or regulation, but it also "reflected the adoption unit's lack of confidence in its own position. Taking advantage of a continuance in the hearing to try to invent a policy that did not exist was an act of desperation." She and Matt had both hoped that the ALJ would be properly revolted by the department's sleazy attempt to influence the hearing decision. But, to their disappointment, she didn't even question Caldwell or the agency representative about the incident.

"Is there anything else, Ms. Gant?" asked the ALJ.

"Mr. Collins has an additional case he would like to offer."

"Very well, Mr. Collins?"

"Our position that P.A. 01–01 does not give state agencies the authority to automatically reject all requests for retroactive payments was upheld in a July 6, 2000, Nevada District Court decision. In the case of *Alsdorf v. the Nevada Department of Human Resources*, the court ruled that the state's policy of automatically denying the adoptive parent's request for retroactive adoption assistance payments constituted an abuse of its discretion and remanded the case back to an administrative hearing to be determined on its individual merits.

"The decision by Nevada's Fourth Judicial District Court for Elko County is significant because a number of states have taken the position of blanket opposition to all requests for retroactive adoption assistance benefits. The implication of the court's ruling is that adoptive parents are entitled to a hearing on retroactive adoption assistance payments based on the specific facts of the their case. A state agency does not have the discretionary authority to automatically reject all claims for retroactive benefits.

"The children in question were placed in 1987. When the family finally applied for adoption assistance in 1998, the state agreed that the children met the eligibility criteria for adoption assistance at the time of the placement. According to the court decision, it was 'also obvious that the agency did not inform the Alsdorfs that benefits were available at the time of the placement or finalization of the adoption. The record further reveals that the State denied the existence of the availability of the benefits when the Alsdorfs continued to inquire throughout the term of the adoption.'

"The subsequent administrative hearing awarded future adoption assistance, but in the court's words, 'neither the State nor the Hearing Officer reviewed or seriously considered the underlying facts and circumstances in this case when deciding not to award retroactive benefits.' A policy which denies 'all claims for retroactive benefits without considering the underlying facts of a case,' in the Court's view is a 'denial of due process and is in violation of the Constitutions of the United States and the State of Nevada.'

"Noting that the Alsdorfs had requested approximately $48,000 in retroactive payments, the judge expressed the opinion that 'by finally granting the adoption benefits 11 years after the placement of the children with the Alsdorfs, the State acknowledged their failures in this adoption. It would therefore appear that if the agency had seriously considered the facts and equities in this case, instead of relying on the "automatic denial policy," and exercised its discretion in this case, the Alsdorfs would have been seriously considered for an award of retroactive benefits.'

"Our contention is that P.A. 01–01 authorizes states to award retroactive payments back to the earliest date of eligibility through the hearing process. We further contend that when adoptive families successfully establish that extenuating circumstances prevented them from receiving adoption assistance, retroactive payments are warranted. Therefore, even if the state's belated attempt to add a policy during the source of a hearing is accepted, we maintain, along with *Alsdorf* that a blanket refusal to consider Ms. Gant's case on its merits violates her due process."

Caldwell looked a little stunned. The ALJ was impossible to read as the hearing ended.

A month went by without a decision. One morning Collins bumped into Cathy Barth at a lecture given by Dr. Greg Keck, a Cleveland psychologist specializing in the treatment of reactive attachment disorder. Barth was the state adoption subsidy supervisor. Collins had known Dr. Keck for years, and they were talking in the bright fall sunshine on the steps of the campus lecture hall when Barth approached. After complimenting Keck on his talk, she turned to Collins.

"I know you think you're helping adoptive families, but the state can't afford to give thousands of dollars to every child. What about the foster children we're trying to get adopted? They're going to need subsidies, too!" she said, her voice rising.

Keck looked at her curiously.

"Federal reimbursement would pay for 60 percent of the cost of retroactive payments in this state," said Collins with a smile. "Don't you think that's a pretty good deal, considering the alternative of not helping these kids? I believe that's referred to as an opportunity cost. You know what happens when they grow up without help—unemployment, jail, stuff like that?"

Keck nodded slowly, which seemed to enrage Barth.

"I've heard your act before. It's so easy for someone like you to bash the department! You don't have to be responsible for compliance with state law. You can be the big hero and tell parents what they want to hear. And we're always the bad guys because we've got a program to run!"

With that she stalked off, high heels clicking on the sidewalk.

"Wait, does that mean the engagement is off?" yelled Collins at her rapidly retreating back.

"What was that all about?" asked Keck in his quiet voice.

"Frustration. I imagine she feels trapped. In some ways, she'd probably like to be more supportive, but she feels pressured by the system to guard the gates against any changes that might cost the state money and get someone up the food chain mad at her."

Collins told Keck about the letter announcing a policy against retroactive payments.

"No matter how many of her superiors told her that she was protecting the general welfare against irresponsible demands by a few troublemakers, at some level Barth had to feel a little bad about playing a dirty trick on a single mom with three handicapped children. But, hey, you're the shrink. What's your read?"

Keck laughed. "Are you kidding? I deal with agencies all the time and it's like we're speaking different languages. To keep from going crazy, I pretend like I'm visiting a foreign country with really strange customs. Sort of like Indiana Jones. Sometimes it helps."

A week later the decision arrived. Nancy stared at the brown envelope as if she could influence the results, then set it on the mantle. She picked it back up, put it down, and then did a slow lap around the house. When she returned, she took a deep breath, snatched the envelope, and ripped it open. Nancy could hardly breathe as she skimmed over the dry statement of facts and recitation of the regulations involved. Finally, she got to the conclusions, and her heart sank to her shoes. The ALJ not only ruled against her, but quoted Caldwell's argument nearly verbatim while ignoring hers. In essence, the decision rejected her claim for retroactive payments because P.A. 01–01 did not explicitly require states to make such payments. If the state had intended to make retroactive payments, she wrote, that intent would be reflected in state law or regulations.

Then came the lowest blow of all. Not only were there no state laws or regulations mandating retroactive benefits, but "a recent letter clearly indicated that the policy of the state Department of Human Services was opposed to retroactive adoption assistance payments." Nancy could not remember feeling so frustrated and powerless. She decided to give up and felt a momentary sense of relief. But as the afternoon wore on, her sense of outrage grew. She would wait until she talked to Matt.

"Man, the ALJ collapsed like a cheap tent, didn't she?" said Collins over coffee that evening. "She neglected to mention that a lot of states don't have any regulations that address retroactive payments one way or another, including this one and the two we cited where back benefits were awarded. I don't think she wanted to be the first one to approve retro—too much risk."

Collins urged her to appeal but warned Nancy not to expect too much. The lawyers in the administrative appeals unit were not exactly known for bold consumer-friendly rulings. "The real decision," he told her, "will be whether you want to appeal to the local court if we lose the next round."

And three weeks later, they did. In reviewing the record, the appeals hearing officer found little fault in the decision. Once again, Nancy felt like throwing in the towel, as Collins explained that the next level of appeal was to request a judicial review of the case from the local court of common pleas.

"Do I need a lawyer?"

"Yeah, probably to file the paperwork and submit a brief reiterating our argument. It's not a hearing, though, just another review."

"I don't know if I can afford a lawyer to do much of anything."

"Well, if we can find one, I'll help with the policy stuff and references to some of the cases. The attorney can handle the legalese."

Nancy had thirty days to file for a judicial review. She contacted legal aide and learned that she was over income for them to represent her. A friend gave Nancy the name of two law firms, and after discussing their fees, she learned that she was way under income to secure their services. With a week left, Nancy was running out of choices. She could probably borrow the money and find a lawyer who wouldn't send her a bill the size of Canada's gross domestic product, but what if the lawyer wasn't any good?

Finally, Collins got a lead and it came from none other than Crazy Dan. Dan was a virtual encyclopedia of successful lawsuits against bureaucracies, having filed several himself. One afternoon, while he was describing the latest "tune-up" he had been forced to administer to the new chief of his section, Dan remembered a case against a school system brought by an agency known as "Protection and Advocacy."

When Nancy contacted them, she learned that Protection and Advocacy, now called the Disability Law Center, were not familiar with adoption assistance cases. Their primary clients were disabled children being denied public school services. After Nancy promised that she and Collins could fill in the policy details, a young attorney named Beth Burns agreed to represent her.

Burns filed the request for judicial review on time, and over the next two weeks, she worked with Nancy and Collins on constructing a brief. She was impressed with the argument they had presented and concentrated most of her attention on placing Nancy's case in a broader legal context. Finally, it was done, and there was nothing to do but wait.

The court's decision arrived on a warm fall afternoon. This time, Nancy called Collins and asked him if he could come over. "I'm too nervous to read it," she said.

Collins arrived about twenty minutes later. As he walked into the living room, he thought of all the places he would rather be, including the urologist's office. What if she lost? What could he say? He would feel bad, of course, but he could walk away. Tomorrow, however, Nancy would get up and still face the problem of giving her kids a normal life—but with a lot less hope of getting the financial resources she needed. Nancy handed Collins the envelope, and he began to scan the pages.

"When you get to the important part, read it out loud, okay?"

"Okay," he said quietly, a bad feeling gnawing at his gut.

"And the state has no regulations that require retroactive payments to be made to adoptive families whose children become eligible for adoption assistance after the final decree of adoption." Collins didn't like the way this seemed to be going, but he was going to keep his mouth shut until he knew for sure.

"However, it is clear from the determination that Sara Gant met the eligibility requirements for adoption assistance before finalization. That being the case, Nancy Gant would have had some amount of adoption assistance payments to help her cover the cost of services necessitated by her daughter's serious medical problems. It is reasonable to assume that Nancy Gant would have applied for assistance had she been adequately informed of the program."

A smile began to shape Collins's craggy features and he reread the section, this time out loud.

"Indeed, the decision to determine Sara eligible for adoption assistance was based on the determination that extenuating circumstances prevented her mother from making an application. Taking all of these factors into account . . ."

Collins handed the paper to Nancy.

"Taking all of these factors into account, it is only fair that the child be granted adoption assistance back to the earliest date of the child's eligibility as defined in federal Policy Announcement (P.A.) 01–01. The state is ordered to make retroactive payments back to the date of Sara Gant's placement for adoption at a rate that it would have paid on behalf of a child with comparable level of medical disability to a family with circumstances similar to the Gants. In considering the circumstances of the family, the state is to be mindful of the income Nancy Gant has voluntarily relinquished to raise three special needs children."

Nancy sat back, happy, exhausted. Collins read parts of the decision over again in a fairly bad imitation of Caldwell. When he looked up, he saw tears on her face.

"I never thought . . . after all this, I can't believe it!"

"It's real all right. At the risk of sounding too sappy, you not only won this for Sara, but you opened the door for a lot of other families. Pretty amazing, huh?"

"Would you mind helping with Mark's appeal? I hate to ask you after all you've done."

"I wouldn't miss it. We've got a winning streak going. Consider it restitution for all of my misspent years as a bureaucrat. By the way, you still have to negotiate the amount of retroactive assistance with the agency, but we can talk about that tomorrow."

"How bad do you think it will be? The subsidy administrator probably won't be too happy?"

"With the court decision behind you, I think you'll be in pretty good shape. Cathy Barth may not be too happy to see you, but the bureaucratic mind is a curious thing to behold. Now that she is forced to comply with a court order, she can't get blamed for making a risky decision. You know, 'the feds made me do it, the court made me do it, the Russian Mafia made me do it.' Plus, in the end, it's not her money, even though she acted like you were asking for a cut of her retirement when you first applied for assistance. So, she might be a little cranky, but don't be surprised if you've suddenly morphed into her best friend. 'Nancy, so nice to see you. You know we were always secretly on your side. Those comments suggesting that you were greedy and unstable were just to throw them off."

Nancy laughed. "We've still got a long way to go."

"Yeah, but you just took a big first step. Well, Nancy, we gave 110 percent out there today," said Collins, now a football coach. "We have to take it to a another level next week and play them one at a time. The state is big, but it puts its pants on one leg a time. You know what I'm sayin', Nancy?"

৩৯ৼ৶

The Negotiation

Aron Brown entered the room and sat down across from the agency social workers. He accepted a cup of coffee and took off his blue blazer while the supervisor of the adoption unit, Janet Hartley, arranged some papers. Aron opened his briefcase and took out a purple file folder marked "Subsidy."

"We're happy to see you again, Mr. Brown," said Gwen Croewl, his adoption caseworker. "This is Ellen Savage, the adoption subsidy specialist."

Aron nodded pleasantly and extended his huge right hand, which swallowed that of Ms. Savage. "Glad to meet you," he offered in a deep baritone that concealed his nervousness.

"As you know, we're here today to discuss adoption assistance for Paul," said Hartley. "Ellen?"

"Paul is eligible for federal adoption assistance," noted Savage, glancing down at a form in her hand. "He received federal foster care assistance, which means that he met the AFDC relatedness test. Do you know what that is, Mr. Brown?"

Brown nodded. "It means that Paul's birthparents met the qualifications for welfare at the time your agency took him out of that home and put him in foster care."

Savage nodded through Brown's recitation like an approving teacher. "That's essentially correct. He is also classified as a special needs child."

"I would hope so, since he has tried to kill himself, not once, but twice," thought Aron.

"And on the basis of those two conditions and the fact that a court determined that it was contrary to Paul's best interests to return home, he meets all of the standards for adoption assistance."

Aron already knew that his would-be adopted son qualified for a federal subsidy, but what kind of subsidy? That's what the meeting was all about. Aron decided to be patient.

"We are prepared to offer a monthly subsidy payment of $375 per month and will cover the cost of psychological counseling that is not covered by Medicaid. Paul, of course, is automatically eligible for Medicaid."

There it was out on the table. It was pretty much what Aron had expected. He nodded once, rubbed his chin, and tried to look a bit puzzled.

"What is the basis for a monthly subsidy of $375?" he asked quietly.

"It's the standard adoption assistance rate for a boy Paul's age with his special needs."

Aron nodded slowly in understanding.

"We have drawn up an adoption assistance agreement," said Savage, handing him a copy. "Why don't we give you a few minutes to read it over?"

The three social workers got up and left the room with a promise to return in fifteen minutes. Most of the agreement contained the standard language, outlining the adoptive parent's responsibility to care for the child as a condition for continued assistance and informing him that the agreement could be amended at any time by mutual consent of the parties. The benefits, including the proposed monthly payment, the provision for Medicaid eligibility, and psychological counseling, appeared on page 2.

"Do you have any questions?" asked a smiling Janet Hartley after the trio returned and seated themselves.

"I guess I see the purpose of this meeting is to put together a plan of support for Paul based on what we know about his situation and what we can project about his needs in the future."

"Yes?" responded Savage, with an intonation that implied "and so what's your point?" Her smile dimmed a few dozen watts.

"I think, for Paul's sake, that I need to discuss a higher adoption assistance rate."

Aron felt the room temperature drop a few degrees.

"I don't know if that is possible, Mr. Brown," said Savage slowly shaking her head. Her two colleagues looked equally grave.

"Did I say something wrong?" Aron asked with feigned innocence.

"Oh no," responded Ms. Hartley. "But I don't see how we can deviate from agency policy in your case and still justify paying other families $375 a month."

"Now I'm a little confused."

"What are you confused about?" asked Savage a little testily. "The policy seems pretty clear to me!"

"Well, for one thing, someone sent me a copy of the federal adoption assistance law and this policy statement—what's it called?" he muttered, rummaging around in a torn cloth briefcase with a broken zipper. "Here it is . . . no . . . wait . . . that's it."

Aron pulled the documents out and turned to an underlined passage. "Yeah, this is what I was thinking about. Federal Policy Announcement 01–01. P.A.— is that what it's called?" Hartley looked slightly uncomfortable. Savage nodded.

"It says here that according to the federal law, adoption assistance rates are to be negotiated based on a consideration of the child's needs and circumstances of the family. Later on it says that consistency is not the goal, that the situations of individual families may vary. After reading this, I assumed that we would talk about the kinds of therapy that Paul is going to need and my own situation before arriving at an assistance plan."

"The subsidy agreement we proposed includes counseling," said Savage.

"And that will help, but it's only one piece of the puzzle. As you know, Paul was born several weeks premature. The docs that have seen him don't know if his reading problems stem from some sort of brain damage or from the maltreatment he later suffered at the hands of his birthmother and her boyfriend. He's going to need a great deal more testing and intensive tutoring to get his reading up to a functional level. I don't want him dropping out of school at 16. As a matter of fact, I'm thinking about enrolling him in a private school that specializes in learning problems."

"We don't use adoption assistance to pay for special education," said Savage. "That's the school system's responsibility."

"Paul may be suffering from bipolar disorder. He needs a great deal of emotional support and individual attention as well as academic work. The schools I have in mind can provide the therapeutic environment that's not possible in a public school."

"What kind of adoption assistance payments did you have in mind?" asked Hartley.

"If I understand this right," said Aron, scratching his head and falling back into the role of the naïve rube in the hands of city slickers, "Paul was in a therapeutic foster home last year, and if he wasn't being adopted, he would be back in some form of specialized care. So I was thinking that it would be nice if his adoption assistance could be about the same as the therapeutic foster care payments. That would allow me to try a lot of things."

"That's out of the question!" said Savage, waving her arms like a referee signaling an incomplete pass.

"Do you have any idea how much you are asking for?"

"Not exactly. I've heard rumors that therapeutic foster care payments start at three times the amount you've offered for my son and go up from there, depending on the severity of the problem. Which reminds me, I meant to ask you for a copy of the foster care rates. You'd be amazed at how tough it is to come by that information! I did find the adoption assistance rates for all the other states in this region at the NACAC web site. Did you know that all of the other states in this region have a tier of rates that go up well past $800 per month?"

"This agency can't afford to make those kinds of adoption assistance payments. What if everyone requested that kind of support? Do you know how many children we have in foster care waiting to be adopted?"

"Correct me if I'm wrong," said Aron, maintaining his infuriatingly amiable tone. "You're the experts, but isn't 60 percent of the cost of adoption assistance payments covered by federal funding in this state?" ("Actually, 61.5 percent," he thought, remembering the figure in the state subsidy profile provided by NACAC.)

"Ongoing adoption assistance still represents a major financial commitment for the state," sniffed Savage.

"I have to say that I am a little surprised and also a little disappointed," interrupted Hartley. "When you expressed an interest in adopting Paul, we were delighted because you had obviously developed a strong rapport with him. Now I have to wonder if you are ready to assume the responsibilities of a parent."

"What do you mean?" asked Aron.

"All parents face uncertainty, Mr. Brown. We all struggle with unexpected expenses. We all make sacrifices. Hearing you talk this morning, I'm not sure that you understand the purpose of adoption assistance. It is not intended to cover all of Paul's expenses. The adoption subsidy is only a supplement; it's not a substitute for your obligations as a parent. Frankly, I'm not sure if you understand that. And that makes me wonder if you understand what kind of a commitment you will be undertaking."

Even though Aron suspected that the veiled threat of "shut up or lose your kid" was coming, it took an enormous effort to maintain his composure. His face felt hot, but he guessed that his dark skin provided sufficient camouflage to hide it from the trio across the table. If he were a white guy, his face would look like a giant beet. After a few seconds of deep breathing, Aron decided not to say anything.

The silence seemed to drag on for several years. Then Ms. Hartley went for the knockout. "Why don't you take some time to think about your commitment to adopting Paul?" she suggested. "We have some other couples that have expressed an interest in him. Perhaps a two-parent family would be better able to meet his needs. Why don't you give us a call next week and we can talk again."

Translation: If you try to be a good parent by advocating for your child, you are behaving in a greedy and irresponsible manner.

Aron doubted that parents were lining up around the block to adopt a bipolar 14-year-old, but he felt off balance. The momentary panic he experienced when the agency threatened to place Paul with someone else made him realize just how committed to the boy he had become. Just now that fear was competing with the belief that the agency was bluffing. A strategic retreat appeared to be the only sensible alternative at the moment.

He rose from his chair and crammed the documents in his brief case. "I'll give this some serious thought and call you. Is next Wednesday convenient?"

"That would be just fine," said Hartley, her smile returning. "Adoption is a serious decision."

"A serious decision," he muttered as he walked down the hall. "Of course! Why didn't I think of that? And here I was thinking that it might be a fun hobby to start collecting psychotic teenagers. You know, maybe start with a bipolar kid and move up to a full-blown sociopath. Maybe collect the whole set."

Aron stopped abruptly and looked around when he realized that he'd been talking to himself at an increasing decibel level. He looked at his watch. His next appointment was at 2:00. There was time to work out some of the frustrations from the meeting.

He drove over to the YMCA and changed into running gear. Twenty minutes later he crested the first hill on the rugged seven-mile trail that ran along the river behind the Y. The fall trees were reaching full color in the October sunshine. Aron picked up the pace to force the whirling thoughts and anxieties out of his head. There was nothing like several long, steep inclines to tap into more basic concerns, like breathing. Maslow was right. By the end of the run, Gatorade and a dry shirt would be his primary concerns.

As gravity pulled Aron down the last hill and into an open meadow, he saw a doe and two small white-tailed deer browsing next to the trail. The fawns had shed their spots for the chocolate brown that would see them through the coming winter. He often encountered deer on his runs, but the sight of their gentle faces and graceful strides always lifted his spirits. Today they were a definite bonus.

After returning to the Y, Aron stretched, lifted a few weights, and then found a side room used for yoga instruction. For the next thirty minutes, he engaged in centering prayer, a form of meditation developed by Catholic monks. Centering prayer was similar to certain Buddhist meditation practices and to transcendental meditation. The participant sought to quiet the mind through relaxed breathing and to encounter God through silence.

Following his 2:00 appointment at the clinic, he went to see Phil Quinn, his supervisor and mentor. Aron had entered the clinical psychology program at Ohio State at the age of 30. An undersized child, ridiculed by his father for his timid disposition, Aron had grown into a 6'2" 190-pound mesomorph by his sophomore year in high school. He reluctantly turned to athletics to earn his dad's respect. Then he discovered the speed and agility that made him excel as a running back and receiver on the football field. By his junior season, he felt more comfortable on the football field and track than anywhere else. As his athletic gifts emerged, Aron was also beginning to wrestle with another issue. Aron could always recall feeling different from other kids, although for years he didn't know why. His confidence grew in high school along with his popularity. He got along well with teammates and dated periodically. But something was missing. Eventually, Aron began to wonder if he was gay. The thought was so terrifying that he tried to avoid it. And yet the question hung on the edge of his consciousness, never completely going away.

To please his father, Aron gave up an academic scholarship to Yale to take an athletic scholarship at Notre Dame. The summer after his freshman year, he met Brian, a graduate student. They began to see each other, and the missing pieces began to fall into place. Aron accepted the fact that he was gay but continued to conceal it from his teammates. Four successful seasons as a wide receiver caught the attention of NFL scouts, and Aron was projected as a second-round draft choice.

In the spring of his senior year, a young man was found beaten to death in a wooded area south of the campus. He was a freshman at the university, and as the story unfolded, the public learned that he was gay. After a sleepless night, Aron joined the vigil outside the administration building. The next day, he attended the young man's funeral and was photographed embracing the boy's parents. Such strange behavior by a star football player was bound to draw attention. During the course of an interview with a local television station, Aron acknowledged his own secret.

The next few weeks brought Aron national attention, but not exactly the kind he'd dreamed of on all those Friday night high school football fields. He saw himself scoring touchdowns and coming out on ESPN and all of the network news shows. A well-known writer from *Sports Illustrated* also came calling, along with several gay and lesbian organizations. Then, suddenly, he was old news, replaced in the headlines by the firing of a venerable old coach and the shooting of a basketball player by his estranged wife. Aron felt some ambivalence about playing pro football even before he publicly outed himself. Now, making his debut as the NFL's first openly gay player was just too much to seriously consider. Football was hard enough without the baggage. Besides, Aron didn't know if he would even be drafted. He decided not to find out and walked away. After some work with an AIDS service agency, he decided to go back to graduate school in clinical psychology.

"How did it go?" asked Quinn as Aron slumped into the customer's chair.

"I don't know. They threatened to place Paul with someone else. I think they're probably bluffing, but it shook me. I don't want to lose Paul. And you know what's funny? I can't even explain it . . . why it's so important. I've never felt so strongly about anything."

"You're the only one to get through to him. Maybe that's it. I've worked with a lot of adoptive families over the years, and the only word that I can think of to describe the commitment to kids who are all challenge all the time is 'calling.' It really is kind of mysterious. It's one of the best reminders for me that God is hanging around."

"You priests aren't supposed to need reminders, are you?" laughed Aron.

"Sometimes it's hard to find God when you've seen children tortured by the very people that they trust to protect them. But then someone comes out of nowhere and dedicates a large chunk of his life to a stranger. And most of the time it works out pretty well. Let's just say that it's easier to see the face of God at some times than others, even for us sky pilots. It's been a long day. I'm starting to sound like a Graham Greene character. What's next?"

"I don't know. It's going to be a few years until I get a practice up and running. I've spent most of my savings on school. Sean's just gone out on his own as a graphic artist. Not the best time to start a family, but Paul is 14 and his chances for any kind of adulthood are running out."

"So you think that you ought to push them for higher levels of adoption assistance?"

"Yeah, but I don't want to lose him. Maybe I'm being selfish. Maybe there are other families that could provide him with a more stable home. Living with two gay guys won't be any picnic."

"Look, Aron. We've been over this. It comes down to a few questions: Do you really believe that you can love Paul and be a positive force in his life?"

Aron hesitated, then blew out a deep breath. "Yes."

"So do I. And one thing that I wouldn't have predicted when I first signed on with the Paulists is that adoption by a gay man and his partner would be in a teenager's best interest. But that was hundreds of abused kids and a lot of gay couples ago. Do you think that you and Sean are equipped to help Paul come to terms with his sexual orientation whether it's gay or straight?"

"Yeah."

"I mean, if Paul turns out to be straight, you're not going to recruit him, make him change sides, turn him queer?" asked Quinn.

Aron laughed. "We'll have to make him gay. It's part of our agenda."

"I'll bet you were one of those guys who woke up one morning trying to decide whether to go gay or straight. Let's see, if I'm straight, then my coach will be proud of me, my friends will like me, and I'll be considered an all-American pillar of the community. On the other hand, if I turn gay, people will hate me, my coach will kick me off the team, and my parents will disown me. Golly, which should I choose? I think I'll go with gay."

"Yeah, I could've gone with straight," said Aron, "but I didn't see any advantages. Who needs family and friends anyway? To me, it was a no-brainer."

"How long have you and Sean been together?" asked Phil.

"Ten years. You know that."

"I'm just reminding you. You've got some tough choices to make about how far to push the subsidy issue, but it sounds to me like you've worked through the doubts about being a worthy family. I mean at least as much as anyone can. There will always be uncertainty."

"That still leaves me with the decision of whether to accept the agency's offer. You know they can place Paul in another home and invent a reason for it after they do it."

"Yes, they can. You're not completely without options, though. You can petition the court directly for adoption if the agency tries to place him with someone else."

"But won't that jeopardize the subsidy by making it an independent adoption?"

"It would make it more difficult, still possible. But I think that you could qualify Paul for Supplemental Security Income (SSI), and then an agency adoption wouldn't be necessary. If a child meets the SSI eligibility criteria, he's just about automatically eligible for federal adoption assistance. It would take some time, but I think it's a pretty sure thing with the recent bipolar diagnosis."

"Hey! I didn't think of that! I can push the agency harder on the amount of assistance. I don't know if I'll win, but now I don't have to be so worried about them taking Paul."

"The *Guardian Ad Litem* would give you pretty strong support with the court, and my testimony as Paul's primary therapist might help. By the way, have you picked up any vibes from the agency on the gay issue?"

"None. I mean, they know. Sean was around every time they came for a home visit. He obviously lived there. We've never tried to hide it. It's never come up. Don't ask. Don't tell. I think they were genuinely impressed by the bond that's formed between Paul and me. The fact that I'm a resident in clinical psych hasn't hurt, either. You know, it's funny, but even though I've been afraid they might try to place Paul with someone else over financial issues, I've never really been worried about them playing the gay card— maybe because I could claim discrimination and file a law suit."

"You still could if they try to place him with another family because of a disagreement over adoption assistance."

"Yeah, but I don't want to put Paul through a public blood letting over gay rights either, so it's kind of a stalemate."

Since becoming his advisor, Phil had filled the void left by Aron's own father's bitter rejection. Turning his back on a chance to play pro football and coming out of the closet were more than his dad could cope with. Maybe that was the connection with Paul. At first he was just one of the kids that Aron saw in the adolescent psych practicum and probably the most difficult one to like. But there was something so forlorn about the kid. Maybe it was the utter abandonment by his family that got to Aron. The kid had been betrayed by every adult in his life, even his original foster parents. Although Aron's parents had never abused him, he knew the devastating pain of rejection. Neither of his parents nor his brother had been able to accept his sexual orientation. You were the same person, but suddenly you were a complete stranger to people you loved.

They certainly didn't hit it off right away. Paul didn't trust anyone and was particularly contemptuous of the big ex-jock who came to his therapy session. The thaw began when they discovered a mutual interest in music. Like most kids, Paul liked contemporary rock and some hip hop, but to Aron's surprise, he had an extensive knowledge of jazz and blues. The two began going to concerts together, and after many months, a friendship began to grow.

Aron didn't know anything about adoption and never thought about it until a court date was set to consider the termination of the parental rights of Paul's biological mother and father. Termination was a foregone conclusion. Paul seemed headed for some kind of long-term foster care, perhaps in an institution. Kids that age and that messed up did get adopted sometimes, but they were long shots.

How had the idea that he might adopt Paul come up in the first place? Was it Phil? Probably, but once the idea planted itself, it not only terrified him—it became an obsession. He learned that gay people did adopt and that a state Supreme Court case made it illegal to discriminate solely on the basis of sexual orientation. On the other hand, the state only recognized adoptions by a single gay adult, even in cases where there was a stable relationship of long standing. There was a case before the state Supreme Court in which the lesbian partner of an adoptive mother was seeking to adopt her daughter. Courts in other states had ruled favorably on similar petitions, but the decision in this case was still pending.

The next week found Aron back at the agency, feeling a noticeable tension in the room as he sat down.

"Let's see," said Hartley with a somewhat strained attempt at cheerfulness, "where were we?"

Aron handed each of the three women copies of a service plan he had put together. Savage frowned as she read in silence. The plan included an intensive program that combined music with psychotherapy. Paul had been bullied and humiliated until he had no confidence in his physical abilities. Aron found a martial arts class that specialized in training young people with serious psychological problems. The program combined physical fitness and discipline with an intensive reading and math program. The rest of the plan included more standard psychotherapy with Phil, along with provisions for respite care.

"I am a second-year resident in clinical psych, and it may be quite some time before I establish a practice. In the meantime, Paul will be growing up, and I want to make sure that he has every chance to function successfully as an adult."

"I'm not sure that the state is responsible for subsidizing your decision to go to graduate school," sniffed Savage. "That was your choice."

"Yes, it was, but without that decision, I wouldn't have even come in contact with Paul. As I understand it, adoption assistance is supposed to be flexible, so as to meet different family lifestyles. I know that the law says that the amount of support is supposed to be based on a consideration of the child's needs and the family's circumstances."

"Family circumstances means situations beyond the family's control," said Savage. "It doesn't include voluntary choices like quitting a job to go back to school."

"I think it does." Aron began to rummage around in the bulging file. "Here it is, Federal Policy Announcement 01–01. I have another copy," he said, handing the document to Savage.

"See, it says

The circumstances of the adopting parents must be considered together with the needs of the child when negotiating the adoption assistance agreement. Consideration of the circumstances of the adopting parents has been interpreted by the Department to pertain to the adopting family's capacity to incorporate the child into their household in relation to their lifestyle, standard of living and future plans, as well as their overall capacity to meet the immediate and future needs (including educational) of the child. This means considering the overall ability of the family to incorporate an individual child into their household.

Savage looked stunned. Hartley looked confused. Aron couldn't be sure, but he thought he saw the traces of a smile on Croewl's face.

He charged ahead before they could recover. "As I said, my goal is a plan that that will help me to get the right programs and services for Paul. I know that federal adoption assistance provides some level of monthly payment and Medicaid. I also know that there is a state-funded subsidy program that pays for services that are not covered by my health insurance or Medicaid. Neither Medicaid nor my insurance is going to pay for the kinds of services that will give Paul a chance of becoming a normal young man. I've checked."

"So what specifically are you proposing, Mr. Brown?" asked Hartley.

"Well, I figure that I might be able to cover his needs with an agreement for adoption assistance that would be equal to the cost of supporting Paul in a foster home. That would be a specialized foster care rate, of course."

"Therapeutic foster care rates range from $1,000 to $1,500 per month!" said Savage, her voice rising.

"I'm requesting $1,000 a month. If I understand the program, federal funding is available up to a child's foster home rate. In this state, the federal financial participation rate is approximately 60 percent. So my proposal would cost the state about $400 a month. I know that services could be provided through the state subsidy program, but if I could pay for the services with Paul's monthly adoption assistance, there would be less paperwork. It would also cost the state less since there is no federal funding for the service subsidy. I think that we would both benefit from a plan with higher payments and fewer provisions for services."

As the adoption subsidy supervisor, Savage arranged most of the adoption assistance agreements. She was not used to dealing with prospective adoptive parents who were so well informed. Savage had worked in adoptions for fifteen years and was sincerely committed to finding permanent families for the children in the agency's care, but she felt a great deal of pressure to keep adoption assistance under control. It wasn't that meeting Aron Brown's request for adoption assistance would break the budget, but his insistence of an agreement outside the normal policy raised the specter of the unknown. Agency bureaucracies operate according to predictable routines. In such an organizational culture, the ultimate fear is the loss of control leading to unpredictable outcomes and costs. Ironically, this fear is particularly strong in child welfare, which has a long history of dealing with families who are dependent on the benevolence of agencies. Savage felt threatened by Brown's behavior, even though she would have been hard pressed to explain why.

"I don't think that we can agree to your request, Mr. Brown," said Savage. "We will talk to the assistant director in charge of fiscal decisions and let you know, but I doubt he'll agree."

Aron nodded slowly.

Hartley spoke up then. "Frankly, Mr. Brown, we may have to consider placing Paul with another family. I'm a little disappointed. We thought that you were committed to adopting Paul. Now, I'm not so sure."

"I'm trying to negotiate the best plan for Paul that I can because I am committed to him," Aron responded.

"We'll let you know in a few days," said Savage. And the meeting was over.

Aron drove home riddled with doubts. Sean tried to assure him that he'd done the right thing, but he couldn't stop worrying that he'd pushed the agency too far. Four days went by without contact. On Thursday afternoon, he was sitting in the office when the phone rang.

"Hey, I heard you were trying to adopt a kid! That's great! You'll make a great daddy!" rasped a voice straight out of west Texas. It wasn't the agency.

Donnie Slaughter was an old teammate who had gone on to become an all-pro middle linebacker in the NFL. He and Aron hadn't been all that close when they played together in college. Donnie was two years behind him and appeared to be a classic redneck. "Listen, Aron, Ah don't know if it would he'p or hurt you, but if I can do anything to support what you're trying to do, you let me know." After an hour, they hung up, agreeing to get together over the Christmas holidays.

After Aron came out publicly and was being shunned by family and people he thought were his friends, he ran into Donnie at a local restaurant. Aron braced for trouble. On the football field, Slaughter was a 250-pound wrecking crew.

He almost fainted when Slaughter walked up, paused briefly, then extended his hand and told Aron how much he admired his courage. They had been friends ever since. Talking with Donnie always made him feel better. He supposed it was because Slaughter was a larger-than-life reminder not to judge people by how they talked or where they came from.

The agency's response came the following Tuesday in the form of letter rejecting his request for adoption assistance. The letter informed Aron that he could appeal the decision by requesting an administrative hearing. There was no word of another placement. Aron wondered if that was next.

Without the support of Phil and Sean, Aron might have caved in and agreed to the agency's demands for a lower adoption assistance agreement. In the end, he requested a hearing. As the weeks rolled slowly by, Paul remained in therapeutic foster care. Finally, the date of the hearing arrived.

"It wasn't anything like I expected," observed Sean as they walked out to the parking lot after nearly five hours of testimony and argument.

"Me neither," said Aron. "What surprised you the most?"

"It's kind of hard to say now that I really think about it. The focus of the hearing was the amount of adoption support that Paul should receive. That was clear. I guess I was struck by the difference in the way the two sides presented their arguments."

"I'm not sure I get what you mean."

"I'm not sure either," laughed Sean. "You and Phil and your witnesses spent most of the time talking about Paul and his future needs. The agency representatives concentrated on whether the regulations required them to provide more assistance than they offered."

"We had to tie our testimony about Paul's problems to federal law, policy documents and state regulations," said Aron.

"Yeah, I know, but you kept coming back to Paul and the general purpose of the adoption assistance program. Maybe that's it. Remember, you talked about how federal policy required the adoption assistance to be negotiated on the basis of the child's needs and family's circumstances?"

"Sure." Paul nodded.

"You were saying, 'what does it mean to consider the child's needs and family's circumstances?' It means looking at what it will take to help this adoption to succeed. The agency, on the other hand, was focusing on a literal interpretation of the law. 'Does it say anywhere that we are required to do it?' On one side, you have the family arguing for a broad, flexible interpretation of federal policy. On the other, you have the agency trying to narrow the issue to words pulled here and there from the law. Am I making any sense?"

"Yes, I was so worried about leaving something out of our testimony that I didn't notice. But, yeah, that makes a lot of sense. Our case is based on the intent of federal policy and the child's needs. The agency is saying that the hearing decision should rest entirely on whether there is any language in the regulations that says they must comply with our request. Let's just hope that the ALJ is not a strict constructionist."

Over the next few weeks, Aron's mood roller coastered between quiet confidence and dark pessimism. If they lost, the next step would be an administrative review conducted by a member of the state Department of Human Services' legal staff. After that, they could request a judicial review from the local Court of Common Pleas. They would need a lawyer to file the paperwork with the court and write a brief outlining their case. From there, they could take their case through the appellate process, all the way to the state Supreme Court. Donnie had offered to pay all of the attorney fees and could easily afford it, but Aron dreaded the thought of a prolonged legal battle. Even if they won, he didn't know if the agency would appeal the decision. For maybe the thousandth time, he thought about calling the agency and accepting its offer. Phil urged him to hang on a little longer.

Sean called him at his office on a Wednesday afternoon. "It's here," he said.

"Do you want to open it?" asked Aron.

"Hell, no. I'll bring it over."

"I'll go get Phil after his class and meet you at his office about 4:30."

Two hours later, the three men gathered around Phil's desk. "Just remember one thing," he said. "If it's bad news, we can always appeal. It's not over."

"So can they," thought Aron as he tore open the envelope. His eyes traveled quickly over the document until they arrived at the familiar passage: "The negotiation shall take into consideration the circumstances of the adopting parents and the needs of the child . . ." Then he started to read aloud. "The county agency determined that the child required a specialized level of foster care and has been paying $1,400 a month to the therapeutic foster home in which he is currently living." Aron's spirits rose.

"There are no specific regulations that require the agency to provide the same level of support in adoption assistance as the child received in foster care." A black cloud descended.

"However, the difference between the child's foster care payments and the amount of adoption assistance proposed by the agency is so great as to be inconsistent with the needs of the child and the circumstances of the family." Now his heart was racing.

"The request for adoption assistance in the amount of $1,000 per month appears to be reasonable, based on the assessments of the specialized level of care needed by the child made by the agency itself, as well as the circumstances of the adopting parent. The agency is ordered to negotiate an adoption assistance agreement with the prospective parent based on the present and projected needs of the child and the current capacity of the prospective parent to incorporate the child into a new family and obtain needed services for him. The minimum amount of the monthly adoption assistance payment shall be $1,000 per month."

After the celebration subsided, Aron wondered if the agency would appeal the decision. Within a week, he had his answer. Julie Croewl called and asked him if he was free to come in and discuss the adoption assistance agreement. He thought about asking her if the invitation meant that there was not going to be an appeal but let it go. The call ended with an agreement to meet with the agency the following morning.

Aron didn't know what to expect when he walked into the agency conference room. Julie Croewl had been friendly over the phone, but she was always friendly. Savage and Hartley were seated at the table when Croewl ushered him inside. He took his time removing his jacket, trying to take the social temperature. He sat down and looked into three smiling faces.

By the end of the meeting, Savage and Hartley had become Aron's new best friends. They readily agreed to an adoption assistance payment of $1,000 plus a service subsidy for respite care twice a month and continued psychological counseling with Phil. There was no mention of an appeal. After completing the adoption assistance agreement, they discussed plans for Paul's adoptive placement within the following ten days.

Aron couldn't help but wonder at the change in attitude, although he kept his thoughts to himself. Then, it hit him. Savage and Hartley, for whatever reason, felt obliged to contest his "irresponsible" demands on the program. Maybe they sincerely viewed themselves as the stewards of public funds. Maybe they really believed that he was not willing enough to make sacrifices on behalf of his future child. Aron didn't know. But now that the issue had been settled by a formal hearing, the pressure was off. They had done their duty. He was still pondering the vagaries of bureaucratic culture as he rose to leave. As Aron paused to accept their congratulations, Savage shook his hand and said, "I'm glad we could bring this to a satisfactory conclusion for Paul's sake."

"Me, too," answered Aron with a smile. But as he walked away, he wondered if Savage really looked at Paul's placement as a happy ending. As pleased as Aron was, he realized that the challenge of building a family had just begun. If agencies were geared to think of adoption as an end rather than a beginning, no wonder adoptive parents and agencies experienced so much conflict.

Aron sighed and shook his head. He figured that there would be plenty of time in the coming years to consider the strange ways of children's services agencies. He felt the tension of the preceding days begin to lift as he walked out into the bright fall sunshine. Aron knew that stormy times lay ahead, but right now, this day, things were looking pretty good.

7

ADOPTION AS JOURNEY

Journey (noun): travel from one place to another, to travel

INTRODUCTION

The bumper sticker says, "Life is a journey, not a destination." So, too, with adoption. At every developmental level, the adoptee experiences it differently. The young child is curious. "What does my birthmother look like? Is my birthfather an FBI agent?" The middle child asks why. "Why me? Why do I have to be different? Why did my birthparents give *me* up?" The teen and young adult is focused in on the how of adoption. "How did this happen to me? How did the adoption system respond? How do I deal with this?"

And eventually, most adoptees return to the curiosity they began with. Many reach out to reunite with birthfamily members not because of anything their adoptive families lack, but in an effort to feel whole. To know. To complete the cycle that begins with loss and ends with acceptance. And the adoptive parents who support them find, to their great joy, that the process does not lessen the bonds of love and loyalty that bind them as a family, but rather, it strengthens them!

The fortunate adoptees have adoptive and biological families who accept the simple facts that an adoptee has two real families and that no one can be loved by too many people. The unfortunate ones remain mired in the emotionally painful tug of war that the American way of adoption has forced on adoptees for the last century.

The journey of adoption is different for each person who lives it. There is no right or wrong way to feel if you are adopted. Therefore, these stories can tell us only about a few individuals. They cannot make any blanket pronouncements except that it is normal and typical for each adoption journey to be completely unique—like the sojourners themselves.

෯෧

The Palm Baby

Jacques Piefort was not surprised to come home and find his wife high again. The whole apartment smelled like crack smoke. Their 2-year-old son needed a diaper change and was hungry. As Jacques saw to his needs, he begged his wife once more to get back into drug treatment.

"Hazel," he warned, "I've had it. Our son needs you, and our unborn child needs you, too! The next time I find you high, I'm taking the baby and going home to Haiti. I can't go on watching you abuse yourself and our second child. You'll never see us again if we leave. If you love your family, stop using!"

Hazel Piefort ignored him. She was high. She was happy. Nothing could bother her. Two weeks later, she came home after a three-day binge to find the apartment emptied of everything except her clothes. "Haiti," she mumbled and then curled up on her pile of clothes and went to sleep.

When she woke up, she was in labor, active labor, and she couldn't remember how many months pregnant she was. But she wasn't very big. She had not yet been to a doctor; she had been planning to go but never got around to it. So she took a taxi to the emergency room. She made only one quick stop along the way, to make a buy and enjoy a small fix. Couldn't face all those nurses sober, she thought. She collapsed in the emergency room, and when she woke up, she knew right away. The baby was gone. She was no longer pregnant.

"Twenty-three to twenty-four weeks gestation," the doctor told her, "and only twenty ounces, a bit more than a pound in weight. Maybe in a few years, we could save him. I've heard that artificial lung surfactants are in development, but in 1986, we don't have the technology. Your son is still technically alive, but his lungs don't work, and we can't do much for that except give him comfort."

Hazel showed little emotion, dressed as soon as the doctor left, and walked out of the hospital, never to be seen again. Neither she nor Jacques were ever found by the Department of Family Services.

Dr. Navreka, who delivered the "extreme preemie," called him a palm baby because his still fetal-positioned body could fit in the doctor's outstretched palm. The nurses in the neonatal intensive care unit, however, wanted him to have a name right away. They poured over a bible that the hospital chaplain loaned them and chose "John James," after two of the apostles. This name was later shortened to "JJ." As one of the nurses put it, "He's too small to have a long name. JJ fits him better."

The hospital chaplain baptized JJ when he was just 6 hours old and then gave him last rites. The nurses tenderly took turns reaching into the bassinet and carefully, very carefully, stroking his tiny arms. His skin tore as easily as wet tissue paper but when he was being touched, he breathed easier. This was a baby who responded well to human contact.

Several minor crises passed, and when Dr. Navreka arrived at work the next day, he was surprised to find JJ still breathing. And still breathing the next day, and the next. No infant that small had ever survived at that hospital or in the entire city. Each hard-fought breath was a miracle.

His wife, Delores Navreka, starting volunteering an hour each evening to sit and hold JJ and rock him in the rocking chair next to his bassinet. Even with tubes and monitors hooked up all over his frail body, it was obvious he loved the rocking. When Delores held him, all of his vital signs improved. So she stayed with him more and more until she was putting in the same number of hours at the hospital as her husband did. Slowly, JJ grew. Black hair started growing in on a previously bald head. His eyes, once too large for such a tiny head, fit better now. And what lovely eyes—they loved to find a human face and just crinkle up with a smile.

JJ was a bit stronger each day and could sometimes even lift his tiny thumb to his mouth for a moment. He had surgery for blocked eye ducts, for an umbilical hernia, and he somehow managed to survive a virus that should have killed a baby so small. JJ was defying all the odds. And everyone who met him was amazed. At age 3 months, which should have been the time he was born full-term, JJ was strong enough and hefty enough, at 3 pounds, to go home. Delores had started the foster parent training a week after meeting him, so he was able to go home with her and Dr. Navreka. They planned to get him healthy and help him transition to a wonderful adoptive home. The Navrekas had two grown children and were not interested in starting over with a baby. They had traveling to do and grandchildren to spoil.

JJ had to have breathing treatments around the clock, and even with those, he would sometimes just quietly stop breathing and turn blue. The foster parents kept monitors on him at all times to make sure he did not die in his sleep. Slowly, his lungs began to mature, but Dr. Navreka still had strong doubts that JJ would live to see his first birthday. On JJ's second birthday, Delores teased him about that dire prediction!

Most babies walk at about 1 year of age. JJ took his first cautious step one month after his second birthday, when he was the size of a 1-year-old. The Navrekas threw a giant party at the hospital to celebrate. The home-made sign said, "JJ WALKS!" But since JJ preferred not to repeat his performance in front of the crowd of well-wishers, Delores showed a video of those first steps, which played again and again throughout the party.

After the celebration, as Delores took down the party decorations, JJ's social worker approached her and said that it was time to prepare JJ for adoption. He was no longer a dying baby. He was now a "waiting child," which is a foster child who cannot be returned to the birthfamily. He was a toddler with special needs. And although he still took four breathing treatments a day, he needed a forever family now.

Delores said nothing but paged her husband, who came on the run from another part of the hospital, fearing that the party had been too much for his foster son's limited lung capacity. Delores nodded to the social worker, who told Dr. Navreka what she had just told his wife.

Up until now, the couple had worked hard to completely avoid talking about the A-word. The idea of losing JJ was too painful to think about, much less discuss. But now it was not only time for a discussion, but for a decision, too. The foster dad looked down at his feet and over to his wife, whose eyes were already shining with tears. It was clear that if JJ was to leave them, it would have to be her husband who spoke the words. She would not; she could not do it.

Dr. Navreka took a deep breath, looked into the social worker's eyes, and said emphatically, "Ma'am, you are looking at JJ's forever family right now. Please, just tell us where to sign!" Delores threw her arms around her husband and screamed with delight. They hugged for several minutes, saying everything in that embrace that they wanted to say to each other without a single word spoken.

The department could not have been happier to lose this family as a foster home and gain them as an adoptive home. A few months later, JJ officially became John James Navreka.

Of course, there was another big party at the hospital. This time, the sign said, "JJ's Really HOME!"

By age 3, JJ was still walking poorly, so he wore a type of modified football helmet to protect his head when he fell. He could only say a few words, and he was nowhere near ready to be potty trained, but his personality was sparkling. Everyone loved JJ. He spread joy like a blanket before him wherever he went.

By age 4, he still needed several breathing treatments a day, but his lungs were definitely improving. He could walk well now and run, and he was out of diapers. His vocabulary was small, but he communicated well with gestures and body language.

Extensive testing concluded that he was mildly mentally retarded with an IQ of 74. None of the experts would make predictions, however, about whether or not his IQ would change.

Developmentally, he was delayed as well, but daily physical and speech therapy was helping. The Navrekas were well prepared for the challenges and never regretted their decision. Adopting JJ was and would always remain the best decision they ever made without any prior verbal discussion.

He went to a lab in school for children with learning disabilities (LD) and flourished. He began reading by second grade and could add and subtract by then, too. He needed eyeglasses, but his hearing was strong and his teeth, strong and cavity-resistant. He was small for his age, looking about two years younger than he was, but he was active and happy.

In third grade, he was diagnosed with attention deficit hyperactivity disorder, but he turned out to be one of those lucky children who responds so well to medication that it is almost a cure. The new increased attention span translated into more academic progress.

Later that year, JJ came home from school one day with a prestigious award called the President's Physical Fitness Award. His parents were a little surprised, since their son had never been the athletic type. The note accompanying the award said that JJ had broken the school record for the number of pushups and chin-ups completed by a third grader. Now that did not surprise Dr. and Mrs. Navreka. They had long marveled at the large biceps in their son's upper arms and at the upper body strength he showed when he played on the jungle gym in the backyard. People had actually asked them if JJ worked out with weights!

Dr. Navreka explained to his wife that researchers following the first "extreme preemies" to ever survive had found that this extra muscle and strength was not unusual among the children. Apparently, the severe prematurity leads to a type of confusion in the developmental patterns of some of the children. The body puts muscle cells where fat cells should go, so the children have less fat and more muscle. "It makes sense," explained Dr. Navreka, "because fetuses lay on almost all of their body fat in the last two months of the pregnancy. JJ was born well before this process even began."

In fourth grade, new IQ testing showed a ten-point gain, which doubled by seventh grade. The breathing machine had been gathering dust for a few years by then and was replaced with a pocket asthma medication inhaler. By eighth grade, JJ's IQ was squarely in the average category, he was making As, Bs and an occasional C in regular classes, and other than the inhaler, a little medication for hyperactivity, and iron for anemia, he was taking no medicines. He had even graduated from speech and physical therapy.

JJ is still on the small side. As an adult, he will probably not be taller than 5'5" or so, but no one knows for sure yet.

The Navrekas call him their walking, talking miracle. They don't fail to give credit to medicine when it's due, but they also know that JJ survived for other reasons. He was a fighter, for one thing, with amazing personal resilience, and he had lots of people who loved him.

JJ's parents are no longer surprised by their son's progress or accomplishments. They are proud but not shocked. The sky is the limit, as far as they are concerned.

JJ is happy to be alive and relatively healthy, but he takes it all in stride. He's too busy with football, friends, and video games to dwell on the effects of prematurity and prenatal exposure to illegal drugs. JJ doesn't feel unique, doesn't think his survival is anything special. He shrugs his shoulders shyly when asked about his life, his family, and his health. That is exactly what adoption is all about—giving kids from dangerous and difficult backgrounds the opportunity to take a normal family life absolutely 100 percent, entirely for granted.

જ્જ

Dual Reunions

Forty-year-old Liz Graves, a never-married college biology professor, could not remember an occasion when she gave or received more hugs. There were more family members at this once-in-a-lifetime Graves family reunion than she had ever met at a wedding, baptism, or funeral. And since each of her parents had come from large families, there was an almost count- less number of nieces, nephews, cousins, and elderly aunts and uncles to greet.

The richest of the cousins, Lena Graves Brown, who built a fortune in direct sales, had made the gathering possible by paying all of the hotel, activity, and meal expenses and by sending plane tickets to all out-of- towners. Liz could have afforded to fly to Missouri from Florida, but the plane tickets Lena sent her and her parents were happily accepted. Never again would there be an opportunity to see so much family for so long under such comfortable conditions. They had taken over most of the lux- urious hotel in downtown St. Louis.

The highlight of the third and final evening together was a formal feast and the distribution of books entitled *The Genealogy of the Graves Family*. Lena had commissioned the research and paid for the hardbound printing. The volume took the family line all the way back to the Revolutionary War. Since it was now 1975, this created a 200-year-old family tree.

Liz, who had always been interested in tracing the family's roots, was very excited to clutch her copy of the research in her hands. She flipped through it immediately. When she reached the page showing her parents and their siblings and children, however, she was surprised to see that her name was absent. Strange that the usually detail-obsessed Lena would forget one of the cousins.

After dinner, as family members retreated to their rooms to pack, Liz approached her cousin and showed her the page in question. She did not even have to ask. Lena's brow immediately furrowed as she grabbed Liz by the arm and pulled over to a quiet corner of the dining room.

"Oh, Liz. I just didn't know how to handle this, er, situation. I hope it didn't embarrass you not to see your name. You are, of course, one of us, and you know I love you, cuz, but you are also, of course, not part of the genealogy, per se. I just wrestled and wrestled with myself about what to do. In the end, I decided that you should be part of the reunion and that you should have a copy of our family history but that your name really does belong in the genealogy of your real family." She paused for a breath, smiled innocently, and then added, "I just knew you would understand!"

Liz could feel her pulse and blood pressure changing. She felt her face grow hot and her knees collapse. She slumped into a chair and tried to absorb the double impact. In one fell swoop, she had just learned that she was adopted and that she was being ejected from the family history because she was adopted.

Now it was Lena's turn to be shocked. As she watched her cousin's reaction, it became apparent that Liz had not "known," after all.

"Oh, no, Liz! Don't tell me you didn't know. Why, everyone knows you were adopted. I just assumed you did, too!"

"No," said Liz, looking up at Lena and speaking in a surprisingly calm voice, "I didn't know. But if I had known, my dear cousin, I would have objected to your decision not to put my name in this book. I am my parents' child, their only child, and I have the same surname as you. And now, if you will excuse me, I am going to find my mother and father, the only 'real' parents I know, and I'm going to ask them about this."

And somehow, Liz found her legs and left. Fortunately, her parents had not yet checked out of their room. Liz's mother burst into tears and held her daughter in her arms. Her father reacted angrily, demanding to know where Lena was at the moment and why she felt she had the right to interfere in such a way. When everyone had calmed down, Liz's mother told her the whole story.

"Well, it was during the Depression, when most of the family lived near Kansas City, when your father and I found out that we could never have any babies. In those days, adoption was kept a secret. There was a young woman in town who asked our doctor to find a good home for her baby, and he found us. We adopted you right after you were born and your birthmother immediately left town. We were so afraid you would find out, we sent your adoption papers to Uncle Ned, Lena's father, for safekeeping. He stored them in the attic until you were 21 years old, and then, at our direction, he burned them in his fireplace . . ."

Liz held up her hand to pause her mother's narrative while she tried to absorb yet another shock. Unknown birthfather, disappearing birthmother, no papers, no link, and the attic—this is how Lena must have found out. She probably saw those papers as a child and shared the big secret with other cousins.

"But, Mom, why burn the papers? I don't understand."

"Because that's what the lawyer told us to do. Once you were 21, your birthmother could not challenge the legality of the adoption, and burning the papers meant the secret was good forever."

"Secret? What's good about this secret? What if I want to know the whole story? What if I need to know? What about medical histories and . . . and . . ." Liz fell into her mother's arms sobbing. It was all too much to take in.

"Charity Renee Nettles," said her mother quietly into Liz' ear. She looked up, as if trying to remember a poem once committed to memory. "Age 22. Birthplace: Columbia, South Carolina. Occupation: seamstress. That's all we knew about your birthmother, my dear, and no one spoke a word about your birthfather. But the doctor seemed to think he might have been married to someone else when you were born. I memorized these facts just in case there would ever be a reason you might need them."

Liz hugged her mother even tighter. "Thank you, Mom." And then she looked at both of her parents. "I don't know what I'll do with this information, but I know one thing—I'm glad to have it. I'm glad you told me. It feels like you've just given me something that was mine all along. I only wish you had felt comfortable telling me this long ago."

"But, Liz," her dad explained, "we were told never to tell you because you might go running back to your birthfamily. Don't you know how much we love you? We were terrified of losing you. Why, when you were 6 and you came home for lunch on the first day of school, you asked us what 'adopted' was. Do you remember that?

"You said some child in your class had called you that. This meant that the secret was no longer a secret in that town. So we packed up that day and moved clear across the country to Panama City just to protect you. We never dreamed you'd find out this way, in such a cruel way. Lena was just plain wrong to tell you, and she was way out of line to take your name out of this book. She had no right!"

"Oh, Daddy," said Liz, wrapping her arms around his neck, "we have to trust love more than that. Nothing can ever change the love we have for each other. We will always be a family. You worried for nothing. And Lena didn't think she was telling me anything new. Apparently, my adoption secret has not been a secret among the cousins for many years. And as for the genealogy, we'll just write my name right in under yours in our copies. Lena can't stop that!"

Charity Renee Nettles would now be 62, and Liz decided the next day that she wanted to meet her. It wasn't difficult to win the full support and enthusiasm of her parents. Together, they spoke to a private investigator who located Charity Nettles Wiley rather quickly. She was living in her birthplace, Columbia, South Carolina. Ironically, there was a large Nettles family reunion taking place the following weekend at a South Carolina lake resort. The investigator thought Charity would be there.

Liz chose to fly to the reunion before contacting her birthmother. She actually checked into a room at the resort and then called the front desk, asking to be connected to the room of Charity Wiley. She had barely leaned back on the bed when the ringing phone was answered by a woman. With a shaking voice, Liz opened the conversation the way the private investigator had suggested.

"Mrs. Wiley? My name is Liz Graves and I was born March 1, 1935, in Kansas City, Miss—"

Her voice was cut off immediately by shouting and screaming at the other end of the phone. She could hear Charity crying out, "Oh, thank you, Lord! Thank you! My prayers have been answered! Praise God!"

Within seconds, they were both crying too hard to be intelligible. But Liz managed to communicate that she was in the very same hotel right now, in room 233, and seconds later, she heard pounding on the door. Charity had run at top speed down the hall from room 239.

Liz opened the door on a woman who looked like an older version of herself—same height, same coloring, same wavy hair. It was the first full five-minute-long hug either of them had ever given anyone, and then they held hands for an hour after that. They talked all night until they were hoarse, grabbed a couple of hours of sleep, and talked some more.

The next few days would be full of introductions, tears, and more long strong southern hugs. Apparently, the entire Nettles family had been trying to find Liz for years, including her three younger sisters and her birthfather, Alan Wiley. Liz had been relinquished at birth because Alan was married to a woman who lived in a mental hospital. After his wife passed away, he and Liz were married and brought three more daughters into the world. When Charity had returned to her aunt's home in Missouri to find out what happened to the baby she gave up for adoption, she hit nothing but dead ends.

Alan had an easygoing personality and a quick wit. Charity laughed at almost everything he said. Her sisters had a million questions about her life in Panama City. And they had plenty of photographs of their children to show her. Charity was instantly an aunt, many times over!

This second family reunion in one month was just as joyous as the first, but without the shock and grief at the end. Liz enjoyed being around people she had so much in common with. At last, she knew why she loved pistachio ice cream so much. Apparently, this was a strong Nettles trait!

And Liz was presented with a book at this reunion, too, but a very different kind of book. It was the small white Bible Charity had owned since she was a little girl. She had faithfully recorded the names of all of the relatives on both sides in the genealogy pages in the center. On the lines that said, "Our Children," she had purposely left the first line blank until she found out the name of her first daughter. Before giving the Bible to Liz to keep, she wrote Elizabeth Graves on that line, and in the margin, she wrote the names of Liz's adoptive parents. "They are a part of our family, now," she explained. "And their names belong in this book, too."

୬ଚ୬

The No-Respect Blues

Robert and Olivia Perry spent fifteen years trying to help their daughter cope with emotional problems. Adopted at age 5 from her seventh foster home, Cathy had already proven that she was a survivor. She had come through infantile neglect at the hands of a birthmother too drug-addicted to respond to her baby's cries, the loss of her father to prison, and the physical abuse of her mother's boyfriend. She had been removed from her first foster home at age 3 because they spanked her for defiance, and foster parents were not allowed to spank. Five more foster homes would ask the social workers to come get the child because of her disobedience and aggression. The last foster home was almost ready to give up as well before the Perrys came along.

They were never given full disclosure about the extent of Cathy's problems and, having no parental experience, they had no way of knowing that her challenging behavior was not typical of 5-year-olds. They finalized the adoption before they ever knew the truth. But when Cathy killed a puppy by playing too roughly with him, they sought psychiatric help.

It was a dual diagnosis of attachment disorder and oppositional defiant disorder. The doctor called AD/ODD the "one-two punch" because it was a difficult combination to treat.

Cathy Perry had trouble trusting anyone and had no desire to be trustworthy either, so her behavior was usually manipulative and deceitful. And she refused to mind, even when obedience was in her best interests. For example, when told to brush her teeth, she would close the bathroom door and make the sounds of brushing, without actually doing so. Eventually, her breath was so bad, she was taken to the dentist for an evaluation. When he told them that she did not have a dental disease but had simply not brushed her teeth in at least three months, the reality of the situation began to hit home.

They started her on mood disorder medication for probable depression and found a child psychiatrist with experience treating AD and ODD. Cathy went through out-patient therapy, in-patient therapy, residential treatment in the summer, and maintenance therapy during the school year. Sometimes she got better, and sometimes she seemed to get worse. The Perrys enjoyed the good days and tried to forget the bad ones. When Cathy was 8 years old, the state called and asked if they would like to adopt her 9-year-old half brother, Paul. They had been separated in foster care due to sibling abuse from Paul, but he was more emotionally stable now and, they felt, ready to be reunited with his sister.

The Perrys showed a copy of the young man's psychological evaluation to Cathy's psychiatrist, who immediately advised against the adoption. Paul had been diagnosed with the exact same conditions, but he was also prone to fits of rage, destruction, and violence. Putting the children together would be a disaster. Robert and Olivia read the file several times and agreed with the psychiatirst. They asked for brief holiday and birthday visits between the children in their home, but even though these went pretty well, they declined the opportunity to adopt Paul. They were quite sure that raising Cathy was a job that required all of their attention.

Paul would eventually be adopted twice, but both placement attempts ended in disruption because of his behavioral problems. He grew up in a residential treatment facility with a weekend foster family visitation home near his birthplace, two states away from Cathy. They kept in contact mainly by phone.

The high school years were particularly difficult for the whole family. Cathy repeatedly rejected her parents and heaped on them the anger she had been holding inside toward the people in her past who hurt her so much. Her parents, on the advice of Cathy's excellent family therapist, Ms. Katy Thomas, M.S., rejected her rejection just as often. They refused to be shut out of her life.

When their daughter yelled, "I hate you!" they reminded her that this did not change their love for her. When she cursed at them, they "grounded" her, restricting her movements to home, school, and church alone. And they always prayed for her. When she said, "You're not even my real parents!" they reminded her that her opinion did not make it so, nor did it change the reality that they would always consider her their daughter. Slowly but surely, taking two steps forward and one step back, Cathy worked through her rage and grew to appreciate her family.

By age 20, Cathy was doing amazingly well. She was continuing in therapy, taking her medication, and staying away from the alcohol she had experimented with off and on in high school. She was not smoking anything anymore.

A very bright young woman, she had completed high school with fine arts honors and had earned a two-year Associate of Arts degree from the local junior college. She had just found a full-time job working as a tour guide in a museum, had moved into her first apartment, and was sharing it with two friends. Her relationship with her parents varied from warm to indifferent and seemed to alter with her mood, not unlike changes in the weather. One week, she was affectionate and fun to be with, and the next, she might be angry and sullen. Lately, she had been more consistent, but Olivia and Robert were relieved that she was still seeing her therapist, Ms. Thomas.

It was about this time that the phone call came. A woman who sounded like she was in her fifties, identifying herself as Mrs. Vaughn, called to ask for the phone number of Cathy Vaughn. That had been Cathy's name, and her birthmother's maiden name, prior to adoption. When Olivia asked her who she was, she replied, "I'm Cathy's grandmother. Who are you?"

Paul, it seemed, had run into his grandmother at a shopping mall, and she recognized him, even after more than a decade had passed. As he was now 21, unemployed, and homeless, he moved in with his grandmother the same day. Paul had remembered the Perrys' phone number but did not tell Mrs. Vaughn anything else. She had assumed this was Cathy's foster family.

Olivia explained that Cathy was their adopted daughter, their only child, and that she had recently left home. Mrs. Vaughn impatiently asked for the new phone number or address. "Paul is living with me now, and I want Cathy back, too," she said.

Olivia was stunned. Obviously Mrs. Vaughn did not regard the adoptive relationship as anything of substance if she could dismiss it so lightly. Cathy may well want to meet her grandmother, but was it not premature to assume that Cathy would want to leave her new apartment and move hundreds of miles away and in with someone she barely knew?

Olivia attempted to explain Cathy's situation, but Mrs. Vaughn would hear none of it. "I'd like her phone number, please," she said sternly. "I *am* her grandmother, after all."

Olivia blurted out, "Then why didn't *you* adopt her fifteen years ago? I'm sorry, Mrs. Vaughn," she replied, "I can't divulge that information without my daughter's permission. But if you will give me your phone number, I will give it to Cathy tonight."

Mrs. Vaughn ignored the question and gave Olivia three different phone numbers and an e-mail address, thanked her, and promptly hung up.

Later, Olivia and Robert were surprised to hear Cathy's reaction. "Yes, I remember her, and I don't want to call her. She had a chance to adopt me and Paul, but she was too busy with her beauty shop business. I have no desire to see her or Paul." Then Cathy impulsively tore the paper with the contact information into tiny pieces. Robert would later be able to fit them together well enough to read the e-mail ID. He sent Mrs. Vaughn the following message: "Dear Mrs. Vaughn, We gave Cathy your message. Her response is that she does not wish to have contact with you or with her brother at this time. This is her decision to make and is out of my hands. I wish you well, Bob Perry."

Two weeks passed without a response. Then one evening, as the Perrys were leaving their home with Cathy to take her out to dinner, they were met on the front porch by two people who resembled Cathy so much, they knew immediately who they were.

Mrs. Vaughn spoke to Cathy first, "We found your address with a CD-ROM phone book. You can tell we are determined to see you again, Cathy. After all, you are my granddaughter. Won't you please come with us for a little visit? You choose the restaurant. It's my treat."

Olivia quietly hoped that Cathy would at least agree to talk to Paul and her grandmother for a little while to make her views clear. And perhaps talking to them would change her mind about seeing them again. This was a golden opportunity for Cathy to learn more about why her grandmother did not adopt her and to, perhaps, start the process of forgiveness and re-connection. Neither Olivia nor Robert felt threatened by any relationship Cathy might develop with her birthfamily. They had long ago dealt with unreasoning fears. Their only concern now was for Cathy's safety and that her wishes, whatever they were, be respected. Olivia never got the chance to encourage her daughter to talk to Mrs. Vaughn. Cathy's eyes immediately flashed with anger, her fists clenched, and her face turned red. It was a reaction the Perrys had seen many times in other situations. "I don't want to see either of you right now. I will let you know when I change my mind. Now please leave me alone!"

Mrs. Vaughn never paused. She nodded toward the Perrys and asked, "Have these people turned you against us? We're blood! What's the matter with you?"

Cathy's response was to turn quickly and go back into the house, slamming the door behind her. Thinking quickly, Robert grabbed a pen from his pocket and a scrap of paper and scribbled an address on it. "Be there tomorrow at noon," he said to Mrs. Vaughn. "Cathy will be there, and we'll figure this out." Olivia stared at her husband. What was he up to?

Paul took the paper and they left, without so much as a good-bye. The address Robert had scribbled was that of Cathy's long-time therapist, Ms. Thomas. He called and told her what he had done, and she was prepared when everyone arrived on time at her office the next day.

Ms. Thomas took them to a conference room. Cathy sat next to her parents and refused to speak to her grandmother. Ms. Thomas picked up a piece of chalk and strode to the chalkboard. She wrote a word at the top in big letters: R-E-S-P-E-C-T. Then she made three columns beneath RE-SPECT, labeling each, "Adoptee," "Bio-Fam," and "Adopt-Fam."

Her lecture was brief and to the point. "If there is ever to be any effective communication between any of the people listed in these columns, each of you must respect the position of the others and the rights and responsibilities of the others. Cathy, your right to have a relationship with your bio family, or not, must be respected, but you have a responsibility to base your decision on the facts. If you feel rejected by your bio family, you may or may not have good reason. But you should at least listen to your grandmother's version of your early years. You might learn something you did not know."

Cathy fidgeted in her seat and stole a glance at her grandmother, who had just mumbled, "Amen!"

"And you, Mrs. Vaughn," continued Ms. Thomas. "I'm an adoptee myself, so I am speaking to you as a therapist, as someone who knows Cathy well and cares about her, and as someone who has personally experienced the tug of war that so many adoptees suffer through. Do you have any idea how it feels? When you have two families, you want to love both and be loved by both. But if someone tries to make you feel guilty for that, or if one family does not respect the role of the other, it feels like your heart is being torn in two. Cathy did not grow up with Vaughn as her last name, as Paul did. She was adopted, and you need to understand that this is just as important as blood. If you can't accept that, you risk Cathy's further rejection of you."

Mrs. Vaughn looked like she was about to object, but then her face melted and she slumped back in her chair. It was as if she had known this all along but was trying desperately to push it aside. She was now giving up the struggle.

But Paul wasn't convinced. "What about me?" he said loudly, jumping up out of his chair and pointing at the Perrys. "What about my rejection? I waited my whole life for the Perrys to adopt *me*. I wanted to live in their fancy house and have a regular mother and father, like Cathy. But they didn't want me and I got stuck at the children's home. And I still don't know why!"

For a moment, it looked as though he might pick up his chair and throw it, because he was banging it on the floor to punctuate his sentences. However, once finished with his outburst, he sat back down.

Olivia and Robert sat speechless, horrified that Paul had felt such rejection at their hands and equally horrified that they had never realized it before. They had focused all of their energies on Cathy and never considered his feelings.

Ms. Thomas spoke first. "Paul, I owe you an apology. There should be four columns on this chalkboard, not three, and I apologize for not realizing that before." She stepped back to the board, made a fourth column and labeled it "Foster Care Graduate."

She explained, "I use this term because Paul's situation is different than that of anyone here. He is one of the tens of thousands of Americans who grow up as nobody's kid in foster care, a system that is designed to be temporary but wasn't in his case. He deserves respect for his position. He has the right to be viewed as the victim of a system that, for whatever reason, failed him. He should have enjoyed some form of permanency, but the state ultimately could not match him to anything lasting. Paul, you must also realize that you, too, may have jumped to conclusions about the Perrys, just as your sister may have done regarding your grandmother. You have the responsibility to listen to the Perrys tell you why they did not adopt you. You have the responsibility to listen to your grandmother, as well, to discover the same thing."

Paul nodded, folded his arms, and leaned back in his folding chair, balancing it precariously on two legs. "Okay, I'll listen," he said, "for awhile." Even in his angry mood, he was hopeful that, finally, he would get the answers to questions he had been turning over and over in his mind for many years."

"And finally," Ms. Thomas said turning to Robert and Olivia, "you have the right to be respected by everyone present as Cathy's other family. You are not babysitters or foster parents but the people who raised her and who will continue to be there for her as long as you live. And you have the responsibility to go on supporting Cathy emotionally as she sorts through all of this. You have the responsibility to avoid interfering with the birth-family as long as their actions do not impact on you personally. You should be congratulated for setting this meeting up, as it may prove to be a valuable clarification for your daughter and for her brother."

The meeting continued for two more hours as each person took turns speaking, or in Paul's case, speaking very loudly. Cathy and Paul were surprised to learn that their grandmother had chosen not to adopt them because her hands were full taking care of their mother. Her drug usage eventually led to a diagnosis of AIDS, and it was Mrs. Vaughn who cared for her until her death five years before.

Paul was surprised to learn how difficult raising Cathy had been for the Perrys and that their rejection of him was not personal, but a matter of limited resources. In other words, all of the adults present had been doing the best they could and the most they could for everyone involved.

Mrs. Vaughn's anger was a result of her guilt that she had not raised her grandchildren. Her guilt was compounded by the fact that she had lived with her own grandmother for several years as a child but was then unable to take in her grandchildren when they needed her. As she was able to let go of that burden of guilt, she found herself embracing Olivia and thanking her and Robert for staying committed to Cathy through thick and thin. Cathy's reaction was to cry tears of relief.

Paul remained angry that he and his sister had been split up and blamed the system for not finding a single home to adopt them both. He also did not remember many of the behavioral episodes relayed by the Perrys and wondered aloud if they were exaggerating. He had a better understanding of the situation at the end of the long session but was not convinced of the severity of his own problems. However, he agreed with Ms. Thomas that he could definitely use some ongoing therapy, and she arranged to refer Paul to counseling colleagues of hers in his hometown.

The next few months had their ups and downs, but in time, respect among the individuals took hold. Cathy became more comfortable with the realization that she was a member of two families, and Paul made steady progress in an anger management treatment group.

The biggest argument was about with which family she would spend the next holiday, which would be Thanksgiving. When Cathy suggested that her birth and adoptive families get together for Thanksgiving, the idea did not go over very well right away.

"Give it a few years," suggested her grandmother. "It could happen."

"Maybe in a year or two," said her father. "Give us all some time. Rome, after all, wasn't built in a day."

❧

Dear Mom . . .

June 2

Dear Mom,

Another day, another diary entry, but this is one of the saddest days of my life. I've been reading some of the old diaries. The one I reread most is from the worst year of my life, when I lost my baby. So many other men and women in the birthparent support group have now had reunions, but not me. Now I know that there will never be a reunion in my life. I finally received a letter back from the adoption agency, from Mrs. Kukle. My baby died shortly after being adopted. Died. All of these years, I have wondered about him, prayed for him, thought of him every single day, imagined his face, his voice. I developed a habit of scanning crowds for him, convinced in my mind that I would know him instantly if I saw him. And now the hope is dead, too.

June 4

Dear Mom,

Like layers of an onion, I'm peeling back every layer of my sorrow, and each one is laced with irony. I survived my birth, the same event that killed you. I survived a childhood without adoption, growing up in seven different foster homes and knowing you only through the memories of others, your single diary, and these journals. But my first child, born easily, born healthy, who did find a good adoptive home, did not survive infancy. It's so unfair.

I'm full of what-ifs. What if his dad had not been killed in Vietnam and we could have been married? What if we had eloped and then conceived him? No one would automatically take a baby away from a widow, even an underage one.

And I get to struggle with guilt as well as grief. Perhaps he would have lived if I had found a way to keep him. Maybe I did not fight hard enough to keep him when the social worker said I had to give him up. "Foster children," she said, "are not allowed to have babies! You will be glad later that we gave this baby to a good family to raise. It is best for him and for you."

What garbage. I don't know who made me angrier—that woman or the lawyer I called and begged for help. He said the law was not on my side, that if I waited until I was 18, it would be different. But I "chose" to become pregnant at 17, and the law said that was that. I'm quite sure that if I went back and looked up that law, I would find out that the adoption was illegal from the start. Yes, it was twenty-one years ago, but I never even got to see a judge! They made me sign him away in the hospital. I was still in pain from the birth; I was crying. It was so wrong. And now, it was all for nothing.

June 10
Dear Mom,

I'm not as angry now. More than anything, I just want all the details. I talked to the agency today and thanked them for the letter. Mrs. Kukle was very kind. She has only been at the agency a short while, but she seems to be ideally suited to the work. She really loves children. She said her best guess was that my baby died of Sudden Infant Death Syndrome (SIDS), since it happened so fast and there were no details in the folder. She said the file was simply marked "baby deceased" on the last page.

SIDS. How devastated those adoptive parents must have been. But did anyone not stop to think that the birthmother would also want to know? It would have helped me to be at the funeral, to have something he had worn, to have a photo. Why was I never told? After all, Mom, doesn't the birthmother stop being a big bad threat when the child dies?

June 15
Dear Mom,

What an odd sensation. Sympathy. I am feeling sympathy for the adoptive mother and father. They had probably tried for years to have children and then lost their baby so suddenly. I feel a deep emotional need that I don't even understand, to call these people, to talk to them. Would that be crazy? I want to ask them for a photo, and I want to show them Kara and Chris. They would be able to see in my two youngest children the beauty and the maturity that they would have seen in our baby, had he lived. I want my kids to meet the adoptive family so that they can have some closure, too. I wonder what Mrs. Kukle would say if I asked her to set this up . . .

June 25
Dear Mom,

There's a mystery here. I heard it in her voice! She said to come right away—she even offered to send me bus fare! What on earth could Mrs. Kukle have to tell me that she can't say over the phone? Why do I have to be there? The cynic in me says that the agency wants to try to make things right with me. But I haven't threatened a lawsuit. The ever-hopeful part of me is praying that she has a memento to give me—pictures, a baby blanket, a pair of knitted booties. What a priceless gift that would be!

June 27
Dear Mom,

I don't know whether to laugh, cry, stomp my feet, or sing songs of gratitude to heaven above. How I wish you were still alive and could share in this moment. Your grandson might, just might, still be alive! It seems another birthparent approached Mrs. Kukle about a reunion, and when she checked the file, it said "baby deceased" on it, too. Mrs. Kukle showed me the last page of mine and half a dozen other files all marked "baby deceased." As she put it, one sudden infant death is awful but no surprise. However, two deaths are. Three is suspicious, and anything more than that is downright bizarre. Either someone was systematically killing every baby adopted by the agency that year, or the files were improperly marked and none of the babies died! She is investigating the whole mess—has made it her top priority and has promised to call the minute she knows.

July 6
Dear Mom,

Alive, alive! He's alive! His name is Andrew, and he lives in this state! Mrs. Kukle found him! None of the babies died! Oh, Mom, I'm drunk with joy, dizzy with excitement, and daffy with hope. The baby I lost twice might still want to know me, might still someday put his arms around me and say, "I love you, too." So much emotion, so many questions!

Mrs. Kukle has spoken to many people associated with the agency in the past. Her theory is that Mr. Broadmoor, the agency director the year I relinquished, had a strong bias against reopening records. No one is sure about why, but it might have been some kind of twisted religious belief on his part. The bylaws of the agency prevented him from burning the records of completed adoptions, so he simply marked them "baby deceased" instead. He knew this would delay, discourage, or stop attempted reunions. And it worked for a while! Thank heavens he did not mark more than twenty files that way before he was fired for general incompetence. Here's a final sad irony. Mr. Broadmoor himself actually is "deceased."

Mrs. Kukle has tracked down Andrew's adoptive family and is setting up a reunion now! Apparently, my oldest child is away at college (COLLEGE, Mom!) but comes home most weekends to do his laundry. (See? He's fastidious about his appearance—just like me!) Every time the phone rings, I jump out of my skin. Kara and Chris are almost as excited as I am. And Jeff is being very supportive. After all, Andrew is his step-son!

July 12
Dear Mom,

Mrs. Kukle tells me that there is a pattern to many reunions. They start off in a sea of euphoria, "honeymoon" for awhile, and then hit a brick wall unless everyone is well prepared. All of us have to be empathetic, she says, and respectful. We have to rally behind Andrew and not make him the center of a human tug of war between families. If we can all do that, Andrew and I can build a relationship based not only on genes, but on friendship, understanding, and mutual interests. Our love might be automatic, but our relationship must be built from the ground up. He is a baby no more.

I'm hitting the support group chat room hard. The other reunited b-moms and b-dads have a lot of good tips to share. I am determined to do this right. I never want to lose him again!

July 15
Dear Grandmom,
Yes, Grandmom! Andrew looks just like you! How I wish you could see him. My first reaction upon walking into the conference room at the adoption agency (with the kids holding me up as my knees felt like jelly from nerves) was the same as his. We both burst out laughing! Mom, we were wearing the exact same watch and sandals! What are the odds of that? He pointed at my watch, I pointed at his shoes, and we just hugged and laughed and hugged some more. He said to me, "Gee, Ma, you have excellent taste in timepieces and footwear!"

Andrew looks more like his brother than his sister, but the resemblance is amazing all around. He has his dad's eyes, God rest his soul. I gave him copies of all the photos I have of his birthfather. And he and Jeff hit it off well. They both like fast cars. We all just talked and talked and talked!

His adoptive parents are wonderful people. I genuinely like them. They had been discussing a possible reunion with Andrew for years. Can you imagine if they had found me instead of the other way around? I would have died from shock to suddenly see my "long-dead" son!

I know we will all be friends. Julie, the other mom, brought me a gift. It was one of Andrew's baby sleepers. It's yellow, with tiny trains embroidered on the sleeves. We both had a good cry over that!

I know that hard work lies ahead, Mom. But I am confident that we will have a good relationship. He is a wonderful young man—smart, kind, funny, and so handsome!

I am a whole person at last, and it feels wonderful. I'm going to be super busy, so if I don't have time to write you again for awhile, don't worry, and don't forget that I love you.
Your loving daughter,
Jennifer

☙❧

The Experiment

By the time Karen and Gene Sandborn found the Happy Cradle adoption agency, they had been through the infertility mill twice. They no longer considered adoption a desperate last resort but had embraced the idea as the single best way for them to become parents. They had looked into domestic adoption but had decided on adoption from China, because they knew they could have a healthy baby in their arms sooner, within a year. The hefty price tag was a little shocking, but not much worse than the cost of the last in vitro attempt. They joined the Chinese adoption support group, completed their homestudy in a record four months, and settled in to wait on some Immigration and Naturalization Service forms and other documents. They were getting close to the assignment phase, wherein they would be shown photographs of newborns at the agency's orphanage in China, when their social worker called them with surprising news.

It was somewhat of a rare occurrence, but a local couple had recently relinquished their newborn daughter to the custody of the Happy Cradle agency. The 1-month-old baby had been in a foster home until the thirty-day waiting period was up on the relinquishment. She was healthy, bright, happy, and ready for a permanent family, and they were offering her to the Sandborns first. The cost of the placement, including the hospital bill, was comparable to what they were expecting to pay to go to China.

Karen and Gene jumped at the chance even before the social worker could tell them that there was just one catch. The birthparents had relinquished to the agency with the understanding that the adoption would be open, that is, a limited amount of birthfamily contact would continue.

The birthparents, a stable employed divorced couple, had relinquished their daughter because neither one wanted to be a single parent or even to be a noncustodial parent. They were young, and each wanted a fresh start that would be childless. But the grandparents on both sides wanted desperately to be able to see the baby once a year or more and to send and receive photographs and letters or videos four times a year. As they explained to Happy Cradle, they did not want to parent the baby girl for a variety of reasons ranging from age to ill health, but neither did any of them want to lose contact with a beloved grandchild forever. Karen and Gene had never considered such an arrangement before, and their own parents were very much against the idea. Gene's mother said, "No baby needs more than two grandmas, does she?" and Gene's father remarked, "How do you know they won't steal her away from you on one of these visits?" Karen's best friend called the whole idea an unproven experiment.

But after meeting the birthparents and grandparents and finding them likeable people, the Sandborns agreed to their terms. No last names or addresses would be exchanged, but the annual day-long visit and the quarterly letter and photos sent through the agency would be fine with them.

Baby Delia adjusted to life with her new family right away. Karen described her as the perfect infant. She was rarely cranky, full of smiles, very aware of her surroundings, and she charmed everyone who came near her lovely brown eyes. By her first birthday, she was walking well and had the vocabulary of an 18-month-old.

The letter and photo exchanges had taken place on schedule, but Karen's letters were each shorter than the last. The more she grew to love Delia, the more uncomfortable she was with the requirement that she give detailed information about her child to people who were, to her, strangers.

The letters from the four birth-grandparents spoke with great anticipation about the first visit. One grandma had knitted an entire winter wardrobe for Delia, and one of the grandpas had made her a wooden rocking horse in his backyard workshop. The adoptive grandparents jealously scoffed at such efforts. No one was happy.

Gene spoke to an attorney a few weeks before the first visit was scheduled to happen. The lawyer told him that open adoption agreements are usually not legally enforceable and that no court in that state had, so far, declared them to be legally binding. As the sole legal parents of Delia, Gene and Karen could make any decision they felt was in her best interests. One week before the visit, the birth-grandparents received a letter from the Sandborns' attorney that the visit would not happen this year, and maybe not ever. It took less than twenty-four hours for the grandparents to hire their own lawyer and file suit. Battle lines were drawn and court injunctions requested by both sides.

Happy Cradle learned of the dual legal actions only after the dispute had turned bitter. The director hired a professional legal mediator to speak to both sides before the court hearing. Delia was left in the care of a friend, and the Sandborns showed up with their lawyer and their four parents to sit across a long metal table from the four birth-grandparents and their attorney. The room was filled with tension.

The mediator was Jonas Kinde, a retired divorce attorney who had been working as a full-time family law mediator for the last fifteen of his eighty years of life. He loved the work, and he was good at it. He came fully prepared to deal with the issue at hand, having read every word of the briefs supplied by both attorneys. He set an enormous pot of coffee in the center of the table and passed coffee cups around the room. "Get comfy, folks," he said with a smile, "because we're going to be here until all of us are thinking of one issue and one issue only—what is best for Baby Delia!"

He chatted with each person present briefly about their opinion of the open adoption agreement. He asked a slightly different question of each person in turn, such as: "What do you think Delia will think of this legal battle when she is 20? When she is 40? How would you feel about it if you were Delia?" After the last person had spoken, Jonas smiled again.

"Folks, until I say different, no one in this room may speak except me, and one person for each side—and I don't mean counsel. Mrs. Maynard, as a birth-grandmother, you will represent the birthfamily, and Mrs. Gray, as an adoptive grandmother, you will represent the adoptive family. Is that clear?"

Everyone nodded. Unbeknownst to the group, Jonas had chosen those individuals based on their responses. He believed them to be the most compassionate, open-minded, and child-centered people in the room. Next, he asked each to make a case for their side, to make one point at a time. Jonas wrote down the major arguments on a large tablet situated on an easel. The list looked like this:

Maynard (Birth Family)	Gray (Adoptive Family)
An agreement is an agreement	Parents must do what they think best
A little contact cannot hurt anyone	No one knows if open adoption is a good idea
Grandparents have rights	No baby needs more than two sets of grandparents
Delia should know that she is still loved by us	Delia is too young to understand "adoption"
It's cruel to everyone to exclude us from her life	They can meet Delia eventually

Jonas studied the list silently for several minutes. "I'll begin," he said slowly, sipping his coffee, "by tossing any argument that I know to be factually incorrect. I did a little research on this subject yesterday, and apparently, I learned more than you folks know."

He rose and crossed out Mrs. Gray's second and third arguments. "Open adoption, as we call it, is common in other cultures, and there's no evidence that it's harmful when everyone involved is law abiding and decent."

He continued. "Most U.S. states didn't seal adoption records until well into this century, and a few don't seal them permanently now. Judging from the dozens of books on the market about this subject, a few of which I highly recommend *all* of you read, open adoption is becoming quite common in infant adoption. It would appear that the key to making it work is to develop a little trust and respect on each side. And as far as how many grandparents are optimal, there is no research that has established an exact number. However, it would appear that one terrific grandparent is at least as effective as a dozen mediocre ones."

Then he crossed out arguments number two and three on the Maynard side. "*Any* amount of contact can be harmful if the child's welfare is not uppermost. And I'd like to think grandparents have rights," Jonas drawled, "being a grandpa and a great-grandpa myself and knowing how important we are. But only a few states have laws that agree with that concept and this state is not one of them. Furthermore, in case you missed it on the news, the U.S. Supreme Court recently ruled against grandparent rights."

Now the list looked like this:

Maynard	**Gray**
An agreement is an agreement	Parents must do what they think best
Delia should know that she is still loved by us	Delia is too young to understand "adoption"
It's cruel to everyone to exclude us from her life	They can meet Delia eventually

Jonas continued by handing each grandmother a slip of paper and a pencil. "Write down what you fear the most from this situation. Think carefully about it—and be frank." He wrote their responses at the end of their columns, which now read like this:

Maynard	**Gray**
An agreement is an agreement	Parents must do what they think best
Delia should know that she is still loved by us	Delia is too young to understand "adoption"
It's cruel to everyone to exclude us from her life	They can meet Delia eventually
Fear: Losing Delia forever	Fear: Losing Delia eventually

Jonas added more cream to his third cup of coffee. Smiling, he said, "Looks like we have a bit more common ground than we thought, eh? Everyone's afraid of the same thing. Here's a news flash. Is everyone listening? The best way for all of you to be secure about Delia's love is to make sure she loves all of you! Working together, no one is a threat. Working against each other, each of you is a threat to the others, and only the lawyers will win!"

He paused to allow everyone to whisper among themselves for a minute and continued. "Now the way I see it, all of the remaining statements on the easel are true to some extent, but they are all also immaterial and irrelevant because all that matters is a little girl and how she will grow up feeling about family and about being loved and about giving love.

"Individually and together, you have the power to teach her profound lessons about love, the strength of blood ties, and the eternal miracle of adoption, and alternately, you have the power to teach her about fear, suspicion, and misguided loyalty. Shall we take a vote on which path is best for the child?"

The room fell silent. No one moved for a minute or two.

Jonas said, "All right, now, anyone can talk who wants to."

Gene and Karen stared into each other's eyes as if having a silent discussion. Then they whispered something to their parents, who nodded. Next, Gene quietly turned to their attorney, "We're sorry, but you're fired."

Moments later, the other attorney was discharged as well.

Mrs. Maynard offered her home for the first annual visit, and the Sandborns quickly agreed. "We'll bring the salad, the dessert, and the baby," volunteered Karen.

Jonas rose and stretched. "Just three cups of coffee. Almost a new record in my mediation practice. But while I have one more cup of java, someone show me a photo of this little angel."

Almost instantly, five purses swung open and just as many wallets were retrieved from pockets. Photos were flying all over the table. And laughter filled a room that, just an hour or two before, had been bristling with hostility.

ॐ

Searching for Sienna, a Tale of Two Onlies

Being an only child is just like being a kid in a large family in this respect— there are definite advantages and definite disadvantages. But for most of her childhood, Deanna had felt the sting of the disadvantages more. She just happened to hate being an "only," and what made her feel even more isolated was that the other onlies she knew all loved their special status.

Yes, there were more parental attention and more money to shower her with the resources of a superior education, and the best of everything. But she grew up lonely and feeling alone and daydreaming of a sister to play with.

It's not like she didn't try to change her status. She had always known she was adopted and that her parents could not conceive a sibling for her. But they could adopt again. She asked again and again, she wrote letters to Santa, she hinted, she cajoled, she begged. She often suggested they eat at Wendy's, because this restaurant chain puts adoption information on their paper placemats. But her campaign never bore fruit.

Her parents, who had been in their forties when they adopted her in infancy, simply did not feel that they were of an age to enlarge their family further.

A few weeks after her graduation from law school, while taking a break from her studies for the bar exam, she was browsing an Internet bookstore and happened upon a book about techniques for finding "lost loved ones." Deanna had flirted with the idea of searching for her birthfamily, and her parents were okay with the idea, too, but the timing had never felt quite right. She scanned the list of loved ones the book could help you locate:

- high school friends,
- former coaches,
- neighbors,
- lost siblings

"A long lost sister," Deanna mumbled to herself, "what I wouldn't give to have one of those. . . ." And then it hit her like a bolt of lightning. She sat up arrow straight in her chair and stared open mouthed at the computer screen. *Why*, she wondered, hadn't she thought of the possibility before?! She was *adopted*. That means she could have a biological sibling or half sibling, a real "long lost" sister, or brother, or *both*! Maybe she had two sisters, or three. The possibilities staggered the imagination. Quickly she ordered the book with a few clicks of her mouse and added an extra six bucks for overnight delivery. This was one book she would read cover to cover as soon as she tore it from its wrapping. The techniques described were amazingly simple. The Internet had web sites for private investigators that she could access legally and easily.

Using her original birth certificate, which her mom had given her many years before, she was able to find quite a bit of information on her birth-family. Less than seventy-two hours after receiving the book, the possibility of having a long lost sister had materialized into a factual reality. But the notification was painful.

Deanna found her sister's name in her birthmother's newspaper-printed obituary. It read, "Mrs. Gina Logan is preceded in death by her husband, Maury, and son, Michael. She is survived by Sienna Logan, her daughter." No other relatives were mentioned.

All at once, Deanna found her birthfather, birthmother, and birthbrother and lost them in the same instant. It was almost too much grief for one day. She wept most to think that the obituary was only two months old. If only she had begun the process a little sooner. She would have met her other mother. If only.

Thoughts of searching for Sienna were put on hold while she grieved the loss of a family she would never meet. She tried but failed to get her mind back on her studies and, so, failed the bar exam as well. Her parents were understanding. "Many people take it more than once and are not in deep grief when they fail this test. Give yourself some time, Deanna."

A few weeks passed, and Deanna noticed that she was thinking more and more about Sienna Logan. How she wanted to meet her, to hug her, to stay up all night and talk about sister stuff. She wanted to know how her father and brother died. And she had so many questions about their birth-mother. The obituary said something about a brief illness. How had she died?

Deanna did a little more research and found Sienna Logan's address and phone number. They lived only an hour and a half apart via the interstate. She called her from her parents' living room, with her mom holding her free hand for luck.

"Hello? Is this Sienna, Sienna Logan? Um, my name is, you don't know me. I'm a lawyer, well, almost, I mean. Gee, I'm rambling. Er, my name is Deanna, and, uh, I think, I have reason to believe you might be my sister. My birthparents are Maury and Gina Logan!"

She took a deep breath and waited. And waited. The phone was silent.

"Hello? Miss Logan, are you there?"

"I'm still here," said an exasperated voice on the other end. "But I don't know what to say to you. My parents are both deceased. And if you are calling about the will—"

"No, no, no!" Deanna cried, cutting her off in mid-suspicion. "I don't want any money. This is not about the will. I just want . . . to meet . . . you."

Another pause, and then Sienna spoke slowly, choosing her words with care. "Deanna, please understand that my mother was all I had. My dad and brother were killed in an automobile accident when I was just a baby. She died very soon after the pancreatic cancer was found. I'm still crying every day, know what I mean? I can't do *this* right now. I mean, I knew about you. Mom said she had given up a baby before she and Dad were married, but I have always loved being an only child and I didn't feel the need to, well, you know, to look for you. I don't mean to be rude, but could you give me some time, please?"

"No, no problem at all," said Deanna, fighting back tears of her own. "I'll leave you my number and you call me when you are ready, okay?" Mechanically, she rattled off the numbers typed on the label of her mother's telephone, said good-bye, and then fell into her mother's arms, sobbing. After all of her dreams and hopes, her sister, her only sibling, didn't even want to see her. And what irony, Sienna *liked* being an only!

"Guess I'd better be careful what I ask Santa for, huh, Mom," she managed to say between sobs, "because I just may get it!"

"Give it some time, sweetie," her mother cooed. "Sienna just needs time, that's all. Remember, you are all the family she has left in this world!"

Weeks turned to months, and the weather turned cold as winter approached. Deanna began studying to take the bar exam again, scheduled for mid-January. She had long ago stopped crying about Sienna's rejection, convinced that her sister would call her before the holidays. Surely, she would want to spend Christmas with family, and there was plenty of room at her mom and dad's house, much more than at Deanna's apartment.

The days of December ticked by without word. A hundred times, Deanna picked up the phone to call Sienna, and a hundred times she put it down again without dialing. She wanted to so much to see her, but she knew a reunion could not—should not—be forced.

On Christmas Eve, as she was preparing to go to her parents' house, the phone rang. Deanna dived for it, sure it would be her sister, finally.

It was her mother, and she sounded worried.

"Deanna," she said, "the tree decorations just don't look right to me. I think we need more lights. Can you pick up a box on your way over this evening?"

Deanna stared at the phone for a moment. It was not at all like her mother to wait until the last minute to decorate, but she agreed and left for the store right away, hoping to find one still open.

Her dad opened the front door before she could even knock and practically ripped her coat and neck sweater off of her. He was smiling like the cat who ate the canary. Stranger still, her mother grabbed her elbow and pulled her, still holding the box of Christmas lights, rapidly toward the tree in the living room. Deanna was just about to complain about the poor selection of lights at the store when she noticed a young woman sitting beneath the tree with a big bow tied around her head. She looked at Deanna, grinned from ear to ear, and stood up. She said, "Merry Christmas, big sister. Santa just delivered me here."

And that was all anyone said for the next several minutes, as tears and hugs and more hugs were exchanged. Sienna had plotted the surprise, and Deanna's parents had helped carry it off. The request for more lights was a way to buy time until Sienna could arrive.

Everyone got something special that day. Deanna and Sienna each got a sister, and Deanna's parents unofficially adopted a new daughter.

Deanna was delighted to learn that Sienna had just graduated from college with a bachelor's degree in government and was toying with the idea of going to law school. Deanna suggested the perfect method for helping Sienna make up her mind—"Help me study for my bar exam!"

Perhaps it was a coincidence that Deanna passed it the second time with flying colors, but she credits little sister with the success. And even though Sienna ultimately decided to go into teaching instead of law, the two women share much in common. And they are very good friends.

RESOURCES

BOOKS

Any library or bookstore will have different books about adoption, but the greatest selection, hundreds of titles, is found in the Internet bookstores. Places like www.b&n.com, www.amazon.com, and www.tapestrybooks.com offer adoption titles in every category you can imagine. They also have "adoption bestseller" lists that you can browse if you don't have a particular author or title in mind. To see everything, just use the keyword "adoption" in the search box.

Other Greenwood titles by these authors include *Adoption and Financial Assistance: Tools for Navigating the Bureaucracy* by Rita Laws and Tim O'Hanlon. This book is saving families thousands of dollars and covers:

- subsidy rates nationwide
- negotiating and renegotiating subsidy contracts
- paying for adoption
- fair hearings, appeals, wrongful adoption, etc.
- authors are advocates
- available through your local or online bookstore or call (800) 225–5800 24 hours per day, or (203) 226–3571, or order online at www.greenwood.com.

See also *Adopting and Advocating for the Special Needs Child* by L. Anne Babb and Rita Laws. This book covers:

- the first special needs how-to-adopt guidebook for parents *and* professionals
- saving time, money, and frustration
- authors are long-time adoption professionals, advocates and adoptive parents, too, mothering twenty-four children between them
- available through your local or online bookstore or call (800) 225–5800 24 hours per day, or (203) 226–3571, or order online at www.greenwood.com.

NATIONAL ORGANIZATIONS AND WEB SITES

In previous books, we listed organizations and web sites in separate categories, but, nowadays, every national adoption organization has a web site, and most web sites have an organization behind them. So it makes more sense to merge these into one list. Please note that this is not a comprehensive list, nor is a complete list possible because web sites come and go, URLs change, and new organizations spring up. To find the most up-to-date list of adoption-related web sites and organizations, go to any major search engine or search portal, such as www.yahoo.com, www.webcrawler.com, and www.search.com, and type in the word "adoption." To see a shorter list, use a more detailed search phrase, such as "adoption agency," "adoption support," or "adoption research."

Adoption Policy Resource Center: http://www.fpsol.com/adoption/advocates. A site devoted to advocacy for adoption assistance. The center collects hearing and court decisions, policy-oriented articles, a checklist for adoptive parents interested in exploring adoption assistance, and significant federal policy issuances.

American Adoption Congress: http://www.americanadoptioncongress.org. A web site devoted to advocacy for opening adoption records to adoptees and birth parents.

The Evan B. Donaldson Adoption Institute: http://www.adoptioninstitute.org/policy/intro.html. A good source of information on adoption policy issues, research, and links to other adoption related sites.

Homes for Kids: www.homes4kids.org. This site has a wealth of information on special needs adoption and adoption assistance. It includes the federal law and regulations pertaining to adoption assistance, federal hearing regulations, and a large number of federal policy issuances.

The National Adoption Center: www.adopt.org. Online photolistings of children waiting to be matched to adoptive families right now and lots of information for people interested in adopting waiting children. A one-stop adoption center for families.

AdoptNet: www.adoptnet.org. Part of the National Adoption Center, AdoptNet has an online library of thousands of articles, free book chapters, and expert chat transcripts, free for the downloading or printing. There is also a popular chat room featuring both open forum and topical adoption chats. The chat calendar feature gives you a handy printout, or you can ask to be added to an e-mail list that informs you of upcoming chat events. There is a message board, too, for questions and answers about adoption.

The National Adoption Information Clearinghouse: http://www.calib.com/naic. A comprehensive site that is sponsored by the Children's Bureau, Administration on Children, Youth and Families, Administration for Children and Families, and the Department of Health and Human Services. The clearinghouse publishes fact sheets on a wide variety of adoption topics, lists of international adoption resources, and state-by-state summaries describing access to adoption records and contains separate sections devoted to birthparents, adoptees, and adoptive parents.

The North American Council on Adoptable Children (NACAC): www.nacac.org. NACAC's site features subsidy "profiles" outlining the major feature of adoption assistance programs in all fifty states. No matter which state you adopt a foster child from, that state's profile is *must* reading!

Bastard Nation: http://www.bastards.org. Bastard Nation is a web site devoted to opening adoption records to adult adoptees. The site features profiles of each state and a variety of other advocacy resources.

Joint Council on International Children's Services: http://www.jcics.org. A web site devoted to international adoption maintained by an organization of agencies that place children for adoption from countries outside the United States. A sample news item described the passage H.R. 2883, the Child Citizenship Act of 2000, which was signed by President Clinton on October 30, 2000. The law went into effect on February 27, 2001. The bill grants automatic citizenship to all foreign-born children who are under 18 years of age admitted to the United States as lawful permanent residents and in the legal and physical custody of at least one parent who is a U.S. citizen. Parents would no longer be required to submit an application to have their children naturalized.

INDEX

ABOUT THE AUTHORS

RITA LAWS is the co-author of *Adopting and Advocating for the Special Needs Child: A Guide for Parents and Professionals*, and *Adoption and Financial Assistance: Tools for Navigating the Bureaucracy*. She writes about adoption for various print and online adoption periodicals and trains chat room moderators for the National Adoption Center's AdoptNet web site. A mother of nine sons and two daughters by birth and adoption, she lives in Oklahoma with her seven youngest children and a menagerie of pets. Dr. Laws has been an adoption advocate and activist since 1979 and a NACAC and NAATRIN representative since 1990.

ANN M. MCCABE is the Project Manager for AdoptNet, a program of the National Adoption Center. McCabe is a family therapist in private practice, specializing in working with adoptive and foster families, birth families, and adult adoptees. She is an adoption educator and trainer for parents and professionals. Her writings include a monograph, entitled *Reworking the Burdens of Split Loyalties* as well as many articles on adoption related topics. Ann's work over the last twenty years has focused on helping families and children find the resources needed for personal healing and relational connection. Her experience growing up adopted and her reunion with her birth parents have been her greatest resource in working with all persons connected to the process of adoption.

TIM O'HANLON, a former adoption assistance policy specialist, is the author of *Adoption Subsidy: A Guide for Adoptive Parents* (1998), *Accessing Adoption Assistance After Legalization* (1995), and *Adoption and Financial Assistance: Tools for Navigating the Bureaucracy* (Bergin & Garvey, 1999). In addition to committee work with AFA, training parents, consulting, speaking and writing magazine articles about special needs adoption, he maintains an adoption advocacy web site called the "Adoption Policy Resource Center" at www.fpsol.com/adoption/advocates.html. As a North American Council on Adoptable Children (NACAC) representative, Dr. O'Hanlon has helped many families understand the bureaucracy and their rights as they advocate for their children. Married and the father of a son, Tim makes his home in Columbus, Ohio.